We Took the Train

We Took the Train————

Edited by

H. Roger Grant

NORTHERN ILLINOIS UNIVERSITY PRESS
DEKALB   1990

Published by the Northern Illinois University Press,
DeKalb, Illinois 60115

♾ Manufactured in the United States using acid-free
paper

Design by Julia Fauci

Library of Congress Cataloging-in-Publication Data

We took the train / edited by H. Roger Grant.
     p.   cm.
   Includes bibliographical references and index.
   ISBN 0–87580–156–0
   1. Railroads—United States—History.   2. Railroad
travel—United States—History.   I. Grant, H.
Roger, 1943–
TF23.W4   1990
625.1'00973—dc20   90–41350
                                            CIP

For My Graduate School Mentor: Lewis Atherton *(1905–1989)*

Contents ———————————————————

Preface

   This work began in a different form and for a different purpose. In 1988, I gathered some of these first-hand accounts of railroad travel for a volume sponsored by the National Council on the Aging (NCOA) for its "Discovery Through the Humanities" program for older Americans. That book, *We Got There on the Train: Railroads in the Lives of the American People* (Washington, D.C., 1989), covers a variety of themes, including public disillusionment with the railroad enterprise during the populist-progressive era, the railroad work place, and the prose and poetry associated with the golden age of rail travel. While that book serves the NCOA's educational purposes well, I felt that a publication that features only travel accounts from the 1830s to the present was needed. Such a compilation would be an opportunity to reach a more diverse audience, and it would allow me to make a more comprehensive analysis of railroad passenger transport.

I have benefited immensely from the help of numerous individuals and institutions, primarily, Sylvia Riggs Liroff, Manager, Older Adult Division of the NCOA, and Ronald J. Manheimer, Director of the Center for Creative Retirement at the University of North Carolina-Asheville, who developed the basic idea and involved me in the original project. My colleague and department head at The University of Akron, Keith L. Bryant, Jr., made numerous suggestions. Mary Lincoln, Director of the Northern Illinois University Press, likewise played a key role in this venture. Others, too, assisted: Mark J. Cedeck, St. Louis, Missouri; Arthur D. Dubin, Highland Park, Illinois; Don L. Hofsommer, St. Cloud, Minnesota; Caroline J. Pardee, Akron, Ohio; Charles C. Shannon, Arlington Heights, Illinois; Karen R. Sunderman, Deshler, Ohio; and my wife, Martha Farrington Grant. I also had support from several organizations: DeGolyer Library, Dallas, Texas; Kansas State Historical Society, Topeka, Kansas; Railway & Locomotive Historical Society, Sacramento, California; and the Western Reserve Historical Society, Cleveland, Ohio. Finally, I wish to thank Susan Bean and other talented employees of the Northern Illinois University Press and my able typists, Mia O'Connor, Edie Richeson, and Suzanne Seketa. Edie Richeson unquestionably took major responsibility for this project.

H. Roger Grant
Akron, Ohio

Amtrak's train #132, a Metroliner, pauses at the Trenton, New Jersey, station. (Amtrak)

Introduction

       "Tracks are Back!" crowed officials of Amtrak, the National Railroad Passenger Corporation, in 1971. On May first of that year the federal government assumed control of most remaining long-distance passenger trains in the United States. Yet citizens did not immediately flock to this well-known but frequently forgotten form of transport. In 1985, more than a dozen years after Amtrak's debut, the percentage of travelers who selected trains amounted to a paltry 3.8 percent. Since 1987, however, annoyed with congestion of highways and skyways, Americans have started to return to the rails. Amtrak's small fleet carried 21.5 million riders over a 23,500 route-mile system in 1988, and Amtrak representatives confronted a growing number of angry would-be patrons who failed to find seats on sold-out runs. Seemingly, the long downward trend in intercity rail travel has ended.[1]

In the not-so-distant past, Americans regularly took trains. Railroad stations, whether in large communities or small, were vibrant places as patrons awaited thousands of daily runs. "The depot," observed a midwestern businessman in 1903, "is always a beehive of activity. The hustle-bustle, which is America, can be found there." After-all, the iron horse had shattered the nation's isolation by the turn-of-the-century. No longer did people need to depend upon the always slow travel available on waterways, canals, and roads that were frequently made impassable by vagaries of weather. In 1900, the nation's 1,224 railroad companies operated 193,346 route miles of trackage and carried 576,831,000 passengers. (The country's population stood at only 76 million.) Expansion continued. America's network of steel rails reached its zenith in 1916, with an impressive system of 254,037 route miles, thus making the national map of these steam carriers resemble a plate of wet spaghetti. Also, in 1916, the country saw the heyday of electric interurban railways: 15,580 route miles of intercity "trolley" or "juice" lines laced the nation, particularly in New England, the Midwest, Texas, and California. Passenger volume hit the one billion mark in 1912, and this upward trend generally continued until the Great Depression.[2]

The number of intercity passenger trains peaked in the late 1920s. Not surprisingly, passenger-train density on some corridors became heavy. The

Official Railway Guide of February 1928, for example, gave schedules for eighteen trains that operated daily over the New York Central's Chicago to Buffalo speedway. (Today a lone Amtrak train travels this 528-mile route, now part of Conrail, the Consolidated Rail Corporation.) And the quality of service was unparalleled for the age. Observed one frequent traveler in 1927, "The American passenger train is the embodiment of reliability, comfort, convenience, cleanliness, safety and speed in travel." And he added, "It is the all-year-round, every-day-in-the-year transportation service, which functions adequately regardless of the weather."[3]

Dramatic changes followed the Roaring Twenties. Increased competition from buses, airplanes, and, most of all, automobiles, coupled with the hard times of the thirties, significantly lessened journeys on flanged wheels. The interurban industry, in fact, collapsed. At the same time that quality and frequency were dropping on branchlines and nearly vanishing on juice roads, better trains began appearing on principal routes. Sleek diesel-powered trains excited depression-weary Americans, and the "Streamliner Era" seemed to promise a bright tomorrow.[4]

Except for the years of World War II, when train travel experienced dramatic resurgence due to gasoline and tire rationing and conveyance of troops (more than 97 percent of all organized troop movements were by rail), the downward trend of passenger train service persisted. In 1939, railroads handled about two-thirds of "for-hire" travel; by 1965, they transported less than one-fifth. By then, local and branchline trains had mostly disappeared, and the number of long-distance operations likewise had declined. At times over-all quality fell and patrons complained about "riding to hell in a day coach." Prior to Amtrak, the obituary for the passenger train, with a few exceptions, seemed imminent.[5]

Admittedly, several railroads tried to buck the trend of "vanishing varnish."* One was the Union Pacific. As its former president, Edd H. Bailey, relates in his autobiography, "It has been said that when the passenger service began to decline, and the rail freight improved, railroads let the passenger service become unpleasant. Union Pacific, however, went down fighting. We determined we would give our passengers nothing but the best." But then he added, "We welcomed Amtrack [sic] when it came along. It gave us an open door to get rid of the trains that were costing us a lot of money to operate."[6]

Americans did not seem to appreciate particularly the Union Pacific's and other roads' efforts to maintain passenger service in the 1950s and 1960s despite the increasingly significant deficits. The Interstate Com-

---

*"Varnish" is railroad slang for passenger trains. In the era before all-metal equipment, carriers employed wooden cars, often with oak exteriors and highly polished (varnished) mahogany and walnut interiors; hence the expression.

merce Commission finally allowed the nearly bankrupt Erie Lackawanna Railway to discontinue trains 5 and 6 between Hoboken, New Jersey (New York City) and Chicago in early 1970. These runs lost $1.7 million in 1969 despite Erie Lackawanna's noble efforts to make them profitable. At the time of discontinuance patrons were using only 17 percent of the available seats. Critics, including regulators, habitually believed that carriers intentionally drove away patrons.[7] In some cases this was true, but most were forced to make modifications. Comments a former official of the Southern Pacific:

> The harshest critics . . . envisaged the railroad passenger business as more than simply the transportation of people. To those critics, it was a restful, tranquil, relaxing experience, an adventure in tranquility and nostalgia whose enjoyment required painstaking attention to passenger comfort. The critics didn't simply want to be transported from point A to point B; they expected to be cosseted, comforted, nurtured and stroked by a succession of happy, smiling, ever-attentive railroad employees. SP's perception was different; we felt we were not in the business of creating transcendental experiences, but rather in the business of transporting people. From that perception followed numerous cost-cutting measures, each of which was greeted with strident objections by our critics, who alleged that these measures were a plot to "drive passengers away." Example: SP felt that it was spending too much money for fresh flowers in the dining cars. Perhaps the wisest course would have been to simply cut out flowers and put the vases away and this might have gone unnoticed. Instead, the passenger department sought to perpetuate a gracious image by substituting plastic flowers. The result? Howls![8]

Long before the Southern Pacific got involved in the fresh versus plastic flower fracas, some industry executives viewed passenger traffic as a necessary evil. Early in the century James J. Hill, builder of the Great Northern Railway, observed that "a passenger train is like a male teat—neither useful nor ornamental." Yet Hill would readily admit that first-class trains, most of all his posh Oriental Limited (whose cut flowers came from the Great Northern's own greenhouse), served as powerful symbols of the railway age.[9]

Over the course of a century and a half, a train trip has meant traveling in a wide variety of equipment, usually in some sort of "day coach." During their formative years, America's railroads used the technology of established carriage makers, and understandably these pioneer cars resembled (and rode like) stage coaches. Fortunately for the jostled passenger, carriers soon employed more comfortable rolling stock: most of all, eight-wheel cars replaced the original four-wheel ones, resulting

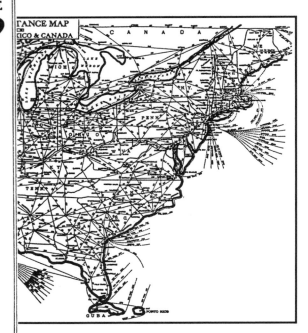

Railroad Distance Map of North America, 1917. Travelers, especially salesmen or "drummers," purchased these and similar maps.

in a better ride. Also, "clerestory" or raised-roof passenger coaches, debuting at mid-century, gave occupants better ventilation, "air pure and sweet."[10]

Cars, too, got roomier and heavier. A Baltimore & Ohio coach in 1835, for example, measured thirty feet in length, seated fifty, and weighed six tons; one owned by the Chicago & North Western fifty years later extended fifty-five feet, accommodated sixty-four passengers, and weighed thirty tons. No wonder an official of the North Western proudly observed in 1885, that "the comfort of the first coaches . . . cannot compare with the pleasures of our modern ones."[11]

Chair-car riders in the twentieth century experienced a host of improvements. For one, they saw introduction of "heavyweight" or "metallic" coaches about 1905. Within a decade thousands of these cars served passengers' needs nicely. They not only rode well, but they were considerably safer. Heavyweights were fire-proof (unless they contained wooden interiors), and they withstood the impact of collision or derailment better than their wooden predecessors, which frequently splintered and burned. Then in the 1930s more betterments occurred. Coaches were likely to be air-conditioned, and increasingly "streamlined," which meant lighter-weight construction. Car builders turned to 'wonder metals" such as aluminum, Cor-Ten® steel, and stainless steel. While these sleek railway coaches pleased passengers as did the companion development of diesel-electric motive power (which increased speed and eliminated grime), total conversion from heavy to light-weight equipment did not occur until the coming of Amtrak. "The best trains were periodically upgraded with a set of new cars, the older ones being reassigned to lesser trains." Even obsolete wooden coaches continued in service long after steel ones arrived. The Chicago & North Western, for example, announced in October 1940, that it would push for retirement of its remaining wooden cars by 1941, but the crush of war-time traffic postponed this noble objective. In recent years, though, streamlining has become universal; today heavyweights serve only patrons of museums and tourist pikes.[12]

An important variation of the standard coach, whether wooden or heavyweight, was the "Jim Crow" car. Early in the railroad age, the races were systematically separated on passenger trains. Carriers assigned African-Americans to specific compartments or cars, called Jim Crow sections. Although this practice ended gradually in the North before the Civil War, it continued in the South until the war's end. When the U.S. Supreme Court ruled in the case of *Louisville, New Orleans and Texas Railroad v. Mississippi* (1890) that states could constitutionally require segregation on carriers, southern and border states enacted legal codes that made racial segregation public policy. Specially made Jim Crow cars had separate sections, usually with a baggage area in the middle, to divide the races (African-Americans rode in front and whites in back). These pieces of segregated rolling stock remained in service long into the twentieth century; Georgia's 20-mile Wadley Southern Railway, for example, operated its Jim Crow Car 12 until the early 1950s.[13]

While three-quarters of riders historically have taken coaches, sleeping cars helped to revolutionize long-distance rail travel. When patrons encountered a night journey, the pleasures they might associate with a daytime trip in a chair-car lessened markedly. Falling into restful sleep became difficult if not impossible; crying babies, talkative and noisy passengers, upright seats, and the commotion of station stops regularly took their toll.

For good reason pioneer railroads experimented with sleeping cars. In the late 1830s Pennsylvania's Cumberland Valley Railroad introduced what allegedly was the nation's first sleeping car, The Chambersburg. As the industry matured, travelers found they could count on more relaxing trips in sleeping cars, usually leased to carriers by private companies. These were firms like the Rip Van Winkle Line, Woodruff Sleeping and Parlor Coach Company, Mann Boudoir Car Company, Monarch Parlor-Sleeping Car Company, Wagner Palace Car Company, and, most notably, the Pullman Company. Eventually Pullman monopolized the field. By 1905, its fleet of 4,138 cars operated over 184,000 route miles and served 14,969,000 passengers. "Pullman" became the synonym for travel by sleeping car. "The name was part of the language, and it was the only name that the public readily associated with railroad car history."[14]

Passenger trains contained more than a locomotive, coaches, and possibly a sleeping car or two. In addition to the "head-end" equipment— namely, baggage, express, and mail cars—the "consist," at least for the better or "name" trains, nearly always included dining, parlor, and observation cars. When the Chicago, Burlington & Quincy happily announced its 12-car diesel-powered Denver Zephyr in September 1937 ("A brilliant new achievement in high-speed travel luxury"), its promotional folder revealed a somewhat typical assortment of equipment types. "Behind [the baggage, express, and mail cars] in consecutive order, are two commodious coaches, a lovely full-length dining car, three 12-section sleepers, . . . and the full-length parlor observation lounge at the extreme end."[15]

Special equipment was added to particular trains. The Denver Zephyr, for one, had an unusual piece, the "all-room car," described as follows: "Especially distinctive is the all-room car, where six bedrooms, three compartments and a drawing room are available. These are so designed that five spacious two-room combinations can be obtained at a moment's notice, by means of a sliding partition. Each room is individually decorated and is equipped with private toilet facilities, illuminated electric clock, individual temperature control, and outlet for personal electrical appliances." Another example could be found on the contemporary Californian, operated jointly by the Rock Island and Southern Pacific railroads. This train of the Great Depression era offered both "economy" rolling stock— "Pullman Tourist Sleepers which are congenial and restful . . . [and] afford a savings of about one-half of standard Pullman charges,"— and a "Special Car for women," described as "a de luxe Chair car . . . reserved for the exclusive use of female passengers traveling alone or accompanied by children."[16]

Luxury trains provided more than transportation. They gave passengers the opportunity to continue the elegance of their daily lifestyles or to experience it for the first time. If a prosperous businessman from Chicago wished to travel to Omaha at the turn-of-the-century, he would leave his handsome house, probably via chauffeured carriage, for a spacious and architecturally pleasing downtown passenger terminal. Since his destination was to be the Nebraska metropolis, he would choose between five railroads, with the Chicago & North Western and the Chicago, Milwaukee & St. Paul railways offering trains of distinction. If the businessman had selected the latter road, he surely would have been delighted. An attractive booklet, "Between Chicago and Omaha," was published in 1900 by the "St. Paul" road to proclaim the benefits of riding the Chicago

The Oriental Limited, Great Northern Railway, ca. 1925.

& Omaha Short Line: "To provide every luxury to which one is accustomed in his home is the first aim of the Chicago, Milwaukee & St. Paul Railway. This perfection is confined not alone to the appointment of its coaches, which are examples of the highest degree of skill in construction and decoration, but extends to every branch of service." The businessman would likely have spent part of his 500-mile journey in the Buffet Library Car, "literally a Man's Club on wheels. In every particular the most fastidious person will find the service of his favorite Club duplicated. . . . The daily papers and periodicals are kept on file, and a carefully selected circulating library is at the disposal of passengers. Favorite brands of cigars, mineral waters and liquors are always kept in stock." When he wished to dine, he would have found epicurean delights, "a meal equal to any served in the best hotels or in one's own home." Unquestionably, riding the Chicago & Omaha Short Line meant that the businessman never had to leave his Windy City environment; he would have traveled along what John R. Stilgore has aptly called the "metropolitan corridor," a route that replicated much of the best that urban life bestowed.[17]

Splendid railroad equipment and service lasted long after the Chicago, Milwaukee & St. Paul withdrew its Buffet Library Car and retired or reassigned its crew. Some name-trains, most of all the extra-fare and all-Pullman streamliners that linked New York with Chicago or Florida and Chicago with California, offered riders until the 1950s every imaginable enjoyment of train travel. When the New 20th Century Limited debuted in 1938, a train running between New York and Chicago that was designed by Henry Dreyfuss in collaboration with engineers from the Pullman Standard Car Company and the New York Central Railroad, it boasted "rich simplicity and ultra-modern conveniences." According to an attractive folder,

> Every unit is provided with special features and all possess innovations peculiar to this celebrated train of trains. A special electrical installation reduced the time of signal transmission between the rear of the train and the locomotive. A telephone system facilitates dining car reservations or the ordering of food from room service. Concealed radio amplifiers in the observation and dining cars inform travelers of the latest world events and together with a record-changing phonograph furnish after-dinner music when the dining car is magically metamorphosed into a night club. . . . A rust, grey and white octagonal barber shop enables busy executives to detrain with no delay, conscious of the same grooming obtainable in a good hotel. Valet and maid are on call, and a train secretary saves time by preparing rush letters or assembling the notes of a speech to be used at destination. Greater privacy is possible than ever before since each passenger is in possession of his own room, there being no open berths on the train.[18]

Although most Americans liked to consider themselves part of an egalitarian society, the gap between rich and poor grew rapidly after the Civil War, a consequence of ever-expanding industrialization and urbanization. While well-to-do travelers likely selected Pullmans and their daytime equivalent, parlor cars, on a plethora of name-trains and less-affluent riders probably opted for inexpensive coaches, the unmoneyed frequently "rode the rods" instead of the "cushions": they stole passage on either freight or passenger trains. Hundreds of thousands of Americans, nearly always men and boys, flocked to the rails during the five-year depression that followed the devastating panic of May 1893. Unemployment figures reached all-time highs and, on a per-capita basis during the winter of 1893–1894, were likely the greatest in the nation's history. "There are countless men from the ranks of the unemployed who are taking to the freights in search of jobs that are not there," reported a Kansas City journalist in April 1894. Of course, hard times did not vanish permanently with the dawn of a new century. Most notably the economic malaise of the 1930s increased the number of "hobos" and other transients who sought a better life down the tracks.[19]

Traveling the "side-door Pullman route" took various forms. Often the ticketless rider sat on a flatcar or inside an empty boxcar or squatted on a freight-car roof. If he actually rode the rods, he placed his "ticket," namely a thick board, between the metal trusses that were once commonly found underneath railroad rolling stock and laid horizontally on it. Another alternative was "riding the blinds." The "bo" stood in the recessed entry-way of a passenger baggage car or coach that was directly behind the locomotive tender or "tank." Occasionally, he dared to make the trip on top of a passenger car— called "decking"—or even aboard the tender, hiding in piles of coal. One adventuresome lad vividly recalled his exciting trip with a companion on the pilot or "cow-catcher" of a Santa Fe passenger locomotive across the Kansas prairie in the late 1890s: "Now the light beam from the headlight, shining on the track, made the rails look like two silver ribbons that were being unreeled out of the darkness ahead of us and swallowed up right under the pilot below us and we went sailing along through the dark and gee, we were getting thrills and chills in turn, one after the other."[20]

No matter where a passenger rode, speed of travel served as a major attraction of railroad transport. Americans expected it. They read with pleasure newspaper accounts of the first 100-miles-per-hour passenger train run. On May 9, 1893, the New York Central & Hudson River Railroad's The Empire State Express, powered by the high-stepping 4-4-0 American-type locomotive 999, sprinted at 102 m.p.h. down five miles of mainline track between the New York communities of Looneyville and Grimesville on its way to Buffalo. On the return trip to New York City, the Express reached 112 m.p.h. near Crittenden, New York, establishing a world's record.[21]

Speed, though, caused countless accidents. "Our railroads kill their thousands every month in wreck or trespass," editorialized a national magazine in 1907. "In more than half the cases, the real truth underlying the tragedy is the fact that the train was running at forty or fifty or sixty miles an hour over tracks that were built for trains that never ran but thirty miles an hour. Even in the far South and in steady old New England, the cry is ever for more speed." Not surprisingly, near the zenith of long-distance train usage, the nation's deadliest wreck occurred. On July 9, 1918, two Nashville, Chattanooga & St. Louis passenger trains, running at high speed, smashed head-on near the Tennessee capital. One hundred and one passengers and crew members died. By then most riders, for good reason, considered travel insurance a necessity for protection of self and family.[22]

Railroad companies still remained committed to speed, albeit ever-more mindful of safety. They added better signals, reduced workers' hours (at the federal government's insistence) and created accident-prevention programs. Even though speed advances since the 1940s have come from automobiles and airplanes, especially commercial jets that entered service in the early 1960s, some railroads sought to meet modal competition by cutting running times for their premier trains. A widely heralded response came from the Pennsylvania Railroad in the late 1960s. This financially troubled company, which once called itself the "Standard Railway of the World," courageously introduced a fleet of "Metroliners" on its superbly engineered and generally well-maintained line between New York City and Washington, D.C.; these electric-powered trains whizzed along at 125 m.p.h. The Pennsylvania's investment in high-speed service understandably challenged the assumption of many that the passenger train was dead. More recently, dramatic speeds obtained by French TGV trains (more than 160 miles per hour) and experimental magnetically levitated trains, "Meglevs" (more than 250 miles per hour), suggest a new era in rail travel.[23]

Historically those who took trains did not always have fast travel. Mainline locals stopped frequently, attaining high speeds only intermittently. Branchline trains also paused repeatedly, and because they rolled over inferior track compared to a mainline's "high iron," their rates of movement were modest at best. Also slow were passenger trains operated by the first cousins of the branchlines, the ubiquitous "shortlines." These were small, independent companies that dotted the landscape, especially in the Midwest and South. Trains on branchlines and shortlines commonly moved over light rail, untreated ties, and dirt or cinder surfaces, rights-of-way hardly designed for "ballast scorching." Frequently, passengers who traveled branchlines or shortlines encountered a poky "mixed" train, namely a passenger coach (usually an old one) or a caboose (sometimes fitted with extra seats) attached to the rear of a freight train. Thus a company could economically haul both "hogs and humans" on a single, leisurely trip. Railroads customarily published timetables for their local branchline and special operations, although they might warn patrons to "consult agent for [schedule] details," particularly when they involved mixed trains.[24]

The public's attitudes about slow trains varied. Some seemed resigned

THE NEW 12-CAR
DENVER ZEPHYRS

America's Distinctive Trains

OVERNIGHT EVERY NIGHT *between*

CHICAGO *and* DENVER

SCHEDULE

Westbound		Eastbound
5:30 pm	Lv. Chicago Ar. ↑	8:50 am
1:15 am	Ar. Omaha . Lv.	12:59 am
1:20 am	Lv. Omaha . Ar.	12:55 am
2:15 am	Ar. Lincoln . Lv.	11:58 pm
8:30 am ↓	Ar. Denver . Lv.	4:00 pm

DIESEL POWERED • STAINLESS STEEL

The Chicago, Burlington & Quincy Railroad issued this combination timetable and postal card for its crack Denver Zephyr, ca. 1940.

to the service; others protested, usually in letters to railroad officials, regulators, and lawmakers. Because slow or late trains were a source of considerable annoyance, they became the butt of frequent jokes. Arkansas became infamous for its unhurried trains, so much so that railroader–turned-publisher Thomas W. Jackson (1867–1934) made a profitable career selling his *On a Slow Train through Arkansaw* humor books. One of his classic tales is as follows:

> It was down in the state of Arkansaw I rode on the slowest train I ever saw. It stopped at every house. When it came to a double house it stopped twice. They made so many stops I said, "Conductor, what have we stopped for now?" He said, "There are some cattle on the track." We ran a little ways further and stopped again, I said, "What is the matter now?" He said, "We have caught up with those cattle again."[25]

*J*ackson's story reflected reality. For example, the woebegone Missouri & North Arkansas Railroad, a "big shortline," operated its train Number 1 between Eureka Springs and Helena, Arkansas, a distance of 290 miles, at an advertised pace of less than twenty miles per hour in its January 1912 public timetable. Moreover, ". . . it was frequently late." No wonder travelers called the M&NA the "*May Never Arrive.*"[26]

*S*peed or even its absence gave travel by train a romantic flavor. Any trip promised to be an adventure. Edna St. Vincent Millay captured this sentiment well when she wrote in her 1921 poem, "Travel," that "Yet there isn't a train I wouldn't take/No matter where it's going."[27]

Travelers frequently took trains of discovery. After crossing the Atlantic Ocean from the Old World, some boarded emigrant cars at east-coast terminals for destinations in America's interior: a milltown in the Midwest, a farm on the Great Plains, or a lumbercamp in the Pacific Northwest. Others took "specials" for well-orchestrated outings: an annual encampment of the Grand Army of the Republic, a convention of the King's Daughters, or a political or religious gathering. Some made their own arrangements for a rail excursion to a nearby spa or a distant resort, perhaps for health reasons—"to take the waters"—or to escape winter's snows, ice, and brutal cold. Or they might seek genuine adventure; for example, prospectors from the time of the California Gold Rush of 1849 onward made part or all of their journey to the fields of "color" by steamcars. Still others entrained for war or returned from one, possibly finding the horrors of battle or an altered hometown.

No matter the destination, an element of anticipation, even apprehension existed in trips to either unknown or unfamiliar destinations. "This train will take us to a new tomorrow," reflected an Illinois farmer in 1915, bound for a homestead on the eastern Wyoming prairie. "I can hardly contain my excitement . . ., yet I will miss what I have known so well and for so long and what has been a good life." Even those who traveled with regularity might also experience thrilling moments. "Surely there were drummers [traveling salesmen] who frequented the same trains over and over again, and didn't see much adventure in most trips. . . . [Nevertheless] they might have expectations of making a big deal or finding that beautiful, accommodating lass at the next stop."[28]

Heightening the romance and fascination with train trips were the widespread published accounts of such happenings. Stories of travel bombarded the public. Newspapers, especially in small-town America, fully reported individual and group journeys and outings. The *Crawfordsville* (Indiana) *Review* in August 1889, noted in its weekly personal column, strategically placed on the front page, that "Wednesday morning Father Dinneen assisted in the marriage of Thomas Dewitt and Miss Nora Kelly. A special train was run from this city to Indianapolis to accommodate the people."[29]

Surely the physical appearance of trains themselves markedly contributed to the sense of romance. Most of all, the power at the head-end stimulated the observer. While sleek diesel-powered trains gained admirers after their introduction in the mid-1930s, unquestionably those pulled by steam locomotives excited on-looker and traveler alike for generations. In the late 1920s, the *New York Tribune* pondered the attraction generated by steam locomotives: "Breathes there a man with soul so dead that he does not thrill at the sight of a modern steam locomotive at work? Somewhere in the breast of every normal homo sapiens there stretches a cord that vibrates only to the sight and sound of a fine steam locomotive. Even now, with airplanes and motors to bid against it in its own fields of romantic interest, the steam locomotive retains its fascination." Similarly, novelist Sherwood Anderson, recalling his boyhood in Clyde, Ohio, remembered well the daily Lake Shore & Michigan Southern varnish. "There was a passenger train going away into the mysterious West at some twenty minutes after seven in the evenings and, as six o'clock was our universal supper hour . . ., we all congregated at the station to see the train arrive and depart, we boys gathering far down the station platform to gape with hungry eyes at the locomotive."[30]

While the sight of hot, steaming locomotives enhanced the romance of the rails, the presence of well-known personalities who patronized trains had a similar impact. Jack Benny, the comedian, for one, always preferred trains to planes, and his appearance and those of other celebrities made urban terminals especially good places for people watching. And, too, "sure enough big shots," including railroad executives, investment bankers, and "whistle stopping" politicians, rode the rails, usually in their posh private cars coupled to the ends of scheduled trains. "There [was] . . . an excitement about seeing the famous at a train station or on a train," recalled an Ohio reporter. "I found this to be a benefit of my job."[31]

The aura of train travel also involved the chance for a different dining environment. Money-conscious passengers commonly brought food. "We always packed our own eats in a large wicker basket when we traveled to California," remembered a former railroad station agent. "My wife fixed quantities of fried chicken, meat sandwiches, cakes and cookies. It was always great fun to munch as we watched the miles fly by." Some bought liquid refreshments and snacks from car attendants or news butchers, "butches," boys who also peddled reading materials, including copies of Thomas Jackson's famous humor books, and oddments. But dinner in the diner was a high point for many. Observed a Maine businessman, "I always think of a good meal when I think of a train trip . . . for me, that's the romance of the rails." Meals, usually comparably priced with the better restaurants, were often elegant and delightfully presented. For example, dinner onboard the crack North-Western Limited for Saturday, June 29, 1907 (the railroad printed a new menu daily), offered a choice of caviar on toast, littleneck clams, potage Richmond and Consomme en Tasse for appetizers; fried lake perch, boiled Orange Blossom ham, prime roast of beef, or roast crystal spring duckling for the main course; and neapolitian ice cream, assorted cakes, cheeses, or cherry pie for dessert. The wine list was extensive as was the variety of beverages. The menu noted that "After-dinner Coffee Served in Composite Car if Desired." Dining on the Missouri-Kansas-Texas Railroad was so popular in the late 1940s that residents of San Antonio, after church, boarded the Katy Limited for the 83 mile, two hour and twenty-five minute ride to Austin, so that they could enjoy a tasty Sunday meal in a leisurely, pleasant manner; diners returned home on the southbound Texas Special, which conveniently left the capital city at 3:20 P.M.[32]

*I*f they were to take the train, riders needed to know how to use the services provided. Travel could be made simple. The local depot agent commonly planned itineraries and supplied timetables and travel folders, which were distributed at no charge by the railroad companies. At first roads were small and their schedules appeared on printed cards or on broadsides posted on station walls. As railroads grew with "system building" following the Civil War, so did the size of their timetables. Publishers, too, exploited the ever-increasing rail-travel market to sell guide books and timetable directories.[33]

The most popular and enduring travel aid was the *Official Guide of the Railways.* Launched by the New York-based National Railway Publishing Company in June 1868, this monthly compendium of railroad schedules, carriers, and stations served both the active and armchair traveler. Readers found more than the practical in the thick publication, richly illustrated with maps; readers could easily fantasize about trips on the Chicago & Eastern Illinois's Dixieland and Dixie Flyer, the Lackawanna's Pocono Express and Owl, or the Norfolk & Western's Cavalier and Poca-hontas. Many individuals admitted the quiet pleasures that they received from browsing through "the" *Guide.* Alfred Hitchcock, the movie direc-tor, once remarked that if he were stranded on a desert island, he wanted a copy.[34]

As with other forms of transport some rail riders relied heavily on word-of-mouth for instructions on how to take a trip. Certain advice seemed universal. Parents continually warned their children not to speak to strang-ers. Young women, most of all, were told to avoid drummers (traveling salesmen), soldiers, or others who might seduce them. Older travelers, too, might receive caveats about pick- pockets, con-artists and the like, espe-cially on crowded trains or in congested terminals. And the elderly might be urged to take a walking cane, whether needed or not, "so they will receive special consideration from fellow travelers."[35]

Written instructions, too, were common, particularly before long-dis-tance telephone service. On January 22, 1882, Julia Pardee, who lived in Carrolltown, Louisiana, wrote to her sister in Wadsworth, Ohio, about how best to make the 1,150 mile, forty-six hour trip from Ohio to Louisi-ana. As Julia Pardee said:

> I suppose the best route will be by way of Penn. & Ohio R.R. [New York, Pennsylvania & Ohio] to Cincinnati, leaving in the morning, you should reach Cincinnati about 5 P.M. Before getting there a baggage man passes through the cars when you can buy omnibus tickets for the Little Miami depot, and he will tell you the number of the omnibus to take. You must also get of him transfer checks for baggage. After getting into the 'bus you will be jolted and bounced quite a long distance over to the other depot, and will get out very near a little eating house opening toward the car tracks where we almost always stop, instead of going upstairs to the ladies waiting room. It is more convenient to the ticket office, sleeping car office, baggage, etc. You can get supper there and then some of the waiters will kindly direct you where you can find these offices where you will find the trunks and the sleeping car. You ought to telegraph to Cincinnati in the morning for sleeping car accommodations. A section comprising an upper and lower birth will be $12 from Cincinnati to N.O. [New Orleans]. If not very large two people can sleep on lower berth. Don and Peter have slept on the upper berth and Belle and I in the lower, but we generally take a section and a half. From Cincinnati probably you had better come via the Louisville & Nashville R.R. That is, by way of Mobile [Alabama]. If you can get through tickets and through checks for trunks from Akron, of course you would be saved some trouble and if you get excursion tickets I suppose they will be through tickets. I wrote to Don this morning that Father Pardee talked of coming and I think he will write to him concerning route, etc. There will be so many of you in the party that I think you

would find great comfort in an alcohol lamp, and so make your own tea. You will find very miserable tea and coffee along the way, and if the train gets behind as it often does you may not get any breakfast before ten or dinner before 3, and then a lunch basket is very convenient, and the porter will set up a table for you. You must be sure to have the sleeping car, otherwise there will be changes and great discomfort.[36]

The Pardee letter correctly suggests that carriers by the 1880s had developed internal support mechanisms to make trips by rail less stressful. Not only did major stations provide ever-present and ever-courteous "red caps," but they housed personnel of omnibus and transfer companies to facilitate ease of movement between terminals and other facilities. Some railroad and union station companies furnished attendants in specially designed "Ladies' Waiting Rooms" and in emigrant reception centers, and all railroads supported the work of the Traverler's Aid Society. In the age of streamliners, leading trains, for example, the City of San Francisco and the Twentieth Century Limited, included uniformed nurses or similar personnel to assist passengers, particularly the very young and the very old.

Although the elegance of intercity trains faded after the 1950s, some of the amenities historically associated with first-class rail travel remain. Amtrak recently experimented with the return to china and linen in some dining cars, and it has introduced movies and telephones on some trains. But, most of all, the public took delight in the fall of 1989, when luxury dining and sleeping cars, with their pampering crews, appeared as the American-European Express, which runs five times per week between Chicago and Washington, D.C.[37]

The railroad corridor once contained a variety of eating and lodging facilities designed for the pleasure of patrons. Likely the best remembered are the Harvey House restaurants that were found in or near the larger depots along the principal lines of the Atchison, Topeka & Santa Fe (Santa Fe) and the St. Louis-San Francisco (Frisco) railroads. The Fred Harvey Company, named after the founder Frederick "Fred" Henry Harvey, developed, in the 1880s, a chain of establishments that served good food with expert service. "Harvey Girls," the firm's neatly dressed and well-trained waitresses, pleased the public and ultimately became the subject of a popular Hollywood film of the 1940s. Other carriers also provided food services ("e" for eats marked the public timetables) or relied on nearby cafes and hotels to feed the hungry. A few stations, usually the largest, followed the European practice of offering sleeping space within their structures. Even country villages had a boarding house or two, and most towns had at least one hotel conveniently located to trackside.[38]

Most Americans could afford trips by train. Of course, frequent, long-distance ones might be beyond the reach of many pocketbooks. But for shorter rides, costs were usually inexpensive. Popular agitation for rate reductions from the 1870s into the early part of the twentieth century led to stringent governmental regulation of maximum ticket prices, and increased competition among carriers further reduced charges. In 1929, at the height of rail usage, the average revenue per passenger mile was 2.808 cents, then it sank to a low of 1.753 cents in 1941, and slowly climbed back to 2.880 cents in 1958. So, three decades later, railroads continued to use essentially their 1929 tariffs even though their costs soared in the post-World War II period.[39]

Other factors also produced travel bargains. Railroads commonly provided cheap excursion rates or offered other travel incentives for special runs. They usually advertised these marked-down prices in local newspapers or even on broadsides tacked to depot walls or adjacent poles and trees. The Toledo & Ohio Central announced with handbills its "Home-Going Excursion" of Sunday, May 13, 1906, between the Ohio communities of Toledo, Bucyrus, Mt. Gilead, Centerburg, and Thurston. A special train would leave Toledo at 7:30 A.M., arriving in Thurston at 12:40 P.M. and leaving there at 5:30 P.M. with a 10:15 P.M. arrival back in Toledo. Round-trip tickets from Toledo to Bucyrus cost $1.00, Centerburg, $1.25, and Thurston, $1.50, and the company noted that "Excursion Tickets [will be] sold from intermediate stations at above rates, except where regular rate between any two stations is less—then regular tickets will be sold for this train."[40]

For regularly scheduled passenger trains, companies often offered "coupon books." Usually these were sold for 1,000 miles of travel on lines of cooperating carriers. The advantages, especially to commercial travelers were several: coupon books were customarily sold at a discount; they reduced the need to carry large amounts of cash (this, after-all, was the pre-credit card era); and they permitted holders to alter their itineraries easily.[41]

At times, free trips were available without the need to ride the rods. Prior to enactment of the Elkins Anti-Rebate Act of 1903, railroads gave free annual or trip passes to shippers, politicians, journalists, ministers, and other friends. Admittedly, the favored appreciated, even expected this practice, but carriers regarded it as a nuisance and a cash drain. (After 1903 only railroad employees, active and retired, enjoyed the benefits of complementary travel.) Even if one were not properly connected to a railroad, as incentives to shoppers, merchants might pay all or part of a ticket to their communities. In 1893, a Kansas City, Missouri, businessman, for example, announced that he would give free transportation to every person within a 100-mile radius who purchased five dollars' worth of merchandise in his store.[42]

Whether taking a trip to buy a suit of clothes or to visit relatives, travel by train once captivated and involved Americans. Rails could be "magic carpets," or as George Stephenson, the English railroad inventor, rightly prophesied early in the nineteenth century: "[They] will become the great highways for the King and all his subjects." While the nature of railroading has changed markedly during the past several decades—for one thing, it is no longer possible to reach most destinations by flanged wheel—passenger trains continue to be part of the nation's transportation picture. "Train time" still causes the heart to quicken, and love of this transport form seemingly knows neither geographical nor generational bounds.[43]

NOTES

1. *New York Times*, March 13, 1989; *Cleveland Plain Dealer*, September 5, 1989.

2. H. Roger Grant and Charles W. Bohi, *The Country Railroad Station In America* (Sioux Falls: Center for Western Studies, 1988), pp. 1–15.

3. S. T. Bledsoe, "Santa Fe Passenger Service," *The Santa Fe Magazine*, 21(February 1927):33.

4. Richard C. Overton, *Burlington Route: A History of the Burlington Lines* (New York: Alfred A. Knopf, 1965), pp. 393–98.

5. David P. Morgan, "Who Shot the Passenger Train?" *Trains*, 19(April 1959):14–51; Peter Lyon, *To Hell in a Day Coach: An Exasperated Look at American Railroads* (Philadelphia: J. B. Lippincott Company, 1968), pp. 179–82, 239–43.

6. Edd H. Bailey, *A Life with the Union Pacific: The Autobiography of Edd H. Bailey* (St. Johnsbury, Vermont.: Saltillo Press, 1989), pp. 123, 124.

7. *DERECO, Inc., Annual Report, 1969* (Cleveland, 1970), p. 6.

8. J. M. Smith to Don Hofsommer, March 29, 1985, copy in possession of author.

9. Lyon, *To Hell in a Day Coach*, p. 223; Ralph W. Hidy et al., *The Great Northern Railway: A History* (Boston: Harvard Business School Press, 1988), pp. 121–30.

10. John H. White, Jr., *The American Railroad Passenger Car* (Baltimore: The Johns Hopkins University Press, 1978), pp. 3– 20, 26–30; *American Railway Review*, May 31, 1860, p. 328.

11. White, *American Railroad Passenger Car*, p. 35; Chicago & North-Western public timetable, April 1, 1885.

12. White, *American Railroad Passenger Car*, pp. 117–200 (quotation on p. 185); *Evening Huronite* (Huron, S.D.), October 16, 1940.

13. C. Van Woodward, *The Strange Career of Jim Crow* (New York: Oxford University Press, 1966), pp. 18–19, 70–72; Lucius Beebe, *Mixed Train Daily* (Berkeley, California: Howell-North, 1961), p. 32.

14. White, *American Railroad Passenger Car*, pp. 203–85 (quotation on p. 245).

15. Chicago, Burlington & Quincy Railroad, "America's Distinctive Trains: The New 12 Car Denver Zephyr" (1937), n.p.

16. Ibid.; Rock Island and Southern Pacific railroads, "On the Californian" (1937), p. 2.

17. Chicago, Milwaukee & St. Paul Railway, *Between Chicago & Omaha*: *The Chicago & Omaha Short Line* (Chicago: C.M.&St.P Ry., 1900), pp. 2, 4; John R. Stilgore, *Metropolitan Corridor*: *Railroads and the American Scene* (New Haven: Yale University Press, 1983), pp. 51–71.

18. New York Central System, *The New 20th Century Limited* (New York: Bodley Printers, 1938), p. 3.

19. H. Roger Grant, *Self-Help in the 1890s Depression* (Ames: Iowa State University Press, 1983), pp. 3–22.

20. Roger A. Bruns, *Knights of the Road*: *A Hobo History* (New York: Methuen, 1980), pp. 26–60; Charles P. Brown, *Brownie the Boomer*: *The Life of Chas. P. Brown a Boomer Railroad Man* (Whittier, California: Western Printing Corporation, 1930), pp. 48–49.

21. *New York Times*, May 10, 12, 1893.

22. "The Pace That Kills," *World's Work*, 13(March 1907):85–96; Robert B. Shaw, *A History of Railroad Accidents, Safety Precautions and Operating Practices* (Potsdam, New York: The Vail-Ballou Press, 1978), pp. 125–27.

23. William E. Griswold, "Who Will Ride These Trains?" *Railway Age*, 164(May 20, 1968):25–31; Robert G. Lewis, "Metroliner Diary," *Railway Age*, 166(February 24, 1969):19.

24. Beebe, *Mixed Train Daily*, pp. 1–7. See also Eugene Alvarez, *Travel on Southern Antebellum Railroads, 1828–1860* (Tuscaloosa: University of Alabama Press, 1974).

25. W. K. McNeil, ed., *On a Slow Train Through Arkansas* (Lexington: The University Press of Kentucky, 1985), p. 35.

26. B. A. Botkin and Alvin F. Harlow, eds., *A Treasury of Railroad Folklore* (New York: Crown Publishers, 1953), p. 506; Clifton E. Hull, *Shortline Railroads of Arkansas* (Norman: University of Oklahoma Press, 1969), pp. 54–112.

27. Norma Millay, ed., *Collected Poems of Edna St. Vincent Millay* (New York: Harper & Row, 1956), p. 78.

28. Chicago & North Western, *Taking the Chicago & North Western Railway* (Chicago: Poole Brothers, 1915), pp. 4, 11.

29. *Crawfordsville* (Indiana) *Review*, August 24, 1889.

30. Clipping (undated) from the *New York Tribune*, 1927, in possession of author; Sherwood Anderson, *Sherwood Anderson's Memoirs* (New York: Harcourt, Brace & Company, 1942), p. 36.

31. *Akron Beacon Journal*, June 28, 1978.

32. Dan Knight to author, September 14, 1985; Will C. Hollister, *Dinner on the Diner* (Corona del Mar, California: Trans-Anglo Books, 1965).

33. H. Roger Grant, "The Railroad Station Agent in Small-Town Iowa," *The Palimpsest*, 64(May/June 1983):93–102.

34. Botkin and Harlow, *A Treasury of Railroad Folklore*, pp. 518–20.

35. Erie Railroad, *Your Trip to New York City* (Cleveland: Erie Railroad Company, 1937), p. 2.

36. Julia Pardee to Carrie Pardee, January 22, 1882, in possession of author.

37. *New York Times*, September 8, 1989; *Washington Post*, November 15, 1989.

38. Keith L. Bryant, Jr., *History of the Atchison, Topeka and Santa Fe*

Railway (New York: Macmillan Publishing Company, 1974), pp. 109–22; Frank P. Donovan, Jr., "The Minneapolis & St. Louis Railway," *The Palimpsest*, 32(July 1951):264.

39. Morgan, "Who Shot the Passenger Train?" p. 44.

40. Toledo & Ohio Central Railroad, "Home-Going Excursion," May 13, 1906.

41. Erie Railroad, "Using a Coupon Book" (ca. 1915).

42. Lewis Atherton, *Main Street on the Middle Border* (Bloomington: Indiana University Press, 1954), pp. 230–31.

43. Morgan, "Who Shot the Passenger Train?" p. 14.

We Took the Train

SUMMER ARRANGEMENT.

Cleveland to N. York.

Cheapest, and Most Comfortable Route;

TO

NEW YORK & BOSTON

And as quick as by any other Route, and the only sure route of making connections,

BY THE

Lake Shore & New York & Erie

RAIL ROAD

Via Dunkirk,

Over one of the finest Roads in the United States, being six foot guage, with wide, roomy cars, and more than one-third of the Road DOUBLE TRACK.

Five Daily Passenger Trains Leave Dunkirk, (except Sundays.)

1ST. TELEGRAPH DAY EXPRESS TRAIN,	- -	leaves at 5.00 A. M.
2ND. LAKE ERIE "	" "	" 5.00 "
3RD. MAIL TRAIN,	- - - -	" " 9.30 "
4TH. NIGHT EXPRESS TRAIN,	- - - -	" " 3.00 P. M.
5TH. CINCINNATI AND CHICAGO LIGHTNING TRAIN,	"	" 9.45 "

Only one Train on Sunday, Evening Express, at 3,00 P. M.

Fare from Cleveland to New York, $11.00.
Fare from Cleveland to New York, Second Class, - - 7.60.

Lake Shore Rail Road Trains leave Cleveland as follows,
(SUNDAYS EXCEPTED.)

1st. EXPRESS MAIL TRAIN, 7.30 A. M.

Connects at Dunkirk with 3.00 P. M. Night Express, and arrive in New York at 9.00 next morn.

2d. Cincinnati and Chicago LIGHTNING EXPRESS, 3.45 P. M.

Connects at Dunkirk with the Lightning Express at 9 45 P. M. Passengers by this Train arrive in New York at 2.20 P. M.

In Advance of any other Route.
3d. NIGHT EXPRESS TRAIN, 8.15 P. M.

Connects at Dunkirk with the 5.00 A. M. Telegraph Day Express, arriving in New York at 10.00 same evening.

Passengers for Boston have the choice of 3 different Routes from N. York, by Steamer or R. R.

This being the only Route by which Passengers from Cleveland at 3.45 P. M., on Saturdays, go through direct and arrive in New York Sunday, at 2.20 P. M.

Passengers taking the Boat from Cleveland will connect at Buffalo with the 8.00 A. M Lightning Express Train, on the Buffalo & N. Y. City, and N. Y. & Erie Rail Road, and arrive in New York at 10.00, same evening.

Fare from Cleveland to New York, Meals & Berths Included on Steamboat, $10

Passengers that wish to go by the way of Niagara Falls, can procure through Tickets that way, for 50 cts. in addition to the regular fare.

The cars of the Lake Shore Road run into the Depot of the N. Y. and Erie Rail Road at Dunkirk.

Baggage checked from Cleveland to Dunkirk, and from thence to New York. NO CHARGE FOR HANDLING BAGGAGE.

Passengers will procure Through Tickets at the Office of the Lake Shore Rail Road, or at the Company's Office, foot of River Street.

Merchants will please call on J. H. MOORE, No. 1 Courtland street, with whom they can contract for Transporting Merchandise on the most favorable terms.

J. NOTTINGHAM.	**CHAS. MINOT,**
WESTERN AGENT, CLEVELAND.	SUPERINTENDENT.
Office foot of River Street.	

The
Iron
Horse
Arrives

Broadside "Summer Arrangement" for
through service between New York City
and Cleveland, Ohio, via the New York &
Erie (Erie) and Cleveland, Painesville &
Ashtabula (Lake Shore) railroads, ca. 1855.

Broadside timetable from New York State's Ithaca & Owego Rail Road (subsequently part of the Delaware, Lackawanna & Western), July 20, 1838.

Below. This photograph, taken in Washington, D.C. in May 1936, shows America's most remembered early steam locomotive, the one-ton Tom Thumb. Built by Peter Cooper in New York in 1829, this engine was tested on the Baltimore & Ohio Railroad in 1830.

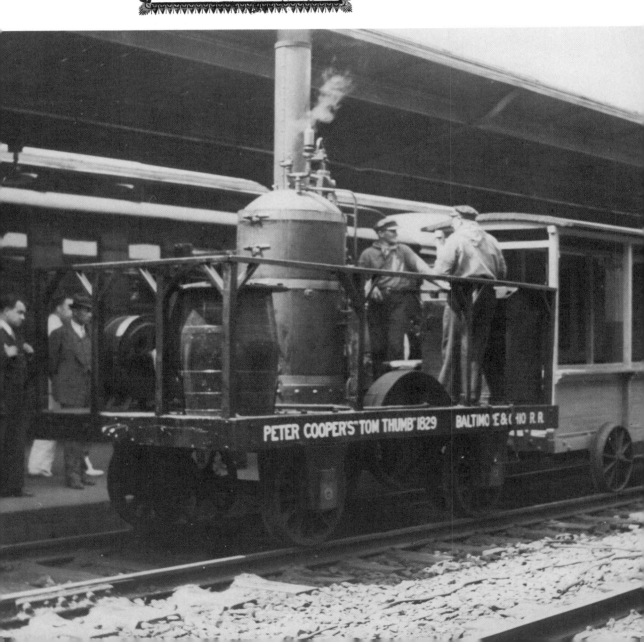

GREETINGS FROM HISTORIC ALBANY

THE FIRST RAILROAD TRAIN IN AMERICA. RUNNING BETWEEN ALBANY AND SCHENECTADY IN 1831

The Mohawk & Hudson Railroad's DeWitt Clinton, a replica of which is shown in a picture-postal card from the early twentieth century, was the third American-built locomotive. Produced by New York's West Point Foundry, this much-heralded "teakettle" made a trial run in July 1831 and began pulling trains of stagecoach-like cars a month later.

Below. Card-type timetable from the Boston & Worcester Rail Road (later Boston & Albany), December 25, 1852.

BOSTON & WORCESTER RAIL ROAD.

NOTICE.

AN EXPRESS TRAIN FOR

NEW YORK

May be expected to leave Boston, to-morrow, SUNDAY,
At 4 P.M., reaching Worcester at 5,
Springfield at....6.20,
New Haven at.....7.50,
New York at...10 P.M.

G. TWICHELL, Sup't.

Boston, Dec. 25th, 1852.

Narrative of an Excursion on the Baltimore & Ohio Railroad

1

Author Unknown

At the dawn of the railway age enormous interest centered on all aspects of this novel and exciting means of transport. "How fast do trains go?" "What can you see?" and "What are your impressions?" were some of the questions people asked of the earliest travelers.

One of America's pioneer pikes, the Baltimore & Ohio Railroad (B. & O.), began passenger service between Pratt Street in Baltimore and Ellicott's Mills, Maryland, 13 miles to the west, in May 1830. And on December 1, 1831, track reached Frederick, Maryland, 61 miles west of Baltimore. Initially, the company operated horse-drawn freight and passenger trains like other contemporary railroads, but the line acquired a steam locomotive, the 7 1/2 ton Atlantic, in the summer of 1832. Animal power soon disappeared.

The comments of an unknown traveler on the newly opened road in 1832 describe vividly the condition of the primitive Baltimore & Ohio. He was especially interested in the firm's operations; its over-all construction, particularly its bridges; and, of course, the scenery. Resembling other early rail riders, he noted the road's timetables and rates of charge. Like others, too, this traveler was optimistic about the future of transportation by flanged wheel. He had every reason to be so sanguine. In this case, the B. & O. grew rapidly and became a giant corporation by the end of the nineteenth century. By the 1890s the B. & O. sported a 3,200-mile system that linked thirteen eastern and midwestern states, and it operated some of the nation's finest and fastest passenger and freight trains.

Started from the office of the Railroad Company, in Pratt Street, on Thursday morning, 13th March, 1832, at half past nine o'clock, in one of the four cars running together, the number of the passengers amounting to eighty, and each car drawn by a single horse. The atmosphere clear and cool, our course due west for about half a mile on that street, in the middle of which a single rail-track has been laid on granite blocks. Reached the old depot, at the upper extremity of the said street, where we changed our course to a south-west direction. This depot stands sixty-six feet above tide water, and forms the commencement of the first section of the road.* For the distance of eight miles, the location of this road runs on a perfect level, except that through the three deep cuts, where small summits are introduced to secure the drainage from the road, the remainder of the road lies on various grades. This part of the section of the road was the most expensive, owing to the hilly surface of the ground. Passed by the scales on which cars are weighed when carrying burdens, to ascertain the tonnage of their loads. This ingenious construction deserves notice.

We rode on the first embankment of this road, to the left of which we noticed a house, of somewhat Gothic construction, where sulphur waters are found. We passed through the first cut of the road, and soon rode over the Carrollton Viaduct, about one mile and a half from Pratt Street.

CARROLLTON VIADUCT

This viaduct, of which a handsome view is here given, has but a single arch of 80 feet span, sprung over Gwynn's Falls, or Creek, and forms a solid and beautiful superstructure of granite stone, 65 feet high, and 300 feet long. Entered soon after on another excavation, and came in sight of a wooden bridge, of a new and ingenious construction, laid on abutments resting on the said excavation, which serves for a passage to the turnpike road from Baltimore to Washington, and we found, thus far, that this mode of travelling, sometimes over ridges, at other times in deep artificial chasms, now over bridges, and soon after under them, was quite a novelty, and highly interesting.

After awhile we again changed our course to the west, and some distance further we entered the largest cut on this road. Its height is 70 feet perpendicular, on which account it is not improperly called the Deep Cut. It forms the most expensive portion of the works on this gigantic undertaking. Immediately after, we passed over the two highest embankments of this route; the largest of the two is on Gadsby's Run, at the end of which we again crossed the Washington Turnpike; but this time on a level. A little further, being accounted six miles from Pratt Street, which is the distance fixed for the relay, the horses were changed in the short space of two minutes. Refreshments are here kept for the

---

*Although the laying of the first stone on the Baltimore & Ohio Railroad occurred on July 4, 1828, track did not appear until October 1829. On May 24, 1830, passenger service began over the thirteen miles of line between downtown Baltimore and Ellicott's Mills, Maryland.

accommodation of travellers. From this part of the road an extensive view is obtained over the country below, of mills, and a forge on Patapsco River, and farther down, of Elk Ridge Landing. One mile further on we passed in sight of the Avalon Iron Works, on the small, but beautiful Patapsco River. Here the eight miles of the dead level ends; and we began to ascend, at the grades of 13 to 17 feet per mile. Having reached the borders of the river, we had on our right several abrupt and rocky hills, the bases of which have been cut to open a passage for this road; and soon came in sight of the noted Buzzard Rock, the summit of which is at least 100 feet above the river. Still further on, we entered the hand-some—

PATTERSON VIADUCT

This viaduct is built across the river. It has four arches, forming a super-structure of fine granite stone, of 360 feet in length. Its height is 40 feet above the water mark.

After having passed this viaduct, we found ourselves on the left bank of the stream, and we never lost sight of handsome scenery. On the right, we had in view the Thistle Cotton Factory, the property of the Messrs. Morris. To the left, a fine prospect of woodland scenery delighted our eyes, consisting of gigantic oaks, luxuriantly growing on the several hills, inclining towards the river, the ascent of which begins at both banks, right and left of the stream, and progressively rise, by unequal steps; and whilst these hills extend about 3 miles from the river each way, and when at the highest elevation they are about 300 feet above the water mark of the stream; they form a considerable hollow or valley, 6 miles in breadth and 300 feet deep, having the stream in the centre along its course.

Met, here and there, as we proceeded, several considerable cuts, made into the large masses of granite rocks, for the passage of the road, from which Baltimore is partly supplied, and by being worked by many artificers, the scene was considerably enlivened. Now to the right, we viewed another cotton factory, remarkable for the height of one of its buildings, and for having a handsome artificial fall of water. It is situated like the preceding, on the other side of the river, and belongs of Mr. Edward Gray.

ELLICOTTS' MILLS

Arrived at Ellicotts' Mills, 10 miles by the turnpike from Baltimore, where a relay was waiting for us. We travelled the distance, from the place of our departure to this spot, in one hour and thirty minutes, nearly 14 miles, which is at the rate of about 9 miles an hour. From the three arch stone Oliver's Viaduct, built here through an embankment, raised on the site of this place, for giving passage to a run, as well as for the Baltimore and Frederick Turnpike, we had the pleasure of observing the difference between the slow paced vehicles passing below us on the turnpike, and the easy and rapid movement of our cars. This spot of ground, as containing an academy for classical education, several large stone houses, stores, two splendid hotels, a number of flour, merchant, linseed, and other mills, richly deserves the name of town. Indeed, laying aside the immense worth of these useful establishments, the neatness of the handsome group of buildings of different sizes, forms, and colours, located at the intersection of the river Patapsco, and of the rail and turnpike roads; the two great thoroughfares of the west of this vast continent, and at the foot of a high and picturesque scenery, attract the attention and admiration of the traveller.

Leaving, with regret, this romantic spot, we immediately entered the second section of this road, the grades of which are various, but none higher than 21 feet per mile; and as soon as we reached the banks of the river again, our eyes were feasted with the sight of more splendid scenery than before. To the right, we viewed the covered bridge of the turnpike, and we could but admire, at a few rods upwards, a most brilliant sheet of water formed by a dam, which, rising the stream, pours its argentine contents from the brims of its smooth surface into the rugged one below. This dam turns part of the water of said river into a canal, which glides through the lower part of the town, and imparts motion and life to the machinery it meets in its course. The scenery, on progressing a few steps farther, is new and striking, by reason of the sight of a large opening, cut through a solid and rocky spur, which opposed the passage of the road. The east side, called the Tarpean Rock, stands isolated on the banks of the river, the bulky head of which, projecting several feet out of the perpendicular, menaces destruction. The other side has nothing remarkable but its height, which is about 80 feet, and for having the name of the constructor of the work chiseled on its large forehead.

To the left, after the passage through the above chasm, our eyes were immediately fixed on a magnificent cascade, making the greatest contrast imaginable with the stable looking establishment adjoining, which is a rolling-mill, situated on the very banks of the opposite side of the river, and belonging to the Messrs. Ellicotts.

Pursuing our course about a quarter of a mile further, the splendor of another artificial water-fall, indicates the good purpose for which it was formed. It sets in motion the machinery of the Union Cotton Factory, belonging to a company in Baltimore; which, with some surrounding buildings, constitutes a handsome landscape. The view farther up the river offers a very different aspect. We entered a woody and narrow defile, and found ourselves hemmed, as it were, within the enclosure of hills and steeps, cut asunder for the passage of the road, and in vain, alas!

should we have looked here for a retreat—none could we have obtained but under the shelter of the trees. However, we were at last relieved, by our course, from that painful situation, by the agreeable sight of the industry of man. It is a new building, situated in this forlorn forest on the banks of the purling stream, and prepared for a cotton factory. This untenanted building owes its mushroom birth to the railroad. Farther up the stream we met, with delight, a cottage where man dwells. Could it be otherwise? Every object around him seemed to smile! To our astonishment we met here among these steep hills what is seen only on flat and good soil. I mean lime stone and lime kiln, they belong to Judge Dorsey; they will be of great service along the course of the railroad and to Baltimore.

Two wooden bridges are seen on this river, and at some distance apart. One of them nearly worn out by age—the other, probably a temporary one, and the property of the individual who owns the woodland on the opposite side of the river. This conclusion is drawn from a rail track, laid on said bridge, and from some piles of fire-wood, lying along side of this road, prepared for the Baltimore market, which, without this railroad, had never been removed from its natural soil.

Opposite to this place the river forks at a small distance from the road— the left fork is called the Western, or Poplar Spring Branch. It is opposite to this fork that the second section of the road ends. The third section we enter after this ascends at various grades, but none higher than 37 feet per mile. At this place the horses are changed, being 12 miles from Ellicotts' Mills; and at a small distance therefrom, passed the said branch over a stone viaduct, where it now runs to our left.

HALF-WAY HOUSE

Arrived at the half-way house, where we stopped for dinner. Here the ground is 368 feet above tide water, and 31 1/4 miles from Baltimore depot, in Pratt Street, near the basin, and 30 miles from Frederick. Both the tavern and plantation belong to Mr. Sykes, hence the name Sykesville has been given it. It is well situated, having its front immediately on the road, and its opposite side on the borders of the stream. A merchant mill is seen at a little distance from it. Two miles further we changed horses; and here, on account of the country being high and healthy, one feels emerged from the heavy atmosphere of a narrow and deep valley through which we have pursued our course, and on account of the surface being less inclined than the side of the hills, at the foot of which we passed, man is encouraged to pursue the useful and noble employment of the culture of the soil. At this part of the road they have raised a small embankment, which, by barring the too meandering course of the branch, causes it to follow another channel, and having lost a portion of its strength, and with it the power of erosion, instead of corroding, as it does below the forks, the crust of our globe, and having formed by degrees, in the course of ages, the deep valley through which we passed, serves here to enliven the scene, by forming mill ponds and cascades, as well as passing among the fields, and watering the meadows in its course.

We passed two mills, separated by no great distance. The small falls, as well as the reservoirs they form above them, give an agreeable zest to the view. At the distance of 38 miles from Pratt Street, a change of horses takes place, where stabling has not yet been provided. About this part, granite rocks no more delight the prospect; owing to the approach of a ridge in front of us, the stones of which generally partake of those standing on mountains, called quartz, forming the heads of streams. Here the sight of a handsome farm strikes the view with delight. It is the property of Mr. Cornelius Mercer.

Being now near the head of the branch, which we have followed closely so far, we rode over an embankment, crossing, nearly at right angles, the Baltimore and Frederick Turnpike; at the end of which we arrived at the foot of the inclined plane. A viaduct has been erected through this embankment, for the passage of the said turnpike.

Here two horses are added to each car, to effect the ascent over the plane. We thought the expense, in regard to this mode, too great, on account of the quantity of horses and attendants required for such an arduous undertaking. However, it ought to be observed that the present arrangement is to be considered merely on a temporary footing, until the power of a stationary engine is applied at the head of the inclined plane, which will draw up and let down the cars.*

FOOT OF THE PLANE

From the foot of this plane we changed our course in a westerly direction, and ascended the inclined plane, which is upwards of 1 1/2 miles long, by several steps or grades. The height of this plane is 179 feet. Arrived at the summit of the plane, called Parr Spring Ridge, where an area is found 600 feet diameter, and on which the stationary engine is to be located. We stayed here for a minute or two, to fix the breakers under the body of the cars, for preventing too precipitous a descent. For this purpose, a trusty man is placed behind the car, to assist in the regulation of the wheels, by bearing on them, in proportion to the grades of the descent of the plane; this area is the highest place on the route, being

---

*Use of inclined planes on America's early railroads was commonplace. In this case the Baltimore & Ohio constructed inclined planes west of Ellicott's Mills, for the grade exceeded 2 percent, much steeper than the ruling grade of 0.6 percent. In 1834 the B. & O. discovered, quite by accident, that a steam locomotive could ascend the inclined planes with a moderate load. "The event really ended the use of horse power on the Baltimore and Ohio," concludes the company's historian John F. Stover.

813 feet perpendicular above tide water, and forms the end of the three sections. From this, the prospect is extensive, chiefly to the west side, where it is terminated by both the remote sight of the Cotoctin and Blue Ridge, about 18 miles distant, and of the South Mountain, this last being about 6 miles further to the west, and being 1,200 feet above tide water, or 200 feet higher than the Cotoctin Ridge, it is, of course, perceived above the latter. Below the summit of this ridge, there is a valley; the name of which is commonly taken from the river which waters it, and it is called Monococy. This stream probably formed that valley, by the assistance of its collateral branches, the rains being both the mechanical and chemical agents, as I will presently show. This valley is at the present time about 700 feet deep, in the lowest place, and will become still deeper on account of the rains, which wash away the earth from its surface into the various branches. These convey it into the Monococy, and at last it reaches the sea, where it is deposited. Whilst the top of the mountains, at the same time as being composed of a rocky substance, cannot be depressed, of course they remain nearly entire, and of the same height. The same depression takes place in the beds of streams, although they be composed of a solid stony substance, as they nearly all are on this side of the Allegheny mountains; because the fragments of hard matter, detached from the summit of ridges by the frost, the water being then the chemical agent, causing a separation of the parts, they roll on the bed of the said streams, and scrape and file them off, according to the degree of velocity, given by both the bulk and gravity of the water received in them in time of floods; hence the Monococy, as receiving in its bosom both the waters, as well as the corroding agents of its collateral branches, must grow deeper in due proportion.

DESCENDING FROM THE PLANE

We now descend 240 feet in the distance of 1 1/2 miles, by various steps or grades—having the turnpike road at no more than 500 or 600 feet from us, and we followed it, always in sight nearly in a parallel line, for the above distance. Arrived at the foot of the plane, where the man, weighing on the breaker, left the cars. We then descended towards Monococy River, 11 miles distant, by various grades, but none exceeding 37 feet per mile, except in two instances where the descent is 52 feet per mile, and we followed the valley of Bush Creek nearly as far as its mouth, which is into Monococy River between the viaduct of this road, on that river and the bridge on the turnpike of Frederick to Washington city.

On this side of the ridge, the prospect changes, on account of the view being no more intercepted by woodlands. Of course it becomes more interesting and owing to the greater inclination of the surface of the road, than the other side of the ridge, we went at the rate of 10 miles an hour. Two miles further, met a train of cars, loaded principally with flour, and having but one track on the road, we were obliged to retrograde from some distance, until we arrived at a turn-out—a circumstance far from being pleasing, but this will not happen when the road shall have two tracks.

Reached the bed of Bush Creek, over which we passed by means of a stone viaduct. From this spot, the railroad recedes from the turnpike, until it reaches the Monococy; at which place they are 2 1/2 miles apart— but the railroad approaches it gradually, until it again joins it in Patrick Street, Frederick City.

Now several grist and other mills are seen at no great distance from one another, and causes a diversity in the prospect. Here the valley is wider than the one below the forks of Patapsco. This circumstance has given more latitude, than in the former valley, to the engineers of this road. On this account its course is here straighter, and the curves are so well formed, that the eye of the traveller is thereby delighted. Passed by a slate (shistus) quarry, and soon after changed horses, on the very border of the said creek, and on account of the country having, as we approached Monococy, higher features, several rocky spurs are met which have been depressed, and form as many steep cuts, which enhances the beauty of the scenery.

Met at last the river Monococy, and passed it over a handsome wooden viaduct erected on stone piers, and in sight of the Washington Turnpike road bridge. The viaduct is 350 feet long and 37 feet above water mark. The stream is here 296 feet above tide water, and 30 feet higher than the water in the Potomac, at the Point of Rocks. On the other side of the viaduct, we rode over a high embankment of about 300 feet long, at the end of which we reached the fork of this road. The right goes to Frederick—the left to the Point of Rocks, 11 miles from this spot, and passes over one of the most fertile lime stone valleys in the United States. It is nearly on a level, and in sight of handsome mountain scenery. This road is intersected first by Balingers, and after by Tuscarora creeks.

We pursued our journey on the right fork, which is called the lateral road, 3 1/2 miles distant from Frederick over a fertile lime stone soil, in sight of the majestic scenery of the Blue Ridge.

We ascended from the forks for a distance of 1 1/4 miles, at the rate of 30 feet per mile, and descended the remainder of the distance, at the rate of 18 feet per mile; in the pleasing sight of steeples and numerous fine buildings.

Arrived safe at half past 5 o'clock, at the depot, within the limits of Frederick city, on the borders of Carroll's Creek, after having travelled 8 hours, extremely well satisfied with the journey, being the most convenient and agreeable mode of travelling.

It is well to observe, that they are now filling up the space from this depot to Patrick Street, in Frederick—a distance of about 500 feet, and when finished, will cause the road to be so far completed.

Here we stand, 61 miles from the depot in Baltimore, near the basin, and 45 miles by the railroad.

RATE OF TOLLS AND FARE ON THIS ROAD

The toll from Baltimore westerly, which is called going, is $3.60 per ton, the charge of weighing not included. From the west to Baltimore, which is called returning, $2.40 per ton, charge of weighing, as above, not included. Flour in barrels, from Frederick to Baltimore is 26 1/2 cts. each, all charge of deliver, &c. included.

Passenger's fare, going and coming 3 cts. per mile, being $1.80 from Baltimore to Frederick, baggage according to weight.

TIME OF THE DEPARTURE OF THE CARS

Passengers' cars from Baltimore, start now at half past 5 A.M. Stop at Ellicotts' Mills for breakfast—arrive at Frederick about 1 o'clock P.M.

The mail car carrying passsengers, start from Baltimore at 5 P.M., arrives at Frederick at 1 o'clock in the morning.

From Frederick, the passengers' cars start at 9 o'clock A.M. Stop at Ellicotts' Mills for dinner at 3 o'clock—arrive about 5 o'clock P.M.

The mail car starts at 8 o'clock P.M. arrives in Baltimore at 4 o'clock in the morning. The stages from the west take the passengers at the depot, convey them to Mr. Thomas's Hotel, in Patrick Street, where they dine and start immediately after.

HORSE LOADS

A single horse draws 3 cars, loaded with 25 barrels of flour each, being 5,400 pounds for each car, or 16,200 for this load, above 8 tons—equal to the draught of 12 horses on a turnpike. Car's weight not included which is 5,400 pounds more. These burden cars are going at the rate of 3 miles an hour, in ascending and between 4 and 5 descending. Arrangements are making to place on the road, a sufficient number of locomotive steam engines, which will supersede the horse power now in use, being more economical, and admitting greater speed.* Produce and merchandise

---

*Speeds of early passenger trains were inordinately slow by twentieth century standards. The Baltimore & Ohio's "grasshoppers," 0-4-0 type locomotives used by the company in the 1830s, moved at only 10 to 12 miles per hour. On August 16, 1837, the *Atlantic* pulled a six-car passenger train with ninety passengers 82 miles at an average speed of more than 13 miles per hour. But by the 1840s B. & O. passenger trains regularly ran at 18 to 20 miles per hour.

will be conveyed at the rate of 7 or 8 miles an hour, and passengers and the mail from 12 to 15 miles per hour. Steam engines will also be erected on the inclined planes.

COST OF THE RAILROAD

From Pratt Street to Ellicotts' Mills, the expense of the road was $60,000 a mile on an average—from thence to the Point of Rocks, 34 miles further, $20,000 per mile, making $1,400,000 in the whole— but when completed $2,100,000. The lateral road to Frederick cost about $65,000 or $22,000 a mile, less than the cost of a canal on the same ground and distance.*

BENEFIT OF THE RAILROAD

The advantages derived by the inhabitants of Frederick City, and its neighborhood even by Washington County, in the same state, although further west, from the railroad, are manifest. The tenements in that city, which were before unoccupied, have found tenants, and strangers daily arrive there from all quarters. Indeed of late, several stores have been opened in that place, chiefly by strangers—which, but for the railroad would not have been the case. But the real benefits obtained by Frederick County as well as the one adjoining, consist in having their produce conveyed to the Baltimore market, at a cheap rate, (26 cts. per barrel) and receiving therefrom, with the same advantages, the heavy articles of consumption, as well as those for the melioration of the soil, which advances the price of product, and of the land on which it is raised.

---

*During the antebellum period, canal construction expenses generally exceeded those of railroads. Canals commonly cost at least $30,000 per mile. Rail lines were typically in the $20,000 to $30,000 per-mile range.

Letter about the Hudson River and Its Vicinity

2

Freeman Hunt

Railroads, mostly of modest lengths, popped up in mushroom fashion along the eastern seaboard during the 1830s. In this first decade of railroading, New York saw its network of iron rails grow from nothing in 1831 to 374 route-miles by 1840. Of the eleven New England and Middle Atlantic states, only Pennsylvania boasted a larger network, 754 miles. By mid-century, however, the Empire State claimed the region's greatest mileage, 1,361; with second place taken by Pennsylvania, 1,240 miles; and third by Massachusetts, 1,035 miles.

Early on, business-oriented journalists reported with careful attention the development of American railways. One who did was Freeman Hunt (1804–1858), who gained national fame for his Hunt's Merchant Magazine and Commercial Review, *based in New York City. In 1836 his firm, Freeman Hunt & Company, published Hunt's* Letters about the Hudson River and Its Vicinity, *a popular volume that went through three editions. Included in Hunt's* Letters *was this account of his trip over the recently opened Rensselaer & Saratoga Railroad, eventually part of the Delaware & Hudson system. Unquestionably, Hunt liked this new carrier; the Rensselaer & Saratoga's rolling stock, bridges, and employees pleased him greatly. And surely his ride was much more comfortable and faster than had been any trip over the Baltimore & Ohio in 1832.*

MANSION HOUSE, TROY
MAY 11, 1836

Yesterday, I took a seat in one of the passage cars, on the new railroad, for Balston. The road now extends to Saratoga, and will, I venture to predict, become the most fashionable route, as indeed it is the most interesting, to the "Springs."* The arrangements for carrying passengers are

---

*By the mid-nineteenth century, Saratoga Springs, New York, emerged as a popular vacation spa where visitors might "take the waters." Its population reached 4,650 in 1850, due in part to the availability of steamcars.

quite extensive. There are twenty-four cars belonging to the company—at once spacious, elegant, and convenient. They are 24 feet in length by 8 in breadth, and sufficiently high within for the passengers to stand erect, the whole divided into three apartments; the seats of which are cushioned and backed with crimson morocco, trimmed with coach lace; each apartment is surrounded by moveable panels, thus affording the comforts and facilities of either a close or open carriage, to suit the convenience of the passengers. The outside of the cars is painted of a beautiful fawn colour, with buff shadowing, painted in "picture panels," with rose, pink, and gold borders, and deep lake shading; the small mouldings of delicate stripes of vermillion and opaque black. Within the panels are "*transferred*" some of the most splendid productions of the ancient and modern masters, among which are copies from Leonardo da Vinci, Horace Vernet, David (the celebrated painter to Napoleon), Stuart, and many more of the modern school. The whole number of the subjects of the twenty-four cars cannot fall far short of two hundred, as each car averages from six to ten subjects: among which may be enumerated, several copies from the antique, Napoleon crossing the Alps, the two splendid scenes in Byron's Mazeppa, the Hospital Mount St. Bernard, portraits of most of the distinguished men of our own country, among whom Washington (from Stuart's original) stands conspicuous, the wounded tiger, the avalanche, portraits of distinguished women, views of several of our popular steamboats, the railroad bridge near Philadelphia, and several views in the south. The *tout ensemblea*, is more like a moveable gallery of the fine arts, than like a train of railroad cars. The springs of the cars are of Philadelphia make, and bear evenly. The "journals" are on a new plan, obviating all previous objections. The wheels are of cast iron, with patent rolled iron tire, well annealed and wrought, being put on the car wheel while hot. The cooling of the tire, and the contraction of the iron, render it impossible to deviate from its place. The whole is then turned in a steam lathe by machine tools, thus rendering the circle of the wheel perfect from its centre, which is a great desideratum.

The cars were made in Troy by those famous coach builders, Gilbert, Veazie, and Eaton, aided by Mr. Starbuck, a scientific machinist. Connected with the cars are two beautiful locomotives called the "Erie" and the "Champlain."*

The railroad bridge, over which the cars cross the Hudson from Troy to Green Island, on their route to the Springs, is certainly a noble, substantial specimen of this kind of architecture. It is 1,512 feet in length, 34 feet in width, and 17 feet to the eaves. It is supported by stone abutments

---

*Early railroads named their locomotives rather than numbered them. But when companies grew, numbering proved to be easier. This practice, though, destroyed an obvious vestige of individualism and replaced it with standardization.

and piers. The sides are double lattice work, covered with boards on the outside. The floors of plank, and the roof shingled. It has thirty-two sky-lights or scuttles. The roof is supported in the centre by a tier of pillars. The draw on the east end is 104 feet long, 24 feet wide, and 10 feet high. The side draw is 52 feet long and 24 feet wide. A cast iron pipe for conveying water from the main pipe of the Troy Water Works Co. extends along under the roof, the whole length of the bridge. It has sixteen hy-drants, one being placed at every other skylight. After crossing this bridge before reaching the village of Waterford, you pass three bridges besides the main one. The first crosses the Mohawk from Green Island to Van-schaick Island, and is 482 feet long, the second crosses another sprout of the Mohawk from Vanschaick Island to Hawver Island, and is 202 feet long. Three hundred and sixty feet further north, the third or minor bridge crosses the upper sprout of the Mohawk to Waterford, and is 326 feet long. On Hawver Island may be seen the remains of an old fort thrown up in the Revolutionary War. On the Troy bridge there is a side walk for foot passengers, the railroad track, and a passage for common car-riages. A bridge is shortly to be thrown across the Hudson from Green Island to West Troy, and the miserable horse-boats which now convey travellers across the Hudson will eventually fall into disuse.

The passage over the islands to Waterford, and indeed the whole route to Balston and Saratoga Springs is really delightful. Then, too, the agents on the railroad are civil to the passengers, and attentive to the locomotives. The engineers are experienced, and, although "flying as it were on the wings of the wind," one feels perfectly safe from accident. A few miles above Waterford, we pass on our right Mechanicsville, a flourishing little manufacturing village; and within a mile or two of Bemus' Heights, ren-dered memorable as the scene of battle.

3 A Ride from Boston to Providence in 1835

Samuel Breck

Not everyone thought that the coming of railroads was a blessed event. After all, steamcars radically altered often long-established patterns of transport. Stage coaches and their support facilities, including country inns and taverns, began to fade. An older traveler, Samuel Breck, damned the passenger operations of one up-start railroad, the Boston & Providence, later part of the Old Colony, and then a component of the New York, New Haven & Hartford (New Haven). For Breck, this 43 mile trip of July 22, 1835, was much less enjoyable than a comparable one by stagecoach. Undeniably, the quality of railroad service varied and so did public reaction.

JULY 22, 1835

This morning at nine o'clock I took passage in a railroad car (from Boston) for Providence. Five or six other cars were attached to the locomotive, and uglier boxes I do not wish to travel in. They were made to stow away some thirty human beings, who sit cheek by jowl as best they can. Two poor fellows who were not much in the habit of making their toilet squeezed me into a corner, while the hot sun drew from their garments a villainous compound of smells made up of salt fish, tar, and molasses. Bye and bye, just twelve—only twelve—bouncing factory girls were introduced, who were going on a party of pleasure to Newport. "Make room for the ladies!" bawled out the superintendent. "Come, gentlemen, jump up on the top; plenty of room there." "I'm afraid of the bridge knocking my brains out," said a passenger. Some made one excuse and some another. For my part, I flatly told him that since I had belonged to the corps of Silver Greys I had lost my gallantry, and did not intend to move. The whole twelve were, however, introduced, and soon made themselves at home, sucking lemons and eating green apples. . . . The rich and the poor, the educated and the ignorant, the polite and the vulgar, all herd together in this modern improvement of travelling. The consequence is a complete amalgamation. Master and servant sleep heads and points on the cabin floor of the steamer, feed at the same table, sit in each other's laps, as it were, in the cars; and all this for the sake of doing very uncomfortably in two days what would be done delightfully in eight or ten. Shall we be much longer kept by this toilsome fashion of hurrying, hurrying from starting (those who can afford it) on a journey with our own horses, and moving slowly, surely, and profitably through the country, with the power of enjoying its beauty, and be the means of creating good inns. Undoubtedly, a line of post-horses and post-chaises would long ago have been established along our great roads had not steam monopolized everything. . . . Talk of ladies on board a steamboat or in a railroad car. There are none! I never feel like a gentleman there, and I cannot perceive a semblance of gentility in any one who makes part of the travelling mob. When I see women whom, in their drawing rooms or elsewhere, I have been accustomed to respect and treat with every suitable deference—when I see them, I say, elbowing their way through a crowd of dirty emigrants or lowbred homespun fellows in petticoats or breeches in our country, in order to reach a table spread for a hundred or more, I lose sight of their pretensions to gentility and view them as belonging to the plebeian herd. To restore herself to her caste, let a lady move in select company at 5 miles an hour, and take her meals in comfort at a good inn, where she may dine decently. . . . After all, the old-fashioned way of 5 or 6 miles, with liberty to dine in a decent inn and be master of one's movements, with the delight of seeing the country and getting along rationally, is the mode to which I cling, and which will be adopted again by the generations of after times.

4 In America

Charles Dickens

Foreign visitors commonly rode American railroads. One famous Englishman who boarded a train in the United States was novelist Charles Dickens (1812–1870). In his popular work, American Notes for General Circulation, *published in 1842, he related his trip over the 26-mile Boston & Lowell Railroad, subsequently part of the Boston & Maine.*

    The views of foreign observers frequently noted the "classlessness" of American trains, something rare for those in Europe and other parts of the world. At times this egalitarianism troubled Europeans, as it may have bothered some Americans as well. Yet Dickens correctly noted the segregation of the sexes and races. The accounts of visitors like Dickens often bring the nature of passenger-train travel into sharper focus than did those of domestic riders. Dickens, in fact, suggested in his larger study that American society was relatively vigorous, religious, aspiring, progressive, and democratic, but at the same time it was lacking in erudition, unreliable in conduct, crude in manners, and wasteful of materials. He alludes to these same conclusions in this narration of his journey to Lowell.

Before leaving Boston, I devoted one day to an excursion to Lowell. I made acquaintance with an American railroad on this occasion, for the first time. As these works are pretty much alike all through the States, their general characteristics are easily described.

There are no first and second class carriages as with us: but there is a gentlemen's car and a ladies' car: the main distinction between which is that in the first, everybody smokes; and in the second, nobody does. As a black man never travels with a white one, there is also a negro car;* which is a great blundering clumsy chest, such as Gulliver put to sea in, from the Kingdom of Brobdingnag. There is a great deal of jolting, a great deal of noise, a great deal of wall, not much window, a locomotive engine, a shriek, and a bell.

The cars are like shabby omnibuses, but larger, holding thirty, forty,

---

*Charles Dickens's reference to "a negro car" is evidence that segregation was the rule, prior to the Civil War era, on both sides of the Mason-Dixon Line.

fifty people. The seats, instead of stretching from end to end, are placed crosswise. Each seat holds two persons. There is a long row of them on each side of the caravan, a narrow passage up the middle, and a door at both ends. In the centre of the carriage there is usually a stove, fed with charcoal or anthracite coal; which is for the most part red-hot. It is insufferably close; and you see the hot air fluttering between yourself and any other object you may happen to look at, like the ghost of smoke.

In the ladies' car, there are a great many gentlemen who have ladies with them. There are also a great many ladies who have nobody with them: for any lady may travel alone, from one end of the United States to the other, and be certain of the most courteous and considerate treatment everywhere. The conductor or check-taker, or guard, or whatever he may be, wears no uniform. He walks up and down the car, and in and out of it, as his fancy dictates; leans against the door with his hands in his pockets and stares at you, if you chance to be a stranger; or enters into conversation with the passengers about him. A great many newspapers are pulled out, and a few of them are read. Everybody talks to you, or to anybody else who hits his fancy. If you are an Englishman, he expects that that railroad is pretty much like an English railroad. If you say "No," he says "Yes?" (interrogatively), and asks in what respect they differ. You enumerate the heads of difference, one by one, and he says "Yes?" (still interrogatively) to each. Then he guesses that you don't travel faster in England; and on your replying that you do, says "Yes?" again (still interrogatively), and it is quite evident, don't believe it. After a long pause he remarks, partly to you, and partly to the knob on the top of his stick, that "Yankees are reckoned to be considerable of a go-ahead people too"; upon which *you* say "Yes," and then *he* says "Yes" again (affirmatively this time); and upon your looking out of the window, tells you that behind that hill, and some three miles from the next station, there is a clever town in a smart lo-ca-tion, where he expects you have con-cluded to stop. Your answer in the negative naturally leads to more questions in reference to your intended route (always pronounced rout); and wherever you are going, you invariably learn that you can't get there without immense difficulty and danger, and that all the great sights are somewhere else.

If a lady takes a fancy to any male passenger's seat, the gentleman who accompanies her gives him notice of the fact, and he immediately vacates it with great politeness. Politics are much discussed, so are banks, so is cotton. Quiet people avoid the question of the presidency, for there will be a new election in three years and a half, and party feeling runs very high; the great constitutional feature of this institution being, that directly the acrimony of the last election is over, the acrimony of the next one begins; which is an unspeakable comfort to all strong politicians and true lovers of their country: that is to say, to ninety-nine men and boys out of every ninety-nine and a quarter.

Except when a branch road joins the main one, there is seldom more than one track of rails; so that the road is very narrow, and the view, where there is a deep cutting, by no means extensive. When there is not, the character of the scenery is always the same. Mile after mile of stunted trees: some hewn down by the axe, some blown down by the wind, some half fallen and resting on their neighbours, many mere logs half-hidden in the swamp, others mouldered away to spongy chips. The very soil of the earth is made up of minute fragments such as these; each pool of stagnant water has its crust of vegetable rottenness; on every side there are the boughs, and trunks, and stumps of trees, in every possible stage of decay, decomposition, and neglect. Now you emerge for a few brief minutes on an open country, glittering with some bright lake or pool, broad as many an English river, but so small here that it scarcely has a name; now catch hasty glimpses of a distant town with its clean white houses and their cool piazzas, its prim New England church and school-house; when whir-r-r-r! almost before you have seen them, comes the same dark screen; the stunted trees, the stumps, the logs, the stagnant water—all so like the last that you seem to have been transported back again by magic.

The train calls at stations in the woods, where the wild impossibility of anybody having the smallest reason to get out is only to be equalled by the apparently desperate hopelessness of there being anybody to get in. It rushes across the turnpike road, where there is no gate, no policeman, no signal: nothing but a rough wooden arch, on which is painted "When the bell rings, look out for the Locomotive." On it whirls headlong, dives through the woods again, emerges in the light, clatters over frail arches, rumbles upon the heavy ground, shoots beneath a wooden bridge which intercepts the light for a second like a wink, suddenly awakens all the slumbering echoes in the main street of a large town, and dashes on hap-hazard, pellmell, neck-or-nothing, down the middle of the road. There—with mechanics working at their trades, and people leaning from their doors and windows, and boys flying kites and playing marbles, and men smoking, and women talking, and children crawling, and pigs burrowing, and unaccustomed horses plunging and rearing, close to the very rails—there—on, on, on—tears the mad dragon of an engine with its train of cars; scattering in all directions a shower of burning sparks from its wood fire; screeching, hissing, yelling, panting; until at last the thirsty monster stops beneath a covered way to drink, the people cluster round, and you have time to breathe again.

I was met at the station at Lowell by a gentleman intimately connected with the management of the factories there; and gladly putting myself under his guidance, drove off at once to that quarter of the town in which the works, the object of my visit, were situated.

1897

Colorado

RESORTS

THE LOOP NEAR GEORGETOWN

UNION PACIFIC,
DENVER & GULF RY.
"The Gulf Road."

FRANK TRUMBULL,
RECEIVER AND GEN'L MANAGER.

T. F. DUNAWAY,
GEN'L SUPERINTENDENT

B. L. WINCHELL,
GENERAL PASSENGER AGENT.

GENERAL OFFICES, DENVER, COLORADO.

America's — Railroads Mature

Colorado Resorts advertisement by Union Pacific, Denver & Gulf Railway, 1897. The road's scenic "Georgetown Loop" is depicted on the cover (shown here).

PULLMAN'S
Palace Hotel Cars,

VICEROY,
    PRESIDENT,
        CITY OF NEW YORK,
            CITY OF BOSTON,
                PLYMOUTH ROCK, and
                    WESTERN WORLD,

Forming a Daily Line Between

CHICAGO AND ROCHESTER,

Leaving Chicago, daily at 5.15 P. M.

AND

Arriving at Rochester the following

Day,

LEAVING ROCHESTER

DAILY, at 9.20 A. M.,

Arriving in Chicago the following morning.

Tower, Millard & Decker, Printers, 44 Lake St., Chicago.

Pullman's Hotel Car folder, May 1, 1869,
displays names of the company's sleeping
cars.

The pioneer railroad artery across the
West passed through Ogden, Utah, where
trains of the Union Pacific connected with
those of the Southern Pacific (née Central
Pacific). A San Francisco photographer
found considerable activity in 1884: Union
Pacific trains are on the left and Southern
Pacific's are on the right.

Although this photograph of the Chicago & North Western station and passenger train in Oakes, North Dakota, dates from the early twentieth century, this locomotive and its cars were hardly new; they represent nicely American railroading during the Gilded Age. (George Krambles Coll.)

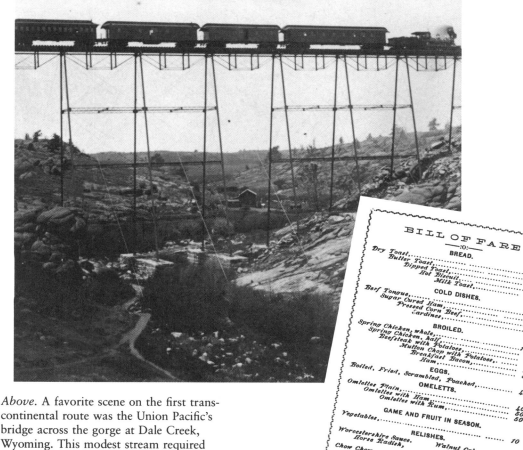

Above. A favorite scene on the first transcontinental route was the Union Pacific's bridge across the gorge at Dale Creek, Wyoming. This modest stream required the most elaborate bridge on the line. Dating from the late 1880s, this view shows the second span. Like the original "stick" version, this bridge caused travelers to experience a quickened heartbeat if they peered out the windows. The Union Pacific dismantled this bridge in 1901.

Right. The Pullman folder also contains the "Bill of Fare."

BILL OF FARE
—:o:—
BREAD.

Dry Toast, ... 10
Butter Toast, ... 15
Dipped Toast, ... 15
Hot Biscuit, ... 15
Milk Toast, ... 25

COLD DISHES.

Beef Tongue, ... 40
Sugar Cured Ham, ... 40
Pressed Corn Beef, ... 40
Sardines, ... 40

BROILED.

Spring Chicken, whole, ... 1.00
Spring Chicken, half, ... 75
Beefsteak with Potatoes, ... 75
Mutton Chop with Potatoes, ... 75
Breakfast Bacon, ... 50
Ham, ... 50

EGGS.

Boiled, Fried, Scrambled, Poached, ... 40

OMELETTS.

Omlettes Plain, ... 40
Omlettes with Ham, ... 50
Omlettes with Rum, ... 50

GAME AND FRUIT IN SEASON.

Vegetables, ... 10

RELISHES.

Worcestershire Sauce,   Walnut Catsup.
Horse Radish,   French Mustard.
Chow Chow and Mixed Pickles.

Fruit in Season, ... 10

Preserves, ... 25
French Coffee or Tea with an order, ... 25
Coffee or Tea without an order, ... 15
.... 25

5 Sketches of Prison Life

A. O. Abbott

The generally inferior nature of railroads in the South became painfully apparent to Union Army prisoners during the Civil War. Southern railroads nearly universally failed to have the same quality of construction, rail, motive power, and rolling stock that characterized their counterparts in the North. Moreover, Dixie's rail network fell short of being integrated with the remainder of the country or, for that matter, even within itself. Gauges varied, several major rivers lacked bridges, and "systems" were mostly unknown. The wartime period merely made a poor network much worse, so bad that Confederate-controlled trains, when they operated, often crept over their routes. These wretched conditions did not change dramatically until the end of the nineteenth century. Eventually, Southern carriers improved: they adopted standardized gauge, acquired modern equipment, and merged into larger, more efficient units.

The battered condition of railroads in the Confederacy did not enhance the dreadful experiences of Allen O. Abbott, a lieutenant in the First New York Dragoons, who found himself in enemy hands in 1864. During that summer he traveled the 280 torturous miles between Manchester, Virginia (near Richmond), and Charlotte, North Carolina, over three carriers, the Richmond & Danville, Piedmont, and North Carolina railroads. Fortunately for future riders, these firms entered the orbit of the dynamic Southern Railway in the 1890s, and such a journey from Richmond to Charlotte would produce positive memories.

We left Manchester at 7:30 A.M., the 31st [sic] of June, just as the battle of Cold Harbor was opening.* We soon found that traveling on a Rebel railroad was very different from what it would be on one in our northern states. Their rolling stock was nearly worn out, the rails broken, splintered, and battered, the ties rotten, and, altogether, it was a dangerous

---

*The Battle of Cold Harbor, fought in June 1864 east of Richmond, Virginia, checked General U. S. Grant's advance toward the Confederate capital. This bloody battle led to thousands of Union Army casualties. Grant then moved his troops toward Petersburg and eventually captured this strategic Virginia city.

matter to ride at all upon them, to say nothing of speed. For greater safety, their fastest trains were limited to 12 miles an hour by Act of Congress. Their stops are frequent, for their wheezy old engines use double the fuel they would if they were in good repair; and their wood and water stations are separate, thus making a stop every 4 or 5 miles.

During this ride we suffered for water, for the day was intensely hot, and we had nothing to get it in, but had to drink it from our hands or from the holes by the side of the track. The stations along this route are not villages such as you find on our northern roads, but consist of five or six houses dignified with a name high sounding enough for a corporation. The depots are small, unpainted buildings, with but few conveniences and much dilapidation.

We obtained a little relief from the oppressive heat in the cars by kicking off some of the boards, thus letting in fresh air.

We arrived at Danville about one o'clock the next (Wednesday) morning. We were not allowed to leave the train till seven, when we were marched to another train in waiting to take us to Greensboro', North Carolina. After we were on board they issued to us a half a loaf of corn bread warm from the oven, and a small piece of cooked bacon, in quality much better than any we had ever received at Libby.* Here our old guard was relieved by some Virginia militia under command of Lieutenant Gay, 3d Virginia Infantry (Hampton's Legion).

Danville is situated on the south side of the Dan River, 148 miles from Richmond, and had at this time a population of about five thousand. It had increased in numbers since the war, many of the refugees from Northern Virginia coming here with their families to escape from the immediate horrors of the battle-field. It had several government hospitals, and at times federal prisoners have been confined here, but at this time nearly all had been sent farther South. It was also a depot for supplies *in transitu* from Georgia and North Carolina.

The road connecting Danville with Greensboro' is a new one built in 1863, '4, by the Rebel government, and we were among the first that went over it. The train did not make over 8 miles per hour. We met several negroes, who said they were on their way to Richmond to work on the fortifications. They were on foot, and carried whatever they had in bags or packs on their backs.

We arrived in Greensboro' about 1 o'clock P.M., and were ordered from the train and marched to a little grove to rest and wait for a train to be made up for us. As soon as we were bivouacked, there began a sharp business in trading. Some of the inhabitants came around with something

---

*Libby prison, located on Belle Isle (a misnamed island in the James River at Richmond, Virginia), was a leading Confederate penal institution. Conditions there, however, were generally much better than at the infamous Andersonville prison in southwestern Georgia.

to eat. Our rations received at Danville were barely sufficient for a single meal, and the sight made us very hungry. Watches, knives, rings, jewelry, pocketbooks, any thing that could be spared, was sold for rations. We paid for onions five dollars per half dozen, scallions at that; bacon, four dollars per pound; crackers, homemade, two dollars per dozen; biscuits, three dollars and fifty cents per dozen. Many of us took a nap, while the enlisted men spent a portion of their time in *skirmishing*, a duty all prisoners soon learn, while several ladies strolled by and watched the process.

Night came, and, there being no prospect of a train, we composed ourselves to rest. About eleven o'clock we were aroused, to take the train at one. After some delay we were marched to the cars, and halted before an old rickety thing with two large holes in the bottom, and ordered to embark. About forty succeeded in getting into the car, when the lieutenant in charge of us was told that the car was full. He said it was *not*, and more should ride there. Ten or twelve more were crowded in, when it was declared that no more *could* ride there. The lieutenant then ordered in two of his guards, and told them to use their muskets in driving the men back, *for the whole sixty-one must and should ride in that car*, no matter what the consequences might be. After a good deal of swearing on his part, and no little grumbling on ours, the whole sixty-one *were* crowded into the car; but for more than one quarter of us to sit down at the same time was out of the question, to say nothing of trying to sleep in that condition; but this was not all of our trouble, *for the guards must ride with us*. They attempted to get standing room near the door, but could not; and finally, referring the case to the lieutenant, he gave permission for four of the officers to ride on top of the car, thus leaving room for the guard, and in that packed, suffocating condition, we were to ride to Charlotte, North Carolina. We finally started from Greensboro' about two o'clock the next morning, ran about 10 miles, then came to a dead stand. The engine was unable to draw us. It was uncoupled and started off to get up steam, and after an hour returned, and we went on at the rate of about 8 miles per hour.

A drenching storm came on during the night, which, though uncomfortable to those on the outside, seemed to cool the atmosphere, and make it more tolerable to us inside.

This morning we found ourselves passing through a low, flat country, but little cultivated, and at nine o'clock crossed the Yadkin River, and arrived at Salisbury, North Carolina. While waiting here for a train to pass, I learned that the town contained about five thousand inhabitants, and was the site of the State Penitentiary, which had been occupied more or less during the war by federal prisoners.

We left Salisbury at 12 M., passing through a wet marshy section of country, interspersed with pine groves. After we left Salisbury, Lieutenant

Gay allowed six or eight more to ride on the top of each car. At one of the stopping-places, permission was given to four enlisted men to climb to the top. Three of them had succeeded in reaching it safely; the fourth one was a sickly, weakly boy, hardly able to walk. The lieutenant, in company with a guard, was watching him, when the whistle blew, and the train started. Instead of leaving him to make his way up alone, as he was likely to succeed in doing, he at once ordered the guard to shoot him, which he did. The poor fellow dropped upon the track, and the cars passed over him. We received no rations till dark that night, being thirty-six hours with nothing to eat.

We arrived at Charlotte about four o'clock in the midst of a rain- storm; but we were very glad to get out of the packed cars, for we felt almost dead. We were then marched to a little grove, and waited patiently for our rations till dark, when we received, for two days, four hard tacks, four inches by six, made of bran and middlings, black, mouldy, and rotten, and one fourth of a pound of bacon.*

---

*Lieutenant Abbott continued to be moved about as a Union prisoner of war. He spent time in Confederate penal camps in Macon and Savannah, Georgia, and in Charleston and Columbia, South Carolina. In February 1865, however, Abbott left the horrors of Asylum prison in Columbia to be part of a "General Exchange" of prisoners that occurred near Wilmington, North Carolina. Soon he returned to the North and his home in Portageville, New York.

A Pleasure Trip from Gotham to the Golden Gate

6

Florence Leslie

Although the quality of service on the Union Pacific Railroad (the eastern two-thirds of the nearly 2,000-mile transcontinental line that stretched through the "Great American Desert" from Council Bluffs, Iowa, to Sacramento, California) lagged behind most of the nation's major railroads until the 1890s, passage over these historic rails held enormous appeal. Indeed, the "wedding of the rails" at Promontory Summit, Utah Territory, on May 10, 1869, meant much to the nation and, for that matter, the world. Completion of the country's first transcontinental artery unmistakably helped to popularize, glamorize, and bring closer the "West."

Some travelers enjoyed first-class accommodations over the Union Pacific. Most took all or part of the "Overland Route," that is they rode on the Chicago & North Western from Chicago to Council Bluffs; the Union Pacific from Council Bluffs to Ogden, Utah; and the Central Pacific (later Southern Pacific) from Ogden to Sacramento. Florence Leslie, (1851–1914) the well-to-do wife of the publisher of Frank Leslie's Illustrated Newspaper, found considerable pleasure and excitement in her 1877 trip from "Gotham to the Golden Gate," as illustrated in this excerpt as she travels from Chicago to Cheyenne, Wyoming Territory.

On arriving at the station, we find that we have exchanged our beloved Wagner Home [sleeping car] for the famous Pullman Hotel Car,* exhibited at the Centennial Exposition,† and built at a cost of $35,000. We are

---

*A "Pullman Hotel Car" was a combination sleeper and drawing-room car. The drawing-room section was available for an extra fare beyond the sleeping-car charge. This equipment belonged to George Mortimer Pullman's (1831–1897) Pullman Palace Car Company. Organized in 1867, the firm 10 years later operated 800 cars on about 30,000 miles of railroad and employed approximately 2,000 workers, many of whom labored in its large car repair and building shops in Detroit, Michigan.

†The Centennial Exposition celebrated the 100th anniversary of American independence. Held in Philadelphia, Pennsylvania, beginning in mid-May 1876, the Exposition attracted

greeted on entering, by two superb pyramids of flowers, one from Mr. Potter Palmer,* and the other with compliments of the Pullman Car Co.; then new-found Chicago friends arrive in rapid succession, to wish us God-speed, and, in the midst of a cheerful bustle and excitement, we are off, and able to look about us at our new home. First, we are impressed with the smooth and delightful motion, and are told it is owing to a new invention, in the shape of paper wheels applied to this car,† and incredible though the information sounds, meekly accept it, and proceed to explore the internal resources of our kingdom. We find everything closely resembling our late home, except that one end of the car is partitioned off and fitted up as a kitchen, storeroom, scullery—reminding one, in their compactness and variety, of the little Parisian *cuisines*, where every inch of space is utilized, and where such a modicum of wood and charcoal produces such marvelous results.

Our *chef*, of ebon color, and proportions suggesting a liberal sampling of the good things he prepares, wears the regulation snow-white apron and cap, and gives us cordial welcome and information; showing us, among other things, that his refrigerator and larder are boxes adroitly arranged beneath the car, secured by lock and key, and accessible at every station. At six the tables are laid for two each, with dainty linen, and the finest of glass and china, and we presently sit down to dinner. Our repast is Delmonican in its nature and style, consisting of soup, fish, *entrees*, roast meat and vegetables, followed by the conventional dessert and the essential spoonful of black coffee.

We are not a late party that night, retiring at ten, and in the morning are startled by an announcement from the "Sultana," a tall, willowy woman, with dark, almond-shaped eyes, who affects brilliant tints, and lounges among her cushions and wraps of crimson and gold, with grace peculiarly her own, and with a luxuriance so Eastern, as to have won for her the *sobriquet* of Sultana. We are startled by the announcement that her rest had been disturbed by the howling of wolves! The young lady who does the romantic for our party turns pale with envy, especially when the brakeman, appealed to as authority, admits that there is a small

---

thousands of visitors. Most marveled at the scientific exhibits, including a demonstration of the telephone.

*Potter Palmer (1826–1902) became one of Chicago's foremost merchants and real-estate promoters. He is probably best remembered as founder of a first-class Chicago hotel, the Palmer House.

†Unquestionably the term *paper wheel* aroused puzzlement and even smiles in most people during the Gilded Age. This product involved use of compressed paper or "strawboard" for wood at the car wheel's center. Notes historian John H. White, Jr., "The paper center, even though greatly compressed and nearly as hard as ivory, was spongy enough to cushion the ride and deaden the sound of the wheel's grinding over the rails." Introduced by Richard Allen in 1869, paper wheels were used widely between 1880 and 1915.

coyote wolf about the prairies, even so far east, which might possibly have been heard. All day, until sunset, we sweep along over rolling prairie lands of a rich, tawny yellow, with here and there a tiny town, and here and there a lonely settler's cabin, with a little winding footpath stretching up to it.

At Dixon, the train stopped for the passengers' supper, and we stole away for a little exercise and solitude. A storm was imminent, the distant thunder muttered ominously, the lightening came in pulses, and from the far, dusky reaches of the prairie, blew a wind stronger and freer, yet softer, than other winds, with a fragrance sweeter than flowers on its breath. Some strange, wild influence in the scene sent a new sensation tingling through one's blood. All sorts of poetic fancies and inspirations seemed hovering close above one's head, when a dash of rain recalled the realism of life, and sent us hastening back to the car, where all the lamps were lighted and the tables laid for dinner.

"What a dismal scene!" exclaimed some one, looking out of the window.

"We are very fortunate to be snugly ensconced, with plenty of lights and dinner in prospect," replied the Sultana, drawing her cashmere about her shoulders.

By breakfast-time the scenery had changed, the rolling prairie giving place to a succession of low bluffs—steep, hilly, brown, and infinitely wild; then came a quiet little lake, dotted over with wild ducks; more hills growing green in the hollows; swamp-willows budding redly; herds of grazing cattle and wild, shaggy horses; until, at last, we roll into a long, flat, straggling town, and are told it is Council Bluffs.

"And why Council Bluffs?" we suavely inquire of the wise man who gives us this information.

"Because, on these bluffs the Indians assembled in council; also because, beneath the shadow of the bluffs in 1853, a little company of enterprising spirits held a council as to the propriety of building the city of Omaha, upon the opposite shores of the Missouri; also because the conductor counsels us to re-enter the car, as the train is about to start; also—"

"Enough! enough! your last reason is conclusive." And a few minutes later we are rolling over the magnificent bridge, said to be one of the finest in the world, and almost a thousand feet in length.* The stream—weak coffee as to complexion, pea-soup as to consistency—rolls sluggishly between its iron piers. As for the bridge itself, its cost, its construction,

---

*The Union Pacific started its massive iron-truss bridge over the Missouri River between Council Bluffs, Iowa, and Omaha, Nebraska, in January 1869, completing it in March 1872. The bridge contained eleven spans, each 250 feet in length, and stood approximately 60 feet above the water. The cost totalled about $3 million. Unfortunately, a cyclone blew away two of the bridge's spans in 1877. Although the Union Pacific made immediate repairs, it replaced the structure in 1887.

its ingenuity, is it not written in all the guide-books, all the travels, all the diaries of all the *voyageurs?* and to these various sources the statistical reader is referred for information.

Arrived in Omaha, the true beginning, perhaps, of our California trip, we took a carriage, and set forth to view the town. We found it big, lazy, and apathetic; the streets dirty and ill-paved; the clocks without hands to point out the useless time; the shops, whose signs mostly bore German names, deserted of customers, while principals and clerks lounged together in the doorways, listless and idle. This depressing state of affairs is, presumably, temporary, for we are told that, two years ago, Omaha was one of the most thriving and busy cities of the West, claiming for itself, indeed, a place as first commercial emporium of that vast section; and, certainly, its position at the terminus of the three great Eastern roads, and the beginning of the one great Western one, would naturally entitle it to that pre-eminence, when aided by the enterprise and the dollars of such men as have, in twenty years, built a great city from a wayside settlement. Doubtless, when the hard times, which seem to affect everybody and everything, from the baby's Christmas toys to the statesman's visions of international commerce, are over, Omaha will shake off the lethargy depressing her at present, and rise to the position her citizens fondly claim for her. . . .

Returning to the station, we found the platform crowded with the strangest and most motley groups of people it has ever been our fortune to encounter. Men in alligator boots, and loose overcoats made of blankets and wagon rugs, with wild, unkempt hair and beards, and bright, resolute eyes, almost all well-looking, but wild and strange as denizens of another world.

The women looked tired and sad, almost all of them, and were queerly dressed, in gowns that must have been their grandmothers', and with handkerchiefs tied over their heads in place of hats; the children were bundled up anyhow, in garments of nondescript purpose and size, but were generally chubby, neat and gay, as they frolicked in and out among the boxes, baskets, bundles, bedding, babies'- chairs, etc., piled waist high on various parts of the platform. Mingling with them, and making some inquiries, we found that these were emigrants, bound for the Black Hills, by rail to Cheyenne and Sioux City, and after that by wagon trains. A family of French attracted attention by the air of innate refinement and fitness which seems to attach to every grade of society in *la belle France*, and we chatted with them for some moments. A great many families claimed German nationality, and Ireland, England, and Scotland were represented, as well as our own country. One bright little creature—perhaps three years of age—was quite insulted at being called a baby, and exclaimed, indignantly:

"No, no, me not baby!"

"What are you, then? A young lady?" we inquired.

"No, me 'ittle woman. Me helps mammy sweep," replied the mite; and apologizing for our blunder, we handed her some silver for candy, which she accepted with alacrity; and as we watched her setting off on her shopping expedition, a neat, pretty old lady, perched upon a big bundle, said, with much conscious pride.

"That's my grandchild, ma'am."

We congratulated her, and passed on, to visit the emigrant lodging-house and outfitting-shop adjoining the station. The shop, although large, was crowded, and the air insufferably close; long counters ran across the room, and upon them, and upon lines stretched above, lay or hung, every variety of equipment desirable for pioneer life—clothes, blankets, mats, tins, hats, shoes, babies' rattles, impartially mixed and exhibited, while some attention to the aesthetic needs of humanity was shown, in various stuffed heads of moose and deer, with quails perched upon their antlers.

In the eating-room we "assisted," by inspection, at a good, substantial, homely dinner, neatly served at twenty-five cents a plate, and a placard informed the guests that children occupying seats at a table would be charged full price; a precautionary measure not unreasonable, as it seemed to us, in view of the swarms of innocents who had certainly never encountered a Herod!

Lodging is the same price as dinner, and the superintendent of this part of the house triumphantly informed us that the sheets were changed every night.

After passing North Bend, we came upon an Indian camp belonging to a portion of the Omahaw tribe. The lodges—five or six in number—were of white skin, and picturesque in shape: their occupants gathered around a small camp-fire—the men, tall, straight, dark, and dignified, wrapped in toga-like blankets; the women, dirty and degraded, with their pappooses bundled on their backs, the queer, little dark faces peeping out like prairie dogs from their burrows. Further on we met a second band—half a dozen men on horseback— carrying their lodges bundled up and driving a little herd of shaggy Indian ponies. It was a wonderfully new picture for us, the great plains rolling away on either side in apparently illimitable extent, clad in their richest shades of russet and tawny gold in the distance, and the tender grass and moist black earth close at hand, a wild mass of thunder-clouds crowding up from the south, and the low-hanging trail of smoke from our engine sweeping away northward, like a troop of spirits, and this little, lonely band of Omahaws riding slowly away into the storm, casting uneasy glances backward at the flying train. A second picture to place beside that of Niagara in memory's gallery, a second proof that the foremost of human artists is, after all, but the feeblest copyist of the Artist whose name is Wonderful.

The old emigrant trail here runs southward beside the track, and we had the luck to pass two real emigrant wagons: one, white-topped and rather neat-looking, had halted for the night, with the horses picketed out to graze, and the camp-fire lighted; while the other, dark, weather-beaten and forlorn, was doggedly making its way forward.

Our train stopped for supper at Grand Island, a considerable place, and, like most western places, confidently expecting to be larger when the time arrived.* We dismounted to look at our first specimens of buffalo grass, a short, dry, tufted herbage, said to be the especial dainty of not only buffalo, but of all grazing creatures, who leave all other food for it, and unhesitatingly as a gourmand accepts fresh truffles. In front of the station was a little enclosure with a most spasmodic fountain, beside which we lingered for some moments and then returned with alacrity to our Pullman home.

Very early in the next morning we were awakened by the stopping of the train, for the gentle and constant motion had already become essential to our repose as that of his ship to the sailor. The conductor presently appeared to warn us that the detention was likely to be one of several hours, as an accident had happened to the freight train some 5 miles in advance, and the track was both encumbered and injured. The prospect was not cheering, as the rain fell in torrents, and the prairie, sodden and gray in the chill morning light, had lost all the beauty of its sunset garb, presenting one flat, dull expanse, innocent of house, tree, shrub, moving creature, or any point of interest—a perfect picture of desolation.

The several hours of the conductor extended to eight, and required all the attractive powers of the Sultana, all the condensed result of her husband's journalistic and statistical studies, all the young lady's romantic fervor about the plains, and all the fun of the Bohemians, to fill them pleasantly. However, "All things come round to him who will but wait," and to us came at last the delightful jerk of the train, as the iron horse straightened his traces and, with a shriek of exultation, started again upon his journey.

Arrived at the scene of the disaster, we could not wonder at the length of the detention, for a herd of cattle, attempting to try conclusions with a steam engine, had been forced to retreat, leaving six of their number on the field of battle; and so inextricably had the poor creatures become wedged in the complicated machinery of the locomotive, that it was hard to decide where the one ended and where the other began, or which had suffered most in the encounter. The cars lay scattered along the track, all more or less wrecked, and the engine, completely dislodged from the rails, lay beside them, a mass of ruin. During our long delay a wrecker

---

*Grand Island, Nebraska, 156 miles west of Omaha on the Union Pacific's mainline to Ogden, Utah Territory, claimed 2,963 residents in 1880. A decade later its population reached 7,536.

train had been engaged in laying a new section of track, and over this we slowly passed, resuming presently our usual rate of speed, which, however, rarely exceeds twenty-two or three miles an hour, that being conceded as the rate best adapted to economy, safety, and comfort in long distances, and certainly resulting in a smoothness and ease delightfully contrasting with the rush, rattle, and jar of the Lightning Express.

Soon after this we passed through our first snowshed, very like a covered bridge or wooden tunnel in effect, and were informed that the U.P.R.R. had been obliged to construct hundreds of miles of these, and stone fences at different points of the road, to obviate the drifting of snow banks, capable of not only detaining, but of burying, a train.

And now, not without some little excitement, we arrived at Cheyenne, as it is styled upon the maps, the Magic City of the Plains, the City on Wheels, the Town of a Day, as romanticists call it, or in yet more vigorous vernacular, H-ll on Wheels, which latter is, perhaps, its most popular name among its own inhabitants.* In view of this reputation, our conductor strongly advised against any night exploration, at least by the ladies of the party, of the streets and shops at Cheyenne, stating that the town swarmed with miners *en route* for, or returning from, the Black Hills, many of them desperadoes, and all utterly reckless in the use of the bowie-knife and pistol; or, at the very least, in the practice of language quite unfit for ears polite, although well adapted to a place which they themselves had dubbed with so suggestive a name. This opposition, was, of course, decisive; and the three ladies, as one man, declared fear was a word unknown in their vocabulary, that purchases essential to their comfort were to be made, and that exercise was absolutely necessary to their health. Under such stress of argument the masculine mind gave way perforce, and not only the sworn beau of the party, but most of the other gentlemen, endorsed the movement and volunteered to act as escort, producing, loading, and flourishing such an arsenal of weapons as they did so that their valiant charges huddled together, far more affrighted at their friends than their enemies, and piteously imploring that the firearms should be safely hidden until needed; the order was obeyed, and at about half-past nine P.M. the exploring party set forth.†

---

*With construction of the Union Pacific westward from the Missouri River in the late 1860s, gangs of workers lived in temporary camps at end-of-track, often in bunkcars. Nearby "camp followers" of all sorts erected portable structures where they supplied railroaders with liquor, card games, sex, and the like. These stop points became popularly known as "Hell on Wheels."

†Fortunately for members of the Leslie party, their sojourn through the streets of Cheyenne, that self-proclaimed "Hell on Wheels," proved to be uneventful. While they were adventuresome enough to visit a local gun shop, "this warehouse of death," these Easterners appreciated the safety and comfort of the train.

7 A Winter Railroad Ride

Linda Thayer Guilford

Although passenger trains usually have been able to operate in difficult winter conditions, occasionally severe cold and heavy snow have drastically slowed or even stopped them. Such was the case of a New York Central & Hudson River Railroad train in upstate New York in January 1879.

A Cleveland, Ohio, educator who served as principal of a local academy, Linda Thayer Guilford (1823–1911), found her return trip from a holiday visit to western Massachusetts highly memorable. The author of several books and short stories, Guilford skillfully captures the flavor of a not-so-pleasant rail journey for chair-car passengers.

On Thursday afternoon January 2d, 1879, the western bound 3-30 train rolled slowly and smoothly out of Albany. Before we were fairly under way, scattering flakes of snow were sifting through the air. "We are half an hour late," remarked a gentleman looking at his watch. "Thirty-five minutes," corrected his neighbor chirply. If the telegraph reported a storm from the west that was the concern of the railroad, not ours. They had put on two engines. As we plodded majestically along by one station after another making deliberate stops, speculation was busy as to where this lost time was to be made up. It began to snow heavily and was growing cold as we passed Fonda.* At this rate when should we be at Rochester? Was it possible the Central would fail to make connection at Buffalo? The fireman brought an extra bucket of coal, punched the stove like a pile driver and jammed the whole of it in. Yet the thick white frost was covering the windows and the conductor had bandaged his ears with a handkerchief. Through the early night hours we could feel the train was laboring over the track but nearly every one had a whole seat to himself, and with a comfortable feeling of pity for the train men, each resigned himself to partial oblivion and the destiny of a three hour delay in his journey. Not far from midnight there was a long stop and much shunting to and fro. We were at Syracuse† and it appeared serious work was before

---

*Fonda, New York, was the third principal station stop west of Albany, a distance of 43 1/2 miles, on the mainline of the New York Central & Hudson River Railroad.

†Syracuse, New York, 147 1/2 miles west of Albany, was the New York Central & Hudson River's major stop between Albany and Buffalo. Passenger trains regularly stayed there for five minutes, and, at times, even longer.

us for three engines were added to our already double headed train. All the passengers outside of the drawing room and sleeping coaches were now notified to enter one particular car which was thus crowded more than full, so that a number must stand. It was an old smoking car [full of] nicotine and unswept, the window in the rear door was broken out and a board fastened temporarily in the hole. Packed like cabbages for market in this conveyance, we started on our way to Rochester.* The throbbing engines pluckily strained every rod and lever plunging to the tracks in the struggle against the fast accumulating, almost irresistible drifts. But we were going on. The keen blast howled above in the telegraph wires and drove in at the broken door. Now and then, some half perishing train man with a face the color of scarlet slipped in for a moment glad of the shelter of the stifling interior from the cutting wind outside. There was no sleep but no noisy outbreak. At the end of some hours a passenger shouted "Rochester" in exact imitation of the legitimate call but after two successes in stirring simple ones to expectation, this ancient joke died and left no success or "Rochester.". . . lookers out could dimly discern up to the car windows the white walls of snow which barred our way. On and on three hours of pushing and dragging slower and slower and then we stopped without signal. The storm was in the height of its fury, it was impossible to see two rods and the windows were solid frost. We were blocked one mile east of Batavia—thirty-six miles from Buffalo. A second train from Rochester soon came up behind and the problem was to get the whole convoy over that mile. Shovels were brought from the distant station and all the employees from the conductor down were soon toiling against the elements. We curled ourselves up and admired their courageous energy in the stinging cold and wind driven snow.

Meanwhile, the gray morning disclosed our fellow travellers. Two emigrant families; five children among them were at the rear end by the broken door. The littlest ones were crying with hunger and thirst in the now chilly car. The patient mothers were doing their best to soothe while the fathers looked on in half-surly impassivity. One finally set out to walk to the station. After an hour's absence he brought to the suffering family some half frozen milk in a pail. Four cattle drivers had established themselves directly opposite us. They had drank their flasks empty and were playing cards spitting at random in all directions and dropping oaths freely. One weather beaten Dutchman solaced himself with a pipe regardless of frowns. . . . At the other end of the car were two insane women under the charge of some officers of an asylum. The poor creatures had been taken to Utica the day before and were now being returned perhaps to

---

*The next-to-last stop for through New York Central & Hudson River trains between Albany and Buffalo was Rochester. This bustling New York city was 228 1/2 miles west of Albany and 68 1/2 miles east of Buffalo.

some county infirmary. One talked continually, mostly in her native tongue but some times in English. A half drunken individual seated near amused himself by exciting her when she poured forth a torrent of mingled profanity, repartee, and obscenity. This went on for some time, the attendant or official apparently acquiescing, till the conductor passing through promptly silenced the wretch who had roused her. The other unfortunate (now and then) only had uttered an "Ach! Gett!" We fancied she was handcuffed. This was too much—we turned over the seat but the incoherent words were never long out of our ears through the day which followed. Directly behind sat a small dark-eyed young woman in the uniform of a Protestant Sisterhood placidly making entries in a note book. . . . This writer was estimating the sustaining power of twenty slices of brown bread, two apples and a doughnut—the only lunch brought from the North Berkshire hills twenty-four hours before.

Meanwhile the bulletins from outside kept up an excitement. "There was no road beyond Buffalo; There was no trouble beyond Batavia; They would go in half an hour; They would not start till tomorrow." One thing was certain, ice covered the rails under the snow. The heating and ringing the pushing and backing of the engines made a din unequalled since the blacksmithy of the Cyclops. By some hocus pocus the seven engines were made to pull together. After three hours toil—there was a tremendous jerk, a forward movement of a few moments and we were abreast of the station. So far so good but no ladies could leave the car.

That day before Batavia lies in memory like a month. All the morning we were without fire or water. How we crowded around the battered stove in the corner when it was filled once more: How delicious the drink from the tin watering can and its grimy cup after our long waiting: On the cramped seats packed hard by years of use we twisted into every lawful position and found each intolerable after the first moment. What to do? To diversion at cards was wanting, a pack, a partner, and the knowledge of a game. Obviously we could not dance like steamboat passengers. Left to our mental resources their shallowness became apparent. Reciting poetry had been a pastime. Tennyson's "May Queen," and Byron's, "Prisoner of Chillon," whiled away a half hour. We brought up on the fifth stanza of Poe's, "Raven," and drifed away into drivelling bits of negro melodies. Efforts to recall Sunday School lessons were shamefully abortive. . . . [Then] we remembered a pair of scissors in our travelling bag. The tired children with some difficulty looked on for a time, while wheels, stars, and nameless four legged creatures were cut out for them from some pieces of wrapping paper. The fun lasted till they began from very weariness to tear those images to tatters.

At noon the conductor appeared with a telegram of good advice. Tell the passengers they are where they can get food and keep. They had better make themselves contented as possible. Three hours after a second message showed a vast improvement in knowledge of the situation. "I will send down a snowplow and pull you through if it can be done." Meanwhile the drovers had gone ashore and come back bringing the odor of whiskey to load the stifling air. . . . The hours wore away. Our ideas were tending rapidly to a vortex. In Queen Victoria's book Her Gracious majesty frequently informs us that she had breakfast as usual. Alas we had not had breakfast as usual nor dinner nor supper. Long we hesitated. Could we ask one of these hard worked train men toiling in the snow to bring us a lunch? By the middle of the afternoon we plucked up courage to address a respectable looking man who strayed into the car from the front. "One of the brakemen will bring you something if you ask them" he said. "One of the brakemen" after forty-eight hours of continuous service had not lost the traits of a gentleman. In half hour he did his best and brought in a piece of newspaper, two slices of hot saleratus bread with a lump of stale butter melting between. . . . The night fell and like the flag "we were still there." But that dispatcher at Buffalo was keeping his word and in the dark at seven we heard the welcome sound of the snow plough and six engines came with giant grasp to our rescue. They drew off from snow covered Batavia feeling their way through piles of impediment over slipping rails five hours for thirty-six miles. At midnight, headed by the plow, thirteen locomotives drew six cars into the station at Buffalo ringing whistling tooting and blowing all at once and together, with a sound which but feebly expressed our jubilation. Then we found that the passengers in the sleeping and drawing room coaches had been provided with warmth and water and obsequious attention and yet they had not been happy.

"No trains to Cleveland" said the ticket agent with characteristic suavity. "How soon in the morning?" "5:30" and he shut the window. On those detestable divided seats in the great station . . . we waited for the day and a Cleveland train. No sign of a train west at nine o'clock, in fact none for twelve hours after, and through the half excavated streets of the city we sent a message which brought the warm hand grasp of a friend and welcome to a lovely and hospitable Buffalo home. Certain convictions have abided with us to the present time. Women are of no use in the emergencies of a stalled railroad train. They cannot dig and to beg are not ashamed. We can take stock of our mental furniture in an astonishingly short time if there is nothing else to do. Heroes and heroines of fiction shall only have our sympathy when they can not get their regular meals.

Another circumstance may be added. A former President of the Lake Shore Road listened in a friendly way to the table talk narrative of this trip. Some weeks afterward this gentleman remarked, "I mentioned your case to Mr. Vanderbilt."* He said it must have been exceptional. It was

---

*"Mr. Vanderbilt" is reference to William Henry Vanderbilt (1821–1885), who did much

against the policy of the road to force passengers to take sleeping cars. From which it appears even that great man did not always have everything go as he wished.

---

to create the modern New York Central system. After the Civil War he united the New York Central & Hudson River, Lake Shore & Michigan Southern, Michigan Central, and Canada Southern railroads.

By the Way of
Council Bluffs

8

Robert Louis Stevenson

Although first-class accommodations existed and received considerable attention in tour-book, press, and magazine accounts during the Gilded Age, the vast majority of travelers utilized less elaborate equipment and services. Thus, for most people, "We took the train" meant riding in wooden chair-cars or the more economical "emigrant cars."

Robert Louis Stevenson (1850–1894), the Scottish writer, made an excursion between the coasts in 1892. He used the Pennsylvania Railroad between Jersey City, New Jersey, and Chicago; the Chicago, Burlington & Quincy Railroad between the Windy City and Council Bluffs, Iowa; the Union Pacific Railroad between the "Bluffs" and Ogden, Utah Territory; and the Central Pacific Railroad between Ogden and San Francisco. The distance totalled approximately 3,400 miles. Stevenson's experiences, more so than those of Florence Leslie, capture the flavor of intercity rail journeys a century ago. He skillfully reveals the seamy side of travel by train, complementing nicely Linda Thayer Guilford's adventure through New York.

The landing at Jersey City was done in a stampede. I had a fixed sense of calamity, and, to judge by conduct, the same persuasion was common to us all. A panic selfishness, like that produced by fear, presided over the disorder of our landing. People pushed, and elbowed and ran, their families following how they could. Children fell, and were picked up, to be rewarded by a blow. One child, who had lost her parents, screamed steadily and with increasing shrillness, as though verging towards a fit; an official kept her by him but no one else seemed so much as to remark her distress; and I am ashamed to say that I ran among the rest. I was so weary that I had twice to make a halt and set down my bundles in the hundred yards or so between the pier and the railway station, so that I was quite wet by the time that I got under cover. There was no waiting-room, no refreshment-room; the cars were locked; and for at least another hour, or so it seemed, we had to camp upon the draughty, gas-lit platform. I sat on my valise, too crushed to observe my neighbours; but as they were all cold, and wet, and weary, and driven stupidly crazy by the mismanagement to which we had been subjected, I believe they can have been no happier than myself. I bought half a dozen oranges from a boy, for oranges and nuts were the only refection to be had. As only two of them had even a pretence of juice, I threw the other four under the cars, and beheld, as in a dream, grown people and children groping on the track after my leavings. God knows they could get little comfort from these balls of yellow fibre. But the touch completes the misery of the picture.

You will tell me, perhaps, that people are jostled, driven, and condemned to wait in the cold and rain, to get upon an excursion train or to see a new piece in a theatre; and that these discomforts are constantly, if not always cheerfully supported. I cannot deny it; but whether it was because the trial lasted so long, or because we were here whole families together, carrying all their worldly goods and bent upon a serious end, I know only that I have never seen fellow creatures so stricken down, nor suffered, in my own person, such complete paralysis of mind. The whole business was a nightmare while it lasted, and is still a nightmare to remember. If the railway company cared—but then it does not, and I should address the winds. The officials, who are to blame for this unnecessary suffering, are without doubt humane men and subscribe to public charities; but when all hands are piped, they may find their duty lay some other way. Kindness is the first of virtues; and capacity in a man's own business the greatest kindness in his reach.

At last we were admitted into the cars, utterly dejected, and far from dry. For my own part, I got out a clothes-brush, and brushed my trousers as hard as I could, till I had dried them and warmed my blood into the bargain; but no one else, except my neighbour, to whom I lent the brush, appeared to take the least precaution. As they were, they composed themselves to sleep. I had seen the lights of Philadelphia, and been twice ordered to change carriages and twice countermanded, before I allowed myself to follow their example.

Tuesday.—When I awoke it was already day; the train was standing idle; I was in the last carriage, and, seeing some others strolling to and fro about the lines, I opened the door and stepped forth, as from a caravan by the wayside. We were near no station, nor even, as far as I could see, within reach of any signal. A green, open, undulating country stretched away upon all sides. Locust-trees and a single field of Indian corn gave it a foreign grace and interest; but the contours of the land were soft and English. It was not quite England, neither was it quite France; yet like enough either to seem natural to my eyes. And it was in the sky, and not upon the earth, that I was surprised to find a change. Explain it how you may, and for my part I cannot explain it at all, the sun rises with a different splendour in America and Europe. There is more clear gold and scarlet in our old-country mornings; more purple, brown, and smoky orange in those of the new. It may be from habit, but to me the coming of day is less fresh and inspiriting in the latter; it has a duskier glory, and more nearly resembles sunset; it seems to fit some subsequential, evening epoch of the world, as though America were in fact, and not merely in fancy, farther from the orient of Aurora and the springs of day. I thought so then, by the railroad-side in Pennsylvania, and I have thought so a dozen times since in far distant parts of the continent. If it be an illusion, it is one very deeply rooted, and in which my eyesight is accomplice.

Soon after a train wisked by, announcing and accompanying its passage by the swift beating of a sort of chapel-bell upon the engine; and as it was for this we had been waiting, we were summoned by the cry of "All aboard!" and went on again upon our way. The whole line, it appeared, was topsy-turvy; an accident at midnight having thrown all the traffic hours into arrear. We paid for this in the flesh, for we had no meals all that day. Fruit we could buy upon the cars; and now and then we had a few minutes at some station with a meagre show of rolls and sandwiches for sale; but we were so many and so ravenous that, though I tried at every opportunity, the coffee was always exhausted before I could elbow my way to the counter.

Our American sunrise had ushered in a noble summer's day. There was not a cloud; the sunshine was baking; yet in the woody river-valleys among which we wound our way the atmosphere preserved a sparkling freshness till late in the afternoon. It had an inland sweetness and variety to one newly from the sea; it smelt of woods, rivers, and the delved earth. These, though in so far a country, were airs from home. I stood on the platform by the hour; and as I saw, one after another, pleasant villages, carts upon the highway, and fishers by the stream, and heard cockcrows and cheery voices in the distance, and beheld the sun no longer shining blankly on the plains of ocean, but striking among shapely hills, and his light dispersed and coloured by a thousand accidents of form and surface, I began to exult with myself upon this rise in life like a man who had come into a rich estate. For we are creatures of the shore; and it is only on shore that our senses are supplied with a variety of matter, or that the heart can find her proper business. There is water enough for one by the coasts of any running stream; or if I must indeed look upon the ocean, let it be from along the seaboard, surf-bent, strewn with wreck and dotted at sundown with the clear lights that pilot home bound vessels. The revolution in my surroundings was certainly joyful and complete. And when I had asked the name of a river from the brakesman, the least surly of his class whom I encountered, and heard that it was called the Susquehanna, the beauty of the name seemed to be part and parcel of the beauty of the land. As when Adam with divine fitness named the creatures, so this word Susquehanna was at once accepted by the fancy. That was the name, as no other could be, for that shining river and desirable valley.

None can care for literature in itself who do not take a special pleasure in the sound of names; and there is no part of the world where nomenclature is so rich, poetical, humorous, and picturesque as the United States of America. All times, races, and languages have brought their contribution. Pekin is in the same State with Euclid, with Bellefontaine, and with Sandusky. Chelsea, with its London associations of red brick, Sloane Square, and the King's Road, is own suburb to stately and primeval Memphis; there they have their seat, translated names of cities, where the Mississippi runs by Tennessee and Arkansas; and both, while I was crossing the continent, lay watched by armed men, in the horror and isolation of a plague. Old, red Manhattan lies, like an Indian arrowhead under a steam factory, below Anglified New York. The names of the States and Territories themselves form a chorus of sweet and most romantic vocables: Delaware, Ohio, Indiana, Florida, Dakota, Iowa, Wyoming, Minnesota, and the Carolinas; there are few poems with a nobler music for the ear: a songful, tuneful land; and if the new Homer shall arise from the Western continent, his verse will be enriched, his pages sing spontaneously, with the names of states and cities that would strike the fancy in a business circular.

Late in the evening we were landed in a waiting-room at Pittsburgh. I had now under my charge a young and sprightly Dutch widow with her children; these I was to watch over providentially for a certain distance farther on the way; but as I found she was furnished with a basket of eatables, I left her in the waiting-room to seek a dinner for myself.

I mention this meal, not only because it was the first of which I had partaken for about thirty hours, but because it was the means of my first introduction to a coloured gentleman. He did me the honour to wait upon me after a fashion, while I was eating; and with every word, look, and gesture marched me farther into the country of surprise. He was indeed strikingly unlike the negroes of Mrs. Beecher Stowe, or the Christy Minstrels of my youth. Imagine a gentleman, certainly somewhat dark, but of a pleasant warm hue, speaking English with a slight and rather odd foreign accent, every inch a man of the world, and armed with manners so patronisingly superior that I am at a loss to name their parallel in England. A butler perhaps rides as high over the unbutlered, but then he sets you right with a reserve and a sort of sighing patience which one is often moved to admire. And again, the abstract butler never stoops to familiarity. But the coloured gentleman will pass you a wink at a time; he is familiar like an upper-form boy to a fag; he unbends to you like Prince Hal with Pions and Falstaff. He makes himself at home and welcome. Indeed, I may say, this waiter behaved himself to me throughout that supper much as, with us, a young, free, and not very self-respecting master might behave to a good-looking chambermaid. I had come prepared to pity the poor negro, to put him at his ease, to prove in a thousand condescensions that I was no sharer in the prejudice of race; but I assure you I put my patronage away for another occasion, and had the grace to be pleased with that result.

Seeing he was a very honest fellow, I consulted him upon a point of etiquette: if one should offer to tip the American waiter? Certainly not, he told me. Never. It would not do. They considered themselves too highly to accept. They would even resent the offer. As for him and me, we had enjoyed a very pleasant conversation; he, in particular, had found much pleasure in my society; I was a stranger; this was exactly one of those rare conjunctures. . . . Without being very clearseeing, I can still perceive the sun at noonday; and the coloured gentleman deftly pocketed a quarter.

Wednesday.—A little after midnight I convoyed my widow and orphans on board the train; and morning found us far into Ohio. This had early been a favourite home of my imagination; I have played at being in Ohio by the week, and enjoyed some capital sport there with a dummy gun, my person being still unbreeched. My preference was founded on a work which appeared in *Cassell's Family Paper*, and was read aloud to me by my nurse. It narrated the doings of one Custaloga, an Indian brave, who, in the last chapter, very obligingly washed the paint off his face and became Sir Reginald Somebody-or- other; a trick I never forgave him. The idea of a man being an Indian brave, and then giving that up to be a baronet, was one which my mind rejected. It offended verisimilitude, like the pretended anxiety of Robinson Crusoe and others to escape from uninhabited islands. Just you put me on an uninhabited island, I thought, and then we'll see!

But Ohio was not at all as I had pictured it. We were now on those great plains which stretch unbroken to the Rocky Mountains. The country was flat like Holland, but far from being dull. All through Ohio, Indiana, Illinois, and Iowa, or for as much as I saw of them from the train and in my waking moments, it was rich and various, and breathed an elegance peculiar to itself. The tall corn pleased the eye; the trees were graceful in themselves, and framed the plain into long, aerial vistas; and the clean, bright, gardened townships spoke of country fare and pleasant summer evenings on the stoop. It was a sort of flat paradise; but, I am afraid, not unfrequented by the devil. That morning dawned with such a freezing chill as I have rarely felt; a chill that was not perhaps so measurable by instrument, as it struck home upon the heart and seemed to travel with the blood. Day came in with a shudder. White mists lay thinly over the surface of the plain, as we see them more often on a lake; and though the sun had soon dispersed and drunk them up, leaving an atmosphere of fever-heat and crystal pureness from horizon to horizon, the mists had still been there, and we knew that this paradise was haunted by killing damps and foul malaria. The fences along the line bore but two descriptions of advertisement; one to recommend tobaccos, and the other to vaunt remedies against the ague. At the point of day, and while we were all in the grasp of that first chill, a native of the State, who had got in at some way-station, pronounced it, with a doctoral air, "a fever-and-ague morning."

The Dutch widow was a person of some character. She had conceived at first sight a great aversion for the present writer, which she was at no pains to conceal. But, being a woman of a practical spirit, she made no difficulty about accepting my attentions, and encouraged me to buy her children fruits and candies, to carry all her parcels, and even to sleep upon the floor that she might profit by my empty seat. Nay, she was such a rattle by nature, and so powerfully moved to autobiographical talk, that she was forced, for want of a better, to take me into confidence and tell me the story of her life. I heard about her late husband, who seemed to have made his chief impression by taking her out pleasuring on Sundays. I could tell you her prospects, her hopes, the amount of her fortune, the cost of her house-keeping by the week, and a variety of particular matters that are not usually disclosed except to friends. At one station she shook up her children to look at a man on the platform and say if he were not like Mr. Z.; while to me she explained how she had been keeping company with this Mr. Z., how far matters had proceeded, and how it was because of his desistance that she was now travelling to the west. Then, when I was thus put in possession of the facts, she asked my judgment on that type of manly beauty. I admired it to her heart's content. She was not, I think, remarkably veracious in talk, but broidered as fancy prompted, and built castles in the air out of her past; yet she had that sort of candour, to keep me, in spite of all these confidences, steadily aware of her aversion. Her parting words were ingeniously honest. "I am sure," said she, "we all *ought* to be very much obliged to you." I cannot pretend that she put me at my ease; but I had a certain respect for such a genuine dislike. A poor nature would have slipped, in the course of these familiarities, into a sort of worthless toleration for me.

We reached Chicago in the evening. I was turned out of the cars, bundled into an omnibus, and driven off through the streets to the station of a different railroad.* Chicago seemed a great and gloomy city. I remember

---

*The transfer in Chicago, which had become the nation's railroad mecca by the 1890s, frequently involved a change of stations, for the city lacked a true union terminal until the creation of Amtrak in 1971. However, Robert Louis Stevenson surely did *not* change

having subscribed, let us say sixpence, towards its restoration at the period of the fire; and now when I beheld street after street of ponderous houses and crowds of comfortable burghers, I thought it would be a graceful act for the corporation to refund that sixpence, or, at the least, to entertain me to a cheerful dinner. But there was no word of restitution. I was that city's benefactor, yet I was received in a third-class waiting-room, and the best dinner I could get was a dish of ham and eggs at my own expense.

I can safely say, I have never been so dog-tired as that night in Chicago. I sat, or rather lay, on some steps in the station, and was gratefully conscious of every point of contact between my body and the boards. My one ideal of pleasure was to stretch myself flat on my back with arms extended, like a dying hermit in a picture, and to move no more. I bought a newspaper, but could not summon up the energy to read it; I debated with myself if it were worth while to make a cigarette, and unanimously decided that it was not. When it was time to start, I descended the platform like a man in a dream. It was a long train, lighted from end to end; and car after car, as I came up with it, was not only filled, but overflowing. My valise, my knapsack, my rug, with those six ponderous tomes of Bancroft, weighed my double; I was hot, feverish, painfully athirst; and there was a great darkness over me, an internal darkness, not to be dispelled by gas. When at last I found an empty bench, I sank into it like a bundle of rags, the world seemed to swim away into the distance, and my consciousness dwindled within me to a mere pin's head, like a taper on a foggy night.

When I came a little more to myself, I found that there had sat down beside me a very cheerful, rosy little German gentleman, somewhat gone in drink, who was talking away to me, nineteen to the dozen, as they say. I did my best to keep up the conversation; for it seemed to me dimly as if something depended upon that. I heard him relate, among many other things, that there were pickpockets on the train, who had already robbed a man of forty dollars and a return ticket; but though I caught the words, I do not think I properly understood the sense until next morning; and I believe I replied at the time that I was very glad to hear it. What else he talked about I have no guess; I remember a gabbling sound of words, his profuse gesticulation, and his smile, which was highly explanatory; but no more. And I suppose I must have shown my confusion very plainly; for, first, I saw him knit his brows at me like one who has conceived a doubt; next, he tried me in German, supposing perhaps that I was unfamiliar with the English tongue; and finally, in despair, he rose and left me. I felt chagrined; but my fatigue was too crushing for delay,

---

depots. He arrived on the Pennsylvania and departed on the Burlington, two companies that shared the same Chicago facility. In the 1890s the city had seven principal stations.

and, stretching myself as far as that was possible upon the bench, I was received at once into a dreamless stupor.

The little German gentleman was only going a little way into the suburbs after a *dîner fin*, and was bent on entertainment while the journey lasted. Having failed with me, he pitched next upon another emigrant, who had come through from Canada, and was not one jot less weary than myself. Nay, even in a natural state, as I found next morning when we scraped acquaintance, he was a heavy, uncommunicative man. After trying him on different topics, it appears that the little German gentleman flounced into a temper, swore an oath or two, and departed from that car in quest of livelier society. Poor little gentleman! I suppose he thought an emigrant should be a rollicking, free-hearted blade, with a flask of foreign brandy and a long, comical story to beguile the moments of digestion.

Thursday.—I suppose there must be a cycle in the fatigue of travelling, for when I awoke next morning I was entirely renewed in spirits, and ate a hearty breakfast of porridge, with sweet milk, and coffee and hot cakes, at Burlington upon the Mississippi. Another long day's ride followed, with but one feature worthy of remark. At a place called Creston, a drunken man got in. He was aggressively friendly, but, according to English notions, not at all unpresentable upon a train. For one stage he eluded the notice of the officials; but just as we were beginning to move out of the next station, Cromwell by name, by came the conductor. There was a word or two of talk; and then the official had the man by the shoulders, twitched him from his seat, marched him through the car, and set him flying on to the track. It was done in three motions, as exact as a piece of drill. The train was still moving slowly, although beginning to mend her pace, and the drunkard got his feet without a fall. He carried a red bundle, though not so red as his cheeks; and he shook this menacingly in the air with one hand, while the other stole behind him to the region of the kidneys. It was the first indication that I had come among revolvers, and I observed it with some emotion. The conductor stood on the steps with one hand on his hip, looking back at him; and perhaps this attitude imposed upon the creature, for he turned without further ado, and went off staggering along the track towards Cromwell, followed by a peal of laughter from the cars. They were speaking English all about me, but I knew I was in a foreign land.

Twenty minutes before nine that night we were deposited at the Pacific Transfer Station near Council Bluffs, on the eastern bank of the Missouri river. Here we were to stay the night at a kind of caravanserai, set apart for emigrants. But I gave way to a thirst for luxury, separated myself from my companions, and marched with my effects into the Union Pacific

Hotel. A white clerk and a coloured gentleman, whom, in my plain European way, I should call the boots, were installed behind a counter like bank tellers. They took my name, assigned me a number, and proceeded to deal with my packages. And here came the tug of war. I wished to give up my packages into safe keeping; but I did not wish to go to bed. And this, it appeared, was impossible in an American hotel.

It was, of course, some inane misunderstanding, and sprang from unfamiliarity with the language. For although two nations use the same words and read the same books, intercourse is not conducted by the dictionary. The business of life is not carried on by words, but in set phrases, each with a special and almost a slang signification. Thus every difference of habit modifies the spoken tongue, and even to send off a telegram or order a dish of oysters without some foreign indirectness, an Englishman must have partly learned to be an American. I speak of oysters, because that was the last example that I came across: in San Francisco, if you ask to have your oysters opened, it means they are to be taken from the shell. Some international obscurity prevailed between me and the coloured gentleman at Council Bluffs; so that what I was asking, which seemed very natural to me, appeared to him a monstrous exigency. He refused, and that with the plainness of the West. This American manner of conducting matters of business is, at first, highly unpalatable to the European. When we approach a man in the way of his calling, and for those services by which he earns his bread, we consider him for the time being our hired servant. But in the American opinion, two gentlemen meet and have a friendly talk with a view to exchanging favours if they shall agree to please. I know not which is the more convenient, nor even which is the more truly courteous. The English stiffness unfortunately tends to be continued after the particular transaction is at an end, and thus favours class separations. But on the other hand, these equalitarian plainnesses leave an open field for the insolence of Jack-in-office.

I was nettled by the coloured gentleman's refusal, and unbuttoned my wrath under the similitude of ironical submission. I knew nothing, I said, of the ways of American hotels; but I had no desire to give trouble. If there was nothing for it but to get to bed immediately, let him say the word, and though it was not my habit, I should cheerfully obey.

He burst into a shout of laughter. "Ah!" said he, "you do not know about America. They are fine people in America. Oh! you will like them very well. But you mustn't get mad. I know what you want. You come along with me."

And issuing from behind the counter, and taking me by the arm like an old acquaintance, he led me to the bar of the hotel.

"There," said he, pushing me from him by the shoulder, "go and have a drink!"

THE EMIGRANT TRAIN

All this while I had been travelling by mixed trains, where I might meet with Dutch widows and little German gentry fresh from table. I had been but a latent emigrant; now I was to be branded once more, and put apart with my fellows. It was about two in the afternoon of Friday that I found myself in front of the Emigrant House, with more than a hundred others, to be sorted and boxed for the journey. A white-haired official, with a stick under one arm, and a list in the other hand, stood apart in front of us, and called name after name in the tone of a command. At each name you would see a family gather up its brats and bundles and run for the hindmost of the three cars that stood awaiting us, and I soon concluded that this was to be set apart for the women and children. The second or central car, it turned out, was devoted to men travelling alone, and the third to the Chinese. The official was easily moved to anger at the least delay; but the emigrants were both quick at answering their names, and speedy in getting themselves and their effects on board.

The families once housed, we men carried the second car without ceremony by simultaneous assault. I suppose the reader has some notion of an American railroad-car, that long, narrow wooden box, like a flat-roofed Noah's ark, with a stove and a convenience, one at either end, a passage down the middle, and transverse benches upon either hand. Those destined for emigrants on the Union Pacific are only remarkable for their extreme plainness, nothing but wood entering in any part into their consitution, and for the usual inefficacy of the lamps, which often went out and shed but a dying glimmer even while they burned. The benches are too short for anything but a young child. Where there is scarce elbow-room for two to sit, there will not be space enough for one to lie. Hence the company, or rather, as it appears from certain bills about the Transfer Station, the company's servants, have conceived a plan for the better accommodation of travellers. They prevail on every two to chum together. To each of the chums they sell a board and three square cushions stuffed with straw and covered with thin cotton. The benches can be made to face each other in pairs, for the backs are reversible. On the approach of night the boards are laid from bench to bench, making a couch wide enough for two, and long enough for a man of the middle height; and the chums lie down side by side upon the cushions with the head to the conductor's van and the feet to the engine. When the train is full, of course this plan is impossible, for there must not be more than one to every bench, neither can it be carried out unless the chums agree. It was to bring about this last condition that our white-haired official now bestirred himself. He made a most active master of ceremonies, introducing likely couples, and even guaranteeing the amiability and honesty of each. The greater the number of happy couples the better for his pocket, for it was he who sold the raw material of the beds. His price for one board and three straw cushions began with two dollars and a half; but before the train left, and I am sorry to say long after I had purchased mine, it had fallen to one dollar and a half. I cannot suppose that emigrants are thus befooled and robbed with the connivance of the Company; yet this was the Company's servant. It is never pleasant to bear tales; but this is a system; the emigrants are many of them foreigners and therefore easy to cheat, and they are all so poor that it is unmanly to cheat them; and if the white-haired leach is not contumeliously discharged in this world, I leave him with all confidence to the devil in the next. As for the emigrant, I have better news for him. Let him quietly agree with a chum, but bid the official harpy from his sight; and if he will read a few pages farther, he shall see the profit of his reticence.

The match-maker had a difficulty with me; perhaps, like some ladies, I showed myself too eager for union at any price; but certainly the first who was picked out to be my bedfellow declined the honour without thanks. He was an old, heavy, slow-spoken man, I think from Yankeeland, looked me all over with great timidity, and then began to excuse himself in broken phrases. He didn't know the young man, he said. The young man might be very honest, but how was he to know that? There was another young man whom he had met already in the train; he guessed *he* was honest, and would prefer to chum with *him* upon the whole. All this without any sort of excuse, as though I had been inanimate or absent. I began to tremble lest every one should refuse my company, and I be left rejected. But the next in turn was a tall, strapping, long-limbed, small-headed, curly-haired Pennsylvania Dutchman, with a soldierly smartness in his manner. To be exact, he had acquired it in the navy. But that was all one; he had at least been trained to desperate resolves, so he accepted the match, and the white-haired swindler pronounced the connubial bene-diction, and pocketed his fees.

The rest of the afternoon was spent in making up the train. I am afraid to say how many baggage-waggons followed the engine—certainly a score; then came the Chinese, then we, then the families, and the rear was brought up by the conductor in what, if I have it rightly, is called his caboose. The class to which I belonged was of course far the largest, and we ran over, so to speak, to both sides; so that there were some Caucasians among the Chinamen and some bachelors among the families. But our own car was pure from admixture, save for one little boy of eight or nine who had the whooping-cough. At last, about six, the long train crawled out of the Transfer Station and across the wide Missouri River to Omaha, westward bound.

It was a troubled, uncomfortable evening in the cars. There was thunder in the air, which helped to keep us restless. A man played many airs upon the cornet, and none of them were much attended to, until he came to "Home, Sweet Home." It was truly strange to note how the talk ceased at that, and the faces began to lengthen. I have no idea whether musically this air is to be considered good or bad; but it belongs to that class of art which may be best described as a brutal assault upon the feelings. Pathos must be relieved by dignity of treatment. If you wallow naked in the pathetic, like the author of "Home, Sweet Home," you make your hearers weep in an unmanly fashion; and even while yet they are moved, they despise themselves and hate the occasion of their weakness. It did not come to tears that night, for the experiment was interrupted. An elderly, hard-looking man, with a goatee beard, and about as much appearance of sentiment as you would expect from a retired slaver, turned with a start and bade the performer stop that "damned thing." "I've heard about enough of that," he added; "give us something about the good country we're going to." A murmur of adhesion ran round the car; the performer took the instrument from his lips, laughed and nodded, and then struck into a dancing measure; and, like a new Timotheus, stilled immediately the emotion he had raised.

The day faded; the lamps were lit; a party of wild young men, who got off next evening at North Platte, stood together on the stern platform, singing "The Sweet By-and-By" with very tuneful voices; the chums began to put up their beds; and it seemed as if the business of the day were at an end. But it was not so; for, the train stopping at some station, the cars were instantly thronged with the natives, wives and fathers, young men and maidens, some of them in little more than nightgear, some with stable-lanterns, and all offering beds for sale. Their charge began with twenty-five cents a cushion, but fell, before the train went on again, to fifteen, with the bed-board gratis, or less than one-fifth of what I had paid for mine at the transfer. This is my contribution to the economy of future emigrants.

A great personage on an American train is the newsboy. He sells books (such books!), papers, fruit, lollipops, and cigars; and on emigrant journeys, soap, towels, tin washing-dishes, tin coffee pitchers, coffee, tea, sugar, and tinned eatables, mostly hash or beans and bacon. Early next morning the newsboy went around the cars, and chumming on a more extended principle became the order of the hour. It requires but a co-partnery of two to manage beds; but washing and eating can be carried on most economically by a syndicate of three. I myself entered a little after sunrise into articles of agreement, and became one of the firm of Pennsylvania, Shakespeare, and Dubuque. Shakespeare was my own nick-name on the cars; Pennsylvania that of my bedfellow; and Dubuque, the name of a place in the State of Iowa, that of an amiable young fellow going west to cure an asthma, and retarding his recovery by incessantly chewing or smoking, and sometimes chewing and smoking together. I have never seen tobacco so sillily abused. Shakespeare bought a tin washing-dish, Dubuque a towel, and Pennsylvania a brick of soap. The partners used these instruments, one after another, according to the order of their first awaking; and when the firm had finished there was no want of borrowers. Each filled the tin dish at the water filter opposite the stove, and retired with the whole stock in trade to the platform of the car. There he knelt down, supporting himself by a shoulder against the woodwork, or one elbow crooked about the railing, and made a shift to wash his face and neck and hands—a cold, an insufficient, and, if the train is moving rapidly, a somewhat dangerous toilet.

On a similar division of expense, the firm of Pennsylvania, Shakespeare, and Dubuque supplied themselves with coffee, sugar, and necessary vessels, and their operations are a type of what went on through all the cars. Before the sun was up the stove would be brightly burning; at the first station the natives would come on board with milk and eggs and coffee cakes; and soon from end to end the car would be filled with little parties breakfasting upon the bed-boards. It was the pleasantest hour of the day.

There were meals to be had, however, by the wayside; a breakfast in the morning, a dinner somewhere between eleven and two, and supper from five to eight or nine at night. We had rarely less than twenty minutes for each; and if we had not spent many another twenty minutes waiting for some express upon a side track among miles of desert, we might have taken an hour to each repast and arrived at San Francisco up to time. For haste is not the foible of an emigrant train. It gets through on sufferance, running the gauntlet among its more considerable brethren; should there be a block, it is unhesitatingly sacrificed; and they cannot, in consequence, predict the length of the passage within a day or so. The meals, taken overland, were palatable; and they were not dear, at least for us. I had the pleasure, at one station, of dining in the same room, with express passengers eastward bound, getting dish for dish the identical same dinner, and paying exactly half the charge. It was an experience in which I delighted, and I began to see the advantages of a state of Emigrancy. Civility is the main comfort that you miss. Equality, though conceived very largely in America, does not extend so low down as to an emigrant. Thus in all other trains a warning cry of "All aboard!" recalls passengers to take their seats; but as soon as I was alone with emigrants, and from the Transfer all the way to San Francisco, I found this ceremony was pretermitted; the train stole from the station without note of warning, and you had to keep an eye upon it even while you ate. The annoyance is considerable, and the disrespect both wanton and petty.

Many conductors, again, will hold no communication with an emigrant. I asked a conductor one day at what time the train would stop for dinner;

as he made no answer I repeated the question, with a like result; a third time I returned to the charge, and then Jack-in-office looked me coolly in the face for several seconds and turned ostentatiously away. I believe he was half-ashamed of his brutality; for when another person made the same inquiry, although he still refused the information, he condescended to answer, and even to justify his reticence in a voice loud enough for me to hear. It was, he said, his principle not to tell people where they were to dine; for one answer led to many other questions, as, what o'clock it was; or, how soon should we be there? and he could not afford to be eternally worried.

As you are thus cut off from the superior authorities, a great deal of your comfort depends on the character of the newsboy. He has it in his power indefinitely to better and brighten the emigrant's lot. The newsboy with whom we started from the Transfer was a dark, bullying, contemptuous, insolent scoundrel, who treated us like dogs. Indeed, in his case, matters came nearly to a fight. It happened thus: he was going his rounds through the cars with some commodities for sale, and coming to a party who were at Seven-up or Casino (our two games) upon a bed-board, slung down a cigar-box in the middle of the cards, knocking one man's hand to the floor. It was the last straw. In a moment the whole party were upon their feet, the cigars were upset, and he was ordered to "get out of that directly, or he would get more than he reckoned for." The fellow grumbled and muttered, but ended by making off, and was less openly insulting in the future. On the other hand, the lad who rode with us in this capacity from Ogden to Sacramento made himself the friend of all, and helped us with information, attention, assistance, and a kind of countenance. He told us where and when we should have our meals, and how long the train would stop; kept seats at table for those who were delayed, and watched that we should neither be left behind nor yet unnecessarily hurried. You, who live at home at ease, can hardly realise the greatness of this service, even had it stood alone. When I think of that lad coming and going, train after train, with his bright face and civil words, I see how easily a good many may become the benefactor of his kind. Perhaps he is discontented with himself, perhaps troubled with ambitions; why, if he but knew it, he is a hero of the old Greek stamp; and while he thinks he is only earning a profit of a few cents, and that perhaps exorbitant, he is doing a man's work and bettering the world.

> "Jerry is working in—. It is a good country. You can get from 50 to 60 and 75 Dollars for cooking. Tell me all about the affairs in the States, and how all the folks get along."

And so ends this artless narrative. The little man was at school again, God bless him! while his brother lay scalped upon the deserts.

FELLOW PASSENGERS

At Ogden we changed cars from the Union Pacific to the Central Pacific line of railroad. The change was doubly welcome; for, first we had better cars on the new line; and, second, those in which we had been cooped for more than ninety hours had begun to stink abominably. Several yards away, as we returned, let us say from dinner, our nostrils were assailed by air. I have stood on a platform while the whole train was shunting; and as the dwelling-cars drew near, there would come a whiff of pure menagerie, only a little sourer, as from men instead of monkeys. I think we are human only in virtue of open windows. Without fresh air, you only require a bad heart, and a remarkable command of the Queen's English, to become such another as Dean Swift; a kind of leering, human goat, leaping and wagging your scut on mountains of offence. I do my best to keep my head the other way, and look for the human rather than the bestial in this Yahoo-like business of the emigrant train. But one thing I must say: the car of the Chinese was notably the least offensive, and that of the women and children by a good way the worst. A stroke of nature's satire.

The cars of the Central Pacific were nearly twice as high, and so proportionally airier; they were freshly varnished, which gave us all a sense of cleanliness as though we had bathed; the seats drew out and joined in the centre, so that there was no more need for bed-boards; and there was an upper tier of berths which could be closed by day and opened at night. Thus in every way the accommodation was more cheerful and comfortable, and every one might have a bed to lie on if he pleased. The company deserved our thanks. It was the first sign I could observe of any kindly purpose towards the emigrant. For myself it was, in some ways, a fatal change; for it fell to me to sleep in one of the lofts; and that I found to be impossible. The air was always bad enough at the level of the floor. But my bed was four feet higher, immediately under the roof, and shut into a kind of Saratoga trunk with one side partly open. And there, unless you were the Prince of Camby, it were madness to sleep. Though the fumes were narcotic and weighed upon the eyelids, yet they so smartly irritated the lungs that I could only lie and cough. I spent the better part of one night walking to and fro and envying my neighbors.*

---

*Robert Louis Stevenson arrived in San Francisco a few days later. He disliked the trip across the alkali deserts and sage brush country of Utah and Nevada, but he rejoiced when he reached California. "Every spire of pine along the hill-tops, every trouty pool along that mountain river, was more dear to me than a blood-relation. Few people have praised God more happily than I did."

Nine Thousand Miles on a Pullman Train

9

M. M. Shaw

A plethora of groups traveled together by rail. These included soldiers who left for war; immigrants who arrived from Europe, sometimes most of the future inhabitants of a single frontier community; and parties of "gay travelers" who wanted to "see the sights." The activities of the latter are depicted in an unusual book, Nine Thousand Miles on a Pullman Train: An Account of a Tour of Railroad Conductors from Philadelphia to the Pacific Coast and Return, *published privately in 1898. The author, Milton M. Shaw, who worked as a passenger conductor for the mighty Pennsylvania Railroad, was joined by fellow train-men and their wives on a pleasant cross-country odyssey in spring 1898. The following excerpt describes their time in Colorado, which by the late nineteenth century had emerged as one of America's most popular states for tourists and source of considerable passenger revenue for the region's railroads.*

MONDAY, MAY 31st

Awakened this morning about six o'clock by Mrs. S. remarking, "I never saw the beat! Who would believe that so much of our country is desert?" I thought she was talking in her sleep, but turning over I find her gazing out of the window at the rapidly-fleeting landscape. We have drifted away from the mountains and rocks and are crossing a level, barren plain. For miles we see no sign of habitation or cultivation, but now in the distance we catch sight of an irrigating canal, with here and there a plot of land under cultivation whose fertility and verdure break the hard lines of the desert monotony. We pass a station and upon the name board we see the word "Fruita," a singular name,* we think, for a station; but in the two seconds' glance we have of its surroundings we can but feel that it is appropriate. Irrigating ditches, fertile fields, thrifty orchards, and bloom-ing gardens are all seen in that fleeting glance, and we are more than ever impressed with the fact that it needs but water to convert these desert

---

*Fruita, Colorado, located ten miles west of Grand Junction, was on the mainline of the Rio Grande Western Railway, which officially joined its partner, the Denver & Rio Grande Railroad, in 1901.

tracts into verdant fields. A number of our people are astir, and we too "turn out." We find we are in Colorado, having crossed the State line at Utaline, a little station 35 miles west of Grand Junction, which we are now approaching, and where we arrive about seven o'clock. We halt here only long enough to change engines, but in our brief stay we can see that Grand Junction is quite a town. It has a population of about 4,000; is located at the confluence of the Gunnison and Grand Rivers, with an elevation of 4,500 feet; it is quite a railway centre, being the terminus of both the broad and narrow-gauge lines of the Denver and Rio Grande, the Rio Grande Western and the Colorado Midland Railways.*

At 9:08 A.M. Eastern (7:08 A.M. Mountain) time we leave Grand Junction, on the Denver and Rio Grande Railroad, with engine No. 522, Engineer "Cyclone" Thompson, Fireman Bert Roberts, Conductor William M. Newman, Brakemen J. Grout and O. McCullough. Conductor Hugh Long, of Salida Division No. 132, and Charles E. Hooper, advertising agent of the Denver and Rio Grande Railroad, met our train at Grand Junction, and we find them a pleasing and entertaining addition to our party. They present us with descriptive time tables, illustrated pamphlets, and souvenir itineraries of our trip over the wonderful scenic route of the Denver and Rio Grande Railroad. From Grand Junction to Glenwood Springs we follow the Grand River through the Valley of the Grand, amid grand and beautiful scenery. As we approach Glenwood Springs and pass the little stations of Rifle and Antlers, Brother Sloane grows very enthusiastic, for this is a noted hunting district, with which our brother is familiar. From Newcastle to Glenwood Springs, a distance of 12 miles, we traverse closely the north banks of the Grand River, and parallel with the tracks of the Colorado Midland Railroad on the opposite side.

Arriving at Glenwood Springs at 9:40 A.M., we go direct from the train to the springs under the escort of Mr. Hooper, who has made arrangements to give our party free access to the bathing establishment, where we are very courteously received, and each one who desires to bathe is furnished with a suit and a dressing room. Steps lead down into the pool, which is about a acre in size and filled with warm, sulphurous water to the depth of four to five feet. The hot water, at a temperature of 120 degrees, gushes into the pool on one side at the rate of about 2,000 gallons per minute, and on the opposite side an ice-cold mountain stream pours in at about the same rate, keeping the water at a pleasant bathing temperature.

We spent an hour in the pool and enjoyed it mightily. How much fun

*The Colorado Midland, organized in 1887, operated a 310-mile mainlane between Colorado Springs and Grand Junction, with through passenger service between Denver and Ogden, Utah. Poor management, decreasing mineral traffic and difficult operating conditions led to the collapse of the "Pike's Peak Route" in July 1919 and its subsequent abandonment.

we had we can never tell, but we know we had fun, and other people knew it, too, for the following item appeared in to-day's *Avalanche*, an afternoon Glenwood Springs paper:—

CONDUCTORS IN THE POOL

The Pennsyvania Railroad conductors who arrived in Glenwood Springs this morning from the West had more fun in the pool than a lot of wild Indians. Their shouts of mirth and their laughter could be heard at Cardiff, three miles south. If the Indians ever had as much fun in that pool as those Pennsylvania Railroad conductors, then, Wampam woopham longheir spookham.

We all feel this item does us great honor, but we are puzzled for awhile to understand the meaning of the closing expression, until one of our party who had made a study of savage classic lore interpreted it as meaning, "Yankem, spankem, daredevil blankem."

After leaving the pool, another hour was spent in visiting the sulphur springs and vapor cave and in writing and mailing letters. The latter we did in the beautiful Hotel Colorado, which is located near the bathing establishment and is said to be one of the finest- equipped hotels between the Atlantic and Pacific. The Grand River separates the baths from the town, and is crossed by a double-decker bridge, the lower deck for vehicles, the upper for pedestrians. We recrossed the bridge and after a short wait for our train to be brought to us we again got aboard, and at 3:00 P.M. Eastern (1:00 P.M. Mountain) time left Glenwood Springs bound for Salida.

For 16 miles we wind through the canyon of the Grand River, and view with feelings of admiration and awe those towering walls of rock of such peculiar construction and varied colors that we wonder what remarkable process of Nature could have ever formed them thus. At Gypsum, 25 miles from Glenwood Springs, Grand River disappears from view and we come in sight of Eagle River, following it for several miles. We pass great beds of lava and can see, away in the distance, a burned and blackened course where the lava had flowed down a chasm in the mountain, perhaps thousands of years ago. On the plateaus, at the foot of towering cliffs, are numerous little farms in a thrifty state of cultivation. We stop at Minturn to change engines, and bid "Cyclone" Thompson and his trusty fireman, Bert Roberts, good-bye.

We leave in a few minutes with engine No. 524. Engineer Al. Philliber and Fireman Charley Wilcox are in the cab, "Billy" Newman and his brakemen remain with us. Conductor Newman is a member of Denver Division No. 44 and an enthusiastic lover of the order. He is a model conductor and an entertaining companion. E. A. Thayer, Esq., superintendent of hotel, dining, and restaurant service, is our guest from Glenwood Springs to Salida, and we find him an interesting gentleman. Brother Dougherty has found an old friend in Brother Hugh Long, and he has much enjoyment in his company. Charley Hooper is everybody's friend and always has an admiring, interested group around him, and if we could only remember all that Charley tells us we could write an intensely interesting companion.

Soon after leaving Minturn we enter Eagle River Canyon, whose sloping, pine-fringed walls rise to the height of over 2,000 feet on either side, almost shutting out the light of day. A heavy shower adds to the gloom, but does not detract from the interest, for these mighty mountain sides are honeycombed with hundreds of mines and dotted with the cabins of miners. It is very curious and wonderful to see a human habitation hanging, as it were, a thousand feet in the air, on the side of a mountain, where it would seem a mountain goat could hardly obtain a foothold; yet there they are, and many of them—in one place an entire village of red and white cottages, so very high up that they look like miniature houses or dove cots suspended in the air. The products of the mines are lowered to the railroad tracks by means of tramways operated by endless chains or cables, and material is conveyed to the lofty residents by the same novel arrangement.

For four miles we wind up through this marvelous mountain ravine, deeply interested in the wonderful sights and scenery of this extraordinary mining industry. A short stop is made at Belden, where extensive gold mines are in operation, but so high up on the mountain side are the shafts or entrances to the mines that it is impossible to visit them in the limited time we have. Since leaving Minturn our course has been gradually upward, and we have Engineer Amberson, with helper engine No. 513, to assist us up the grade. Emerging from the famous and never-to-be-forgotten Eagle River Canyon, we shortly come to the mining town of Red Cliff. It is a lively, thrifty place of about 1,000 inhabitants, has an elevation of 8,671 feet, and is surrounded by grand mountain scenery. From this point Mr. Hooper directs our attention to a view of the Mount of the Holy Cross, but only a glimpse is obtained of the great white cross and then it is lost to view. "Distance lends enchantment to the view," quotes Mr. Thayer. "Do you know," he continues, "were it possible to transport you to the summit of yonder mount, 20 miles away, and set you down, you would see no semblance of a cross? You would only see rugged rocks, desolate peaks, and snow-filled ravines; you would look in vain for the sublime and typical beauty that you so easily discern 20 miles or more away. You would see, were you in a proper location, the conditions and materials that make your beautiful picture. A great valley or ravine extends down the mountain side, into which the snows of many Winters have drifted. This is one of Nature's perpetual ice houses, whose supply never becomes exhausted. Across the face of the mountain, near the summit, crossing this ravine at right angles, is another great depression or fissure, likewise filled with perpetual ice and snow. All the surroundings are rugged, rough, and broken, and you would never think of looking for the likeness of a cross in the wild, bleak desolation of ice-bound, snow-filled mountain chasms. Distance, however, obliterates the rocks and roughness and smooths the rugged features of the mountain side, and the great white cross of snow stands out in bold relief, as though formed of carved and polished marble. It is a pretty picture, and one that the imagination and sentiment of man have almost rendered sacred."

We are now approaching Tennessee Pass, and our engines are working hard as they climb the steep ascent. Our progress is slow, but so much the better, as it gives us an opportunity to contemplate and enjoy the indescribable beauty of this famous mountain scenery. We reach the pass shortly after four o'clock, at an altitude of 10,418 feet, the highest point on the main line of the Denver and Rio Grande Railroad. Here we again cross the Great Continental Divide and enter the Atlantic slope. Mr. Hooper calls our attention to a tiny stream of water flowing near the track, remarking as he does so, "That is the headwaters of the Arkansas River. We follow it for a number of miles and it will be interesting to notice it gradually increasing in size and volume as we proceed." Our course is slightly downward and our rate of speed increases. We soon reach Leadville, where we halt for half an hour. The time is insufficient to allow us to visit the town, but we get out and look around. A train of freight cars is standing on a sidetrack a short distance away, loaded with ore, and the "boys" are told to help themselves. A number avail themselves of the opportunity of procuring Leadville "specimens" for souvenirs. The pieces carried away, I imagine, contain but very little of the precious metal, for I believe, judging from the appearance, that the "specimens" are being obtained from a train load of railroad ballast. I tell Brothers Sparks and Matthews and some of the rest my convictions, but they call me a "tenderfoot" and say I "don't know a good thing when I see it." Maybe I don't, but I have a chunk of that stuff in my pocket that I will take home and exhibit to my friends as a specimen of Leadville gold quartz, and if they know no more about the material than I do they will believe it. If it is but a stone, I will prize it as a souvenir from the most noted mining camp of the West.

Our half hour is up and Conductor Newman and Manager Wyman are shouting "All aboard!" We scramble on and at 7:40 P.M. Eastern (5:40 P.M. Mountain) time our train pulls out and we leave in our rear an interesting, picturesque, and famous town. At Malta, five miles from Leadville, we lay on a sidetrack ten minutes waiting for a train we meet at this point. Leaving Malta, we pass through a fertile valley, through which flows the Arkansas River, that we notice is rapidly growing larger and more turbulent. We are still running parallel with the Colorado Midland Railroad, which for miles is within fifty feet of the Denver and Rio Grande. We notice a severe storm raging on a mountain not far away, and it seems to be snowing hard at the summit.

As we pass Buena Vista, 25 miles west of Salida, the setting sun is shining upon the snow-crowned summits of the collegiate group of mountain peaks, Harvard, Yale, and Princeton, and many are the exclamations of pleasure and delight at the beauty and grandeur of the sight. These three peaks, each over 14,000 feet in height, are a part of the Sawatch Range of the Rocky Mountains. With their cloud-veiled crests wreathed in perpetual snow, those majestic, rugged giants are ever subjects of interest and pleasure to tourists; but this evening the setting sun has transformed their crowns of glistening snow into dazzling diamonds, and the veil of fleecy clouds that hang about their summits into a gorgeous canopy of purple, silver, and gold. It is a scene of transcendent loveliness and grandeur. No wonder our people are in ecstasies of delight. Mrs. Dougherty claps her hands, and Mrs. Matthews exclaims, "Jimmie, look!" Jimmie, Waddie, Oscar, and the Colonel suspend their interesting game of euchre and turn their attention for a moment to the mountains and the clouds. Mrs. Horner has such an expression of intense rapture in her face that Sam, thinking she is about to have a fit, pours a glass of ice water down her back. Mrs. Mattson says she believes she has an artist's soul, for a sight like this makes her nerves tingle and her mouth water, and the Doctor, standing near, is explaining to an interested circle the philosophy of sunshine, clouds, and colors in their relation to towering, snow-crowned peaks. Suddenly mountain views are obstructed and the light of day is almost excluded by massive walls of rock that encompass us. We have plunged into Brown's Canyon, a mighty chasm in the mountain, between whose towering cliffs there is just room enough for the Arkansas River and the railroad. For many, many years the river held undisputed sway and rushed unaccompanied and alone through this rocky, desolate gorge, till then the railroad came. The nerve and daring of the men who brought it were equal to the task. They followed the foaming river into this wild ravine and fearlessly built their tracks upon its spray-bathed banks; and now as train and river rush headlong together through this narrow, dark defile, the snort of the locomotive and rumble of the train mingles with the roar and gurgle of the tumultuous torrent.

We emerge from the canyon as suddenly as we entered it, and the broad, fertile valley of the Arkansas greets our vision. It is a pleasant change. Still following the river, we traverse the valley until at 7:55, as daylight is fading and it is growing dusk, our train comes to a stop in Salida. We are met at the station by Superintendent R. M. Ridgway, Trainmaster G. H. Barnes, and Chief Dispatcher W. Rech, of the Denver and Rio Grande Railroad, who give us a cordial welcome and kindly inform us that arrangements have been made to give us a trip to-morrow over the narrow-gauge road to Marshall Pass and return. Escorted by Mr. Hooper and Conductor Newman, a number of us start out to see the town.

Salida is a quiet, clean, orderly, picturesque little mountain town of about 3,500 inhabitants. It is situated on the Arkansas River, with an elevation of 7,050 feet. We accept an invitation to visit the fine parlors of the Salida Club and are royally treated by the members present. Our bosom friend and life preserver, Tom McDonald, is along, and proves to be quite an expert with the billiard cue, giving his opponent, Dr. Mattson, a hard hustle in the game they play. A party of our ladies get on our trail and overtake us at the club. They present the bachelor brothers of the party each with a miniature souvenir spoon, but give no explanation why this is done. The inference is that it is but an act of sisterly goodfellowship that needs no interpretation. Following the presentation of the spoons the ladies entertain us for half an hour with excellent singing and music on the piano. As it draws near midnight we return to our train and turn in. Some of the "boys," it is noticed, are not with us when we reach the train, and to them I will have to ascribe another line of "unwritten history."

TUESDAY, JUNE 1ST

Everybody is up bright and early this morning, in anticipation of the promised trip up the mountains to Marshall Pass. After breakfast we board a special train on the Denver and Rio Grande Narrow-Gauge Railroad, and at 8:12 o'clock start on a novel and interesting ride of 25 miles over a road that is a marvel of engineering ingenuity and skill. It requires two engines to make the laborious ascent, which in many places is 211 feet to the mile. Our engines are No. 175, manned by Engineer Sam Roney and Fireman W. Brewster; helper engine No. 400, Engineer W.D. Yates, Fireman M. M. Smith. Conductor M. Guerin has charge of the train, and the brakemen are Tom Kelley and F. Duncan.

Five miles from Salida we reach Poncha Junction, and here the winding and climbing commences in earnest. The weather since we started has become unfavorable; clouds obsure the sun and hide the summits of the surrounding peaks. It has commenced to rain, but the rain lasts only for a little while. As we ascend the clouds become lighter, and finally we see the sun and the sky. Looking down, the clouds and mist hide the valleys from our sight—we are above the clouds and rain; looking up, we behold the brightest, bluest sky we have ever seen; and still our course is upward. Our engines snort and cough and puff as they slowly climb and wind the spiral pathway that leads to the wind-swept summit.

As we near the top we have a magnificent unobstructed view of grand, majestic mountain scenery. Near by looms up mighty Mt. Ouray, an extinct volcano, down whose rugged sides, ages ago, the molten lava flowed; fire-scarred and grim he stands, a silent, frowning sentinel guarding the mountain pass. His companion, Mt. Shaveno, is near, his towering summit being crowned with eternal snow. Mounts Ouray and Shaveno were named in honor of the famous Ute Indian chiefs, and are everlasting monuments to the memory of a once powerful tribe.

Far in the distance, many miles to the south, can be seen, mingling with the sky and clouds, the gleaming peaks of the Sangre de Cristo Mountains. . . . All this range of vision, from Ouray to Sangre de Cristo, is filled with picturesque valleys, timbered hills, mountain canyons, towering peaks, and glistening snow. While we are feasting our eyes upon this grandeur, suddenly it is shut out from view, for we have entered a dismal snow shed. The train stops and our journey is ended. We get out of the train, and looking around, we see a door that leads from the shed, which we pass through, and find snowdrifts six feet deep and the wind blowing a gale.

I see Brother Restein snap his Kodak at Colonel and Mrs. Mitchell as they bravely face the wintry blast; the committee is lined up and he also snaps at them. Steps lead to a lofty tower and a number of us ascend. Some start and turn back; the exertion makes your heart beat like a trip hammer, cuts your wind, and makes you dizzy. We who reach the top do not tarry long; the view is magnificent, but the wind is cold. Overcoats and wraps were brought along and they are needed; the thermometer registered eleven last night, and now it stands at thirty-three. It is a bleak, barren, wind-swept place, and yet it is healthy.

A family has been living here for five years. The husband and father is employed on the road and the mother has charge of the station. She has never been absent from the place, she says, since they took up their residence here. The oldest child was an infant when they came, and two have been born since. They are fine, healthy children, and have never been sick. A doctor has never visited them, she says, because one has never been needed. We are ready to leave before the train is ready to take us; a short visit to a place like this is sufficient. Several of the "boys" amuse themselves by snowballing one another and washing with snow the faces of some of the "girls."

Marshall Pass is 10,852 feet above the level of the sea, and is situated upon a point of the Great Continental Divide—on the ridge pole, as it were, between the Atlantic and Pacific slopes. Within the dingy snow shed where our train is standing we notice water slowly trickling down the bank into the ditch along the track; it makes a tiny stream, just large enough to flow, and we can see that it is running in each direction. A number of us place our fingers upon the dividing line, thus literally touching a point of the very comb of the great water shed between the Atlantic and Pacific Oceans.

Our return is made with more speed than our ascent, but in a very careful manner; helper engine 400 is detached and sent ahead. The descent is made by gravity, the air brakes being used to keep the train under control. Engineer Roney deserves great credit for the careful manner in which he handles the train. A stop of five minutes is made at Mear's Junction, where we make the acquaintance of Station Agent Smith, who, along with his duties as station agent and telegraph operator, is an artist of merit; a number of pictures of mountain scenery that he has painted adorn the walls of the station rooms.

When we get back to Salida and to our train it is 2:05 P.M. Eastern (12:05 P.M. Mountain) time. We find our friend McDonald looking for us, with an abundant lunch prepared, which we heartily appreciate and thoroughly enjoy. We are scheduled to leave here at one o'clock, and as it is nearing that time, we bid adieu to the good people of Salida who have shown us such a royal time, and at one o'clock, sharp, we steam away from the pretty little town, bound for Colorado Springs, 142 miles nearer home.

Leaving Salida we have engine 509, in charge of Engineer John Carr and Fireman R. Wilmonger. Our conductor is J. E. Duey, a member of Arkansas Valley Division No. 36, of Pueblo, Colo. Brother Duey enjoys the notoriety of being a cousin to the late Jesse James, the famous bandit and train robber. The brakemen are S. G. Carlisle and William Shoemaker. Charlie Hooper is still with us, and at present is busily engaged in distributing fine photographic pictures of scenes along the picturesque Denver and Rio Grande Railroad. Mr. Hooper's kindness and generosity are greatly appreciated, and the pictures will be highly prized as valuable souvenirs of our trip. In addition to Mr. Hooper we have with us as guests Brothers W. Newman and Frank Smith, of Division 44, and Harry Hart, of Division 36. A short stop is made at Parkdale, 46 miles from Salida, where we meet Rev. John Brunton, who is invited to accompany us to Pueblo. Mr. Brunton, who is an old engineer, retired from active service, is First Division Chaplain, and has charge of the employes' reading room in Pueblo. He is an entertaining old gentleman; says he is employed to fight the devil, who is always sneaking around after railroad men. Brother Houston says, "A man like that is needed on the Schuylkill Division." No one replies to this insinuation, except Brother Reagan, who merely says, "Sure."

Soon after leaving Parkdale we enter the Grand Canyon of the Arkansas, which is 8 miles in length and the crowning wonder of all the marvelous sights we have yet beheld; a mighty pathway, right through the heart of the Rocky Mountains, hewn by Nature through inaccessible towering mountain walls. Through this narrow gorge, whose perpendicular walls rise to the height of over 200 feet, the crowded, pent-up waters of the Arkansas River rush and roar and foam. There is scarcely space for both railroad and river, but with an audacity that knows no shrinking the intrepid engineers entered the walled-up, darksome canyon, and, following the intricate winding of the surging stream, laid their tracks of steel along its foam-flecked bank. Beyond a doubt it is the most daring feat of railroad engineering ever performed. When half way through the awful Royal

Gorge is reached, here the river holds despotic, undisputed sway for a distance of 100 feet. There is no bank to lay the tracks upon; from wall to wall the river surges, leaps and roars. From out the water those mighty walls, but by Nature's hand, run right straight up, 2,600 feet in the air. Ingenuity and nerve solves the problem; a bridge is built parallel with the river's course, one side resting upon a granite ledge, hewn in the side of the cliff, the other side suspended from rods attached to the overhanging wall of the opposite cliff. Over this construction the trains securely pass, while underneath the torrent rushes on.

Before reaching the bridge our train stops, and as many as wish get out and walk over, in order to obtain a good view of the awe-inspiring grandeur of the Royal Gorge. It is truly a wonderful sight, and one we will never forget. We do not tarry long to contemplate the scenery, for a mean, commonplace shower of rain is falling, and we hurry to the train to avoid getting wet.

Issuing from the canyon, we enter a broad fertile valley, through which flows the ever-present Arkansas River, and in a short time pass through Canon City, a town of considerable importance, having a population of 3,000, and the county seat of Fremont County. The State penitentiary is located here, and near by are mineral springs of great value, making it a favorite resort for those in quest of retirement or health. We didn't stop. The sight of the broad, unfettered freedom of the fertile Arkansas Valley, with its hundreds of acres of fine orchards and miles of magnificent grazing land, is a pleasure and relief after so much cramped and rocky glory, and gloomy, walled-up grandeur.

Pueblo is reached at 6:26 P.M. Eastern (4:26 P.M. Mountain) time, and a stop of ten minutes is made for the purpose of changing engines. We have not time to take in the city, but we disembark and take a look about the depot, which is called Union Station, being the joint property of five different roads and used by them all, namely, the Denver and Rio Grande, Sante Fe, Missouri Pacific, Rock Island, and Union Pacific, Denver and Gulf.* The building is composed of red sandstone, a handsome structure, and is commodious and convenient. Pueblo, though situated in a valley or basin surrounded on three sides by distant mountain ranges, enjoys an elevation of 4,668 feet. It has a population of 40,000 inhabitants, is the centre of extensive mining industries and immense railroad traffic. Because of its great, ever-smoking smelters, and glowing furnaces and foundries, Pueblo is often called the "Pittsburgh of the West." The Arkansas River flows through the heart of the city, but is not navigable, and its sloping banks are neatly walled to prevent overflow in time of

---

*The Union Pacific, Denver & Gulf Railway was about to disappear. An amalgam of twelve roads merged in 1890, the "Gulf Line" once revolved in the orbit of the Union Pacific. But in November 1898, not long after Shaw's reference, the Gulf Line went its own way as the Colorado & Southern Railway, later part of the Burlington system.

freshet. Bidding good-bye to our old new-found friend, Rev. Brunton, and waving adieu to the 509 and the gallant men in her cab who brought us safely through such scenes of weird, bewildering, perilous grandeur, we start on our way again with engine 534, in charge of Engineer Henry Hinman and Fireman George Courtly. Conductor Duey and Brakemen Carlisle and Shoemaker go with us to Colorado Springs.

After leaving Pueblo we pass through an extensive oil district, where many wells are in operation, and we are told the yield is very heavy. We arrive in Colorado Springs at 8:20 P.M. Eastern (6:20 P.M. Mountain) time, escorted by Brothers Newman, Hart, Smith, and Mr. Hooper, we start out to see the town. Colorado Springs is a model town. It is quiet, clean, and dry; in fact, it is *very* dry, being entirely and teetotally temperance. But this is a commendable trait; we find no fault, and are all impressed with the morality and good order which prevail. It is a healthy place; the houses are not crowded together. The population is 12,000; the town has an elevation of 5,982 feet, and covers an area of four square miles. It is much resorted to by invalids, and thousands, we are told, are yearly benefited by taking advantage of its exhilarating atmosphere, favorable climatic conditions, and the pleasure and enjoyment derived from interesting and beautiful natural environments.

Soon after starting out we encounter Brother D. F. McPherson, secretary and treasurer of Holy Cross Division 252, of Leadville, who joins us in our rambles. After giving the quiet little city a pretty thorough inspection, we are grouped upon a corner discussing where we shall go next. "We have shown you the most cleanly and orderly town in the State of Colorado," remarks Mr. Hooper, "and now I would like to show you just the reverse; we will take the next car and slip over to Oldtown." In two minutes the car comes, and getting aboard, a ride of two miles brings us to the neighboring town, where it seems every third door is a saloon and gambling resort. Wherever we go there is turmoil and excitement. We see no outbreaks of strife, but in these crowded gambling rooms we visit, the swarthy miner and reckless stockman jostle one another in their eagerness to reach the tempting roulette wheel or alluring faro table. We can see they are excited, although they are calm, but it is the calmness of suppressed emotion, and we are careful as we move among them not to tread upon their toes; not that we are afraid to tramp their toes if we want to, but we don't want to; we didn't come out West to make trouble, so we are always careful what we do, if we are not so careful where we go.

Getting enough of Oldtown, we board a car and are soon back in sedate Colorado Springs and seek our train, that is sidetracked for occupancy near the station. I size up the crowd as they file in and find some are missing; they have dropped out of the ranks and escaped us, and—more "unwritten history." It is near midnight, all is dark and silent, and we quietly seek our berths.

Young hoboes ride Chicago & North Western's trains #703 near South Elgin, Illinois, on August 10, 1933. These lads likely climbed onto the milk-car in West Chicago for a thrilling twelve-mile trip to Elgin. (George Krambles Coll.)

Traveling without Tickets

John W. Barriger III, who headed the
Railroad Division of the Reconstruction
Finance Corporation from 1933 to 1941,
photographed this forlorn hobo while
touring the Missouri, Kansas & Texas
Railway in April 1935. On the print
Barriger noted simply, "Old Negro at
Muskogee [Oklahoma]." (John W.
Barriger III; Barriger Railroad Coll., St.
Louis Mercantile Library)

HARVEST HANDS
LEAVING MITCHELL
ON A NORTH BOUND
FREIGHT.

JULY 1916

L. E. STAIR
PHOTO.

"BOES" BEATING THEIR WAY TO N. DAKOTA
ON A C. & N.W. FREIGHT TRAIN AUG. 13–1914

PHOTO BY
HERSEY & HERS...
HECLA, S.D.

Shortly before World War I, commercial photographers in Mitchell and Hecla, South Dakota, caught "boes" on freight trains as they passed through their communities. These "ticketless" riders were headed for the annual wheat harvests on the northern plains via the Milwaukee and Chicago & North Western railroads. (Left: Center for Western Studies; Above: Don L. Hofsommer Coll.)

10 "Brownie"

Charles P. Brown

Not all travelers paid fares. Some received complimentary annual or trip passes until the government outlawed free franks to most individuals, except railroad employees. But many more simply stole rides, usually aboard poky freight trains. One who hopped freights was a poor, Missouri-born lad, Charles P. "Brownie" Brown (1879– 19??). Although he later became an itinerant railroad brakeman and fireman, a "boomer," he initially toured sections of the Midwest and West in search of work and excitement by "riding the rods." Brownie's experiences on the Chicago, Milwaukee & St. Paul and Northern Pacific railroads in the late 1890s are typical of those of thousands of young men.

Now, I remember it was in the latter part of July, and the weather was hot and dry, when one day Pat and I hopped a freight train on the C. & E. I. and beat our way to Chicago.* (Beating your way means stealing a ride on a train without paying any railroad fare.) Well, when Pat and I got to Chicago it was in the night time and we went to a cheap rooming house for men only, on State Street, and got us a bed, that is, we each got a little cell-like room with a very narrow cot in it to sleep on. Now the partitions of these little rooms were just a little higher than a man's head and the whole works was covered with heavy wire netting.

I remember that Pat and I almost backed out when we saw this layout, for we thought that we had busted into some kind of jail or other, but as we had paid our money, we had to make the best of it for we were pretty short as it was, so we piled onto the cots and went to sleep and they were not so bad after all.

Now these sleeping places are known to the roving classes of working men as flop houses, and you will find them in all big cities where there is many homeless working men, and they are a pretty good thing for the men at that.

Well, the next day Pat and I walked around and took a look at the town, for it was the first time that either one of us had been in Chicago

---

*Charles P. Brown and his friend, Patrick Kelly, lived in Hoopeston, Illinois, 99 miles south of Chicago on the mainline of the "Evansville Route," the Chicago & Eastern Illinois Railroad.

before, and we wanted to see all we could before proceeding on our journey.

I remember we went up on top of the Masonic Temple and took a look at Lake Michigan, and boy, as it was the first big body of water that I had ever seen, it sure gave me a thrill. Then we went out to Lincoln Park and gave things the once over, and from there we went over to Ferris Wheel Park right near there, and took a ride on the old Ferris wheel which was one of the great attractions of the Chicago World's Fair in 1893. Then we took in a show, after which we went back to the flop house and slept in our little cells.

Well, Pat and I took a street car and rode out to the Chicago Milwaukee and St. Paul railroad yards, where we caught a freight train and beat it for Milwaukee, where we arrived early the next morning.

And after eating some breakfast, we went to the Old Soldiers Home, and slept on the grass all of that day, in the Soldiers Home Park. And that evening just about dark,we grabbed another C. M. & St. P. freight train headed west for LaCrosse, Wisconsin. (Now I will explain here that Pat and I were headed for Fargo, North Dakota, to make the great wheat harvest.) And there were lots of other fellows, both young and old traveling the side door pullman route, headed for the great Northwest to make a stake in the harvest. (Making a stake means that a fellow will work on a job long enough to make himself some money to carry him over while he is traveling to some other part of the country that suits him better.)

Well, after riding all night and most of the next day, we pulled into LaCrosse, a little city located on the east bank of the Mississippi River in Wisconsin, and it was a division point for the C. M. & St. Paul road, and also the C. B. & Q.

Well, Pat and I did not stick around there only long enough to wash up and get something to eat, then we walked across the river on a wagon bridge and waited for a train on the west side (as the C. M. & St. P. crossed the river there over into Minnesota, where it followed the west bank of the river up to St. Paul), for it was easier to catch a train over there, as the yard bulls (railroad police) were inclined to be hostile to the hoboes in the railroad yards of LaCrosse. And the railroad shacks* were out for the money, and if they caught you hiding on their trains it was either dig up or unload (meaning pay or get off). So that evening a little after dark, a long freight train made up of empty boxcars (known to railroad men as a drag of empties) came across the river and headed for St. Paul, the next division point north of there, so Pat and

---

*A "shack" is railroad jargon for brakeman. The name likely came from the wooden enclosure or shack located on the locomotive tender or "tank." This was where the head brakeman commonly rode.

I grabbed her and climbed into an empty boxcar with several hoboes.

I remember that Pat and I were setting over in one corner of the car trying to get some shut eye (sleep), when one of the brakemen stuck his lantern in through the small end door, and when he saw us in there he climbed through the door and dropped down inside the car (and he was one of them tough, hard-boiled babies too, believe me). So he held his lantern above his head (which railroad men do, as they can see much better in a dark boxcar) and says to us men, where all you bums goin' and what are you ridin' on, and some sap over in a far corner of the car makes a wise crack that is ridin' on this here boxcar, and that crack sort of riled the old boomer brakeman, so he walked over and took a look at the wiseacre, and says, say listen bo, don't try to get funny with me, cause I am bad medicine my self. Then he turns around and says to the rest of us, come on all of you yeggs* and line up here, I wanta see whatcha got. So we all went over to where he was, and he says to the yegg that he had bawled out, what have ya got, and the guy told him that he did not have anything, so the shack says, you will stand a frisk (meaning would he let the brakeman search him) and the fellow said no, then the shack told him to stand over by the door, so he sifted us out and the fellows that gave him some money, he let them ride, but the rest of us that did not dig up had to unload.

Well, as the train was not going very fast it was easy to get back on again, which we did, for it is hard to keep men off a long drag of empties after night when it is dark, so after playing hide and seek with the train crew all night, Pat and I rode the train into the St. Paul yards the next morning.

And after we got some breakfast, we took a street car and rode over to Minneapolis, where we went to a flop house and slept all day. And that evening after we got up and ate some supper, we went out to the Northern Pacific yards and caught a train headed west. And after dodging the train crew all night we rode into a little town called Staples, Minn., which was the next division point west.

So Pat and I went over to a little restaurant near the yards where we washed up and got a good breakfast of ham and eggs and plenty of coffee, after which we went back to the yards, just in time to catch a train pulling out for Fargo, the next division point west of there, and I remember that we climbed up on a flatcar loaded with a new traction engine and that there were many other men setting along the sides of the car with their feet hanging over the edge. So pretty soon along came the head brakeman (and he was a foxy old boomer too), and he says to the men, hello there boys, I suppose you are all going out to the wheat harvest, yes; well

---

*"Yeggs" is a common hobo term that refers to "bad apples," or potentially dangerous individuals. Yeggs frequently robbed fellow, "side-door pullman" riders.

now be careful don't get hurt, and all of you boys with your feet hanging over there, watch out for them cattle guard fences that they don't catch your feet and drag you off while going by, then he says who is going to give me a chaw of terbacker, and one of the big Swedes setting alongside of me offered him a chew of Copenhagen out of his snuffbox, but someone had passsed his plugcut up to the old boy by this time and he took a chaw as he called, then he says, well boys, I have got to be moseying along but before I go, I will pass my hat around and take up the collection, so throw in what you can and help me out, for I am working extra at the present time and am not making much money.

Well he had us all so bulled up by this time, that we would have given him a French kiss on both cheeks if he had of asked us to, for everybody dropped something in his hat as he passed it around.

Well, we rode all the rest of the day, and some time before midnight we pulled into Fargo, and Pat and I had reached our journey's end for the time being anyway, for this was the place that we had started out for, so we went to a cheap rooming house and got us a bed and hit the hay between the sheets, for this was the second time that we had slept in a bed since we left Chicago.

Now the little town of Fargo is located in the Redriver Valley on the west bank of the Redriver, and the Redriver Valley in North Dakota and Minnesota, is known to be one of the greatest wheat growing districts in the world, and there were hundreds of men flocking into Fargo, for this was the distribution point for the great wheat fields, and boy, I never saw so much growing wheat before nor since.

Well, as near as I can remember, it was around the third or fourth of August, 1898, when Pat and I reached Fargo, and the wheat was a little too green to cut as yet, so the farmers were not taking on any help just then, and the outcome of it was, there was a small army of hobo wheat harvest hands waiting for the big works to start, and the most of them were living just outside of the town in hobo camps along the river banks. Now in the slang of the hobo, these camps are known as jungles, and you will always find them located where the men can get fire-wood and water.

Now as Pat and I had taken up with two other boys, we all four went out into the jungles and made us a camp, and we each one would throw in some money and make up a jackpot, then a couple of us would go into town and buy some groceries, and bring them back to the jungles and cook up a big can of mulligan-stew, for we done all of our cooking and eating in the jungles. We only eat two meals a day, but oh, boy, they sure did taste good. No doubt you wonder what we used for cooking utensils in the jungles. Well in all hobo jungle camps, there is all sorts of tin cans, ranging from the well known tomato can, up to the big five gallon square oil cans, and the hoboes cut the tops out of these different cans and use them to cook with, and they also use the big oil cans to boil up with (boil and wash their clothes). We used to take one of the big square cans and cut it off about two inches from the bottom and use it (that is the bottom part) to fry bacon and eggs and potatoes in, just like a skillet or a frying pan, we would use the one gallon fruit cans to boil food in, and the small tomato cans to drink coffee out of.

Now after a guy has bummed around over the country long enough to get wise to himself, after he cooks a meal in a jungle camp, he will always wash up the cans and frying pans that he has used and leave them in good order for the next fellow, for that is the code of the hoboes in the jungles, especially among the old time hoboes.

11

Riding Freights to Jamestown in 1936

Erling Kildahl

"Riding the rods," whether in the 1890s (Brownie's story) or the 1930s, or at any time, was never pleasant. For some, like the impoverished yet ambitious Erling Kildahl (1917–   ), it proved absolutely essential. Here was a young man who lived in Idaho and wanted to attend college in North Dakota, hundreds of miles to the east. Unable to afford either a bus or train ticket, he joined his older brother, Harold (1909–   ), on a trek that left vivid memories more than fifty years later.

The trip of Erling Kildahl involved travel over two of the three "northern" transcontinental railroads, the Chicago, Milwaukee, St. Paul & Pacific (née Chicago, Milwaukee & St. Paul) which had reached Washington state in 1909, and the Northern Pacific, a carrier that had served this territory since 1883. Such roads attracted large numbers of "hoboes," especially during the Great Depression. Many hopped freights in search of work in the orchards of the Pacific Northwest, the wheat fields of the northern Great Plains, or at any task.

The carload of lumber in which I was nestled creaked ominously and woke me. I glanced at my brother, Harold, curled up a few feet away. No break in his breathing meant he was oblivious to the unusual sound. He had warned me when we climbed aboard the loaded flatcar that lumber could shift with little or no warning. Was this a warning? I waited, nervously. Should I shake him awake so we could jump off the train before the load injured us? I still hesitated. Nothing happened. "Huck" slept on. I must have trusted his instinct for survival because my fears subsided.

We had searched for an empty boxcar in the early evening dark, couldn't find one, and settled for the loaded flat. Dangerous, true, but time was precious. We had to go east as quickly as possible. Both of us were exhausted from a long day, the auto trip from Coeur d'Alene, somewhat gloomy good-byes, and nervous, impatient waiting for a suitable train. We had hopped a long freight on the Chicago, Milwaukee, St. Paul and Pacific main line in St. Maries, Idaho, located at the southern end of Lake Coeur d'Alene. And here we were on a stack of wood, comfortable enough if a rider can find a space his body can adjust to. (Old timers claimed, I'd heard, that lumber makes the best ride if you can sit or lie on the soft sides of the boards.) Glancing again at Huck, still sleeping, I realized that a creak is not a shift. I let him sleep and looked at the world around me.

From St. Maries the Milwaukee Road, as it was called, followed the course of the St. Joe River as far as feasible and then worked its way through the Bitterroot Range, a long chain of mountains that mark the Montana-Idaho border, down to Missoula. It was the last trancontinental railroad to cross the northern Rockies (completed in 1909) and was electrified through the mountains. By now, certainly, we were on the eastern slopes of the Bitterroots in Montana and not too far from Missoula. I guessed we had been riding for at least seven hours. The train, moving slowly like a ponderous snake, had been winding its way across ten high steel trestles, some more than 500 feet long, straddling deep gorges and ravines and through numerous tunnels up to the culminating St. Paul Pass Tunnel, 8,771 feet long, which marks the Idaho-Montana border and the high point of the Milwaukee Road through the range. Sometime during the night we had switched to electric engines (at Avery, Idaho) and very gently, too, because the change over had not awakened me. Black night and exhaustion denied me sight of these engineering wonders.

Early morning light revealed an enthralling scene. Spots and splashes of color, courtesy of a few deciduous trees flaunting their early autumn foliage, intruded into the realm of peaks and evergreens. I was off to Jamestown College to enroll as a freshman if the North Dakota school would have me. I might never return to northern Idaho or western Montana. Northern Idaho had been home for three years and I had grown fond of the area, so different from Minneapolis where I had lived my first sixteen years. I drank in the landscape with great gulps as if storing it away should I never see it again. It was September 1936. I was young and, with all that splendor in my eyes, the smell of new lumber in my nostrils, train sounds in my ears, and a splinter or two in my posterior, I was off to seek a new, different life. After all, what's a sliver or two?

My thoughts turned to the family decision to send me to Jamestown College. George, my oldest brother, fourteen years my senior, was employed by F. W. Woolworth Company and had been transferred recently to Jamestown as store manager. He had written us about a fine liberal arts college there, stating that he could help me with my living expenses if I wanted to come. Yes, I wanted to go. But how could I get to North Dakota? We were in the depths of the Great Depression. My father's income was reduced severely and there was no money for train fare. That problem was solved by the arrival of Harold. Before his second year began as a seminarian in St. Paul, he had decided to make a quick visit to Coeur d'Alene. Years earlier he had departed the parental hearth to follow his wanderlust. He had to see the country for himself and he started early.

Eight years older than I, Harold had been jumping freight trains since he was fourteen or fifteen and was always able to take care of himself. He was an old hand at riding the rails; he knew all the lore, tricks, techniques, and dangers of freight hopping. He was willing to escort me to Jamestown if I wanted to travel on the freights.

In 1934, I had been injured in an automobile accident that laid me up for a year, and that injury hampered my mobility. Me, on a freight train! I had mixed emotions at the prospect. I had no experience with freights. That was for my brothers, not me. Would it be too demanding for my weakened condition? The more I thought of Harold's offer and listened to his arguments, the more confident I became that I could do it. He would be with me all the way to Jamestown and would see me delivered safely to brother George. If I wanted to enroll for the fall semester I must go with him: I had no other choice. I was lucky to be in Harold's capable hands. And so the decision was made to make the journey. Clothes and my hard-earned $35.00 were sent to George to hold until my arrival and I arranged for my high school records to be sent to the college. I'm sure my wooden foot-locker and Harold's luggage, which he sent to St. Paul, had a more comfortable trip than did we.

Looking back to the day we left home, I know Mother and Dad felt diminished and shamed by our arrangements. They simply did not have enough money to send us off in style, but they were flexible and adapted to the tough economic times. They trusted that I, their youngest child, would be safe, protected by Huck on this adventure. They knew he was thoroughly experienced in riding the freights. He and Phillip (another brother, in age between Harold and me) had always returned safely from their trips west from Minneapolis. Nevertheless, it was with chagrin, worry, perhaps despair, that they had driven us in the Model A from Coeur d'Alene to St. Maries. If so, they showed little of their inner turmoil as they said their last good-byes and started home. I wonder now at their toughness and stoicism.

Huck awoke. We exchanged "good mornings," then shared most of the food Mother had sent along. He stood up and I thought that was a good idea. Now to get my protesting body unfolded and upright. All those protruding lumber butts were getting to me. Between Huck and me we managed the task with some difficultiy, but it was worth the effort. What a relief to work out some of the kinks and cramps while braced on the swaying, moving car! For the first time I saw the front end of the train. Quite a few freeloaders were riding flatcars, which indicated a lack of empty boxcars. Two engines were pulling the long, heavily loaded train at a fairly good clip.

We wanted to get off this perilous load of lumber as quickly as possible. Our chance was Missoula, where the Northern Pacific Railroad main line was just across the Clark Fork River from the Milwaukee tracks. If we were lucky, we would soon board an express, through freight train that would take us all the way to Jamestown, about 1,000 miles east [actually 904 miles]. If we were unlucky, we would be nabbed by railroad police, called "bulls" or "dicks" by all "stiffs" such as we. Our luck held. As the train slowed, Huck kept his eyes forward and told me to watch the rear to see how other riders reacted to these yards. About ten cars back a few were getting ready to jump off, but there didn't seem to be any undue haste or panic motivating them. They were taking their time, gathering themselves for dismounting. Huck observed similar behavior ahead. Nobody was running. We relaxed and prepared ourselves for departure from our well-stacked load of lumber. Later on during the trip I'd wish I were back on that dangerously comfortable flatcar.

We waited until the train came to a full stop accompanied by much grinding, squealing, and screeching. We took our time climbing down, looking around the yards as we did so. No bulls in sight. They must have given up the endless struggle to keep people like us off the cars.

The railroad corporations were concerned about all the non-paying passengers they were carrying. Not only were we free-loaders, but some, a few, caused damage to or stole from cars. Also, once in a while a stiff would be killed by falling under the wheels, caught between the cars, or in boxcar fights, all which caused trouble for the companies. To keep trains from becoming too heavy with rail bums, the companies employed yard police stationed at division and sub-division points. Some of the bulls were mean. Not only did they remove riders from the trains, but they had other ways to make life miserable: delays, questionings, lectures, beatings, arrests, jailing, even killing in rare instances. Clearly, they were to be avoided.

Harold and I gave each other a thorough inspection when we were free of the marshalling yards. We had been on a clean train and were quite presentable. With confidence we shouldered our blanket rolls and started for the other side of the river, eating the last of the stale food. Huck was jaunty—feeling good about the situation, as I was. The trip had gone pretty well—his young brother was, so far, a minimal nuisance and still alive. Definitely, things were looking up, and now we were flexing our muscles, getting some much needed exercise. We were eager for information regarding the NPRR east-bound through freight.

After we had crossed the Clark Fork River, locally called the Missoula, and into NPRR territory, Huck asked a stiff we encountered about a train. He didn't know the answer. Huck told me to scrounge for paper while he would continue to seek information. Paper, I discovered, is the best kind of underwear; it shields the body from drafts and cold when wrapped around legs and torso. Huck learned that "our" train was due in Missoula soon, which suited our needs precisely. Our timing was proving impeccable. We intensified our search for paper and found enough

for both of us, some of it not too clean from blowing about the streets
and yards of Missoula. Now we were ready for the train, the paper folded
and secured under our belts, available when needed.

We did not have long to wait. After the train pulled in, there was a
great deal of shunting, backing, and coupling as cars were detached and
others added. As the train was re-formed we watched our chances and
soon spotted an empty near the middle of the long line of cars. When
the train-men's attention was centered elsewhere, we ran for it and hastily
climbed in. We found the boxcar already occupied by three riders who
were keeping an eye out for dicks. Evidently figuring five were enough
for one empty when plenty of others were available, one of them started
to close the sliding door. Without speaking, Huck grabbed hold of it and
helped. The other door was already closed except for about an inch used
as a peep slit. Huck and the other man slid the door almost shut. Then,
on some unseen signal, he crossed to the other while my brother stood
by our entry door. Both remained motionless. I looked at the two other
riders, one of whom quickly held his finger to his lips. I got the message
and held my breath. Voices outside grew louder—were bulls intent on rousting us out? To our relief they passed our car, going about some other
business—members of the train crew checking couplings, looking for
hot boxes, getting the train ready to pull out. Their voices faded. We
were not disturbed, and we soon relaxed as the train resumed its journey
east.

It seemed very easy to me. Was this all there was to it? It was almost
as if there was a conspiracy to help us reach our destinations as quickly
as possible. If this car stayed with the train far enough, we could make
excellent time. Harold thought we could be in Glendive, Montana, by
evening of the next day and in Jamestown in about forty-eight hours,
provided we could ride this freight all the way. But who knew when or
if this car would be uncoupled and shunted to some siding in the middle
of nowhere? We might be thrown off the train by some bulls along the
way. I thought Huck was optimistic. We had come only about 200 miles
and had about 1,000 to go to reach Jamestown. It would be slow going
not only until we reached the Continental Divide, just east of Butte, but
until we were out of the Rockies near Bozeman.

When we boarded at Missoula, it must have been about 7:30 or 8:00
A.M. We were eight or nine hours from St. Maries—pretty slow going I
thought, but of course a lot of those miles were uphill and tortuous. Truly,
though, the Milwaukee freight had made excellent time, Harold pointed
out. If we could average twenty miles per hour for the whole trip, it would
take about sixty hours. We crawled through the mountains, but time was
made up on the plains, where the NPRR was famous for its "highballing"
speed. And we had an excellent chance of keeping this boxcar, he told
me, because of its placement in the string of cars. If it was soon to be

detached, it would be placed nearer either end, simply to save the brakeman steps. If we could stay in this car we would be in Glendive within forty hours.

The three men at the other end of the boxcar paid little heed to us, and we to them. I remember little about them. They were simply three nondescript, unemployed men among many searching for work, any kind of work, without luck. One of the trio was given to whistling between his teeth when he wasn't talking. Once I heard a little of the refrain of "I'm Sitting on Top of the World," a popular tune of the late '20s. Incongruous, but he seemed to be cheerful enough. Occasionally they argued, a voice would get loud but nothing more. When we approached a town of any size, we would all quiet down, taking no chances. We had to be careful about our smoking when the train stopped in daylight, but in the dark it made little difference as long as we guarded against the flares of matches.

Sitting on our blanket rolls, we leaned against the sides or end of the car, changing positions as often as we wished, a luxury denied us on the load of lumber we had abandoned. The floor of the boxcar was comparatively clean—we wouldn't have to dig through rubbish to lie down to rest or sleep.

During that day our only entertainment was occasional conversation and viewing scenery as we climbed to and passed the divide. The colors of autumn, the endless pines, and the peaks of the Rockies claimed my attention.

In the afternoon, we reached Butte, where our three companions left us, hoping to find work in the copper mines or refinery. Their departure attracted no attention to our boxcar by train crew or police. Harold, seizing the opportunity, decided it was a good chance to look for food and drinks. Harold told me to stay put, good advice because my lack of agility would only hamper his search. I didn't like it, but sensibly agreed. He left on his hunt and I watched for bulls.

I don't remember details very clearly, but from what I saw of Butte it seemed to be wholly devoted to the mining, extraction, refining, and shipping of copper. There was a copperish haze in the air and coppery dust everywhere I looked. The Anaconda Copper Mine near Butte evidently dominated the town and the environs. I don't remember if I worried about Huck getting back to the train before it left Butte, but being a born worrier I probably did. No need to, though. During prolonged shunting and backing he suddenly appeared with some bread and a bottle of water. He worked some kind of magic, I thought, but no—he had located a marked house near the yards, mooched food and drink and had not been disappointed. Houses in any town where vagrants would be given a hand-out were well known by the stiff fraternity and were marked.

An "x" or other sign made by clay or chalk on the steps, porch, or fence told all who recognized it that the housewife would not turn anyone away empty-handed. Kind women helped many wayward travelers stay alive during the Depression.

Again, we were not disturbed. Looking back over fifty years I still wonder at the forebearance of the railroad police in Butte, Bozeman, and Billings on that trip. But considering the great number of free riders on the train, their discretion may have been the better part of valor. Faced with overwhelming odds, they prudently looked the other way and left the rousting to others farther along the line.

From Butte to Bozeman is not far as a bird flies, but a train or car must cross the Continental Divide near Butte. The train made slow progress through the mountains and passes, the latter about 6,000 feet high in that area. At that altitude in mid-September we began to feel the chill. It was time to don our deluxe underclothing. We wrapped paper around our chests and torsos. Our shirts, trousers, and belts held it firmly in place. Next, rolling up our pant legs, we wrapped our thighs and calves, tucking the calf tubes into our sock tops to secure them. The arrangement worked out very well.

I don't remember if there was a sign marking the Divide. No doubt there was a marker, but I missed it. Darkness was falling (fast in mountain country) and I was tired. I don't know what we would have done without paper—it was a very chilly night in the boxcar. Cold and uncomfortable, I tossed and fretted, unlike the night before. Sleeping rough on a boxcar floor is no picnic. It wasn't the Ritz—there were drafts accompanying the vibrations, swaying, and cacophony of sounds. I was unhappy with myself that I was unable to adjust to discomfort; but I noticed Huck had trouble too and I felt better. It was only later in the morning that I snatched a little sleep.

Huck must have scrounged more food in Billings, early as it was. I've always suspected he had a little money with him because finding handouts early in the morning has always struck me as improbable. My first real memory of that day was a stop in the barren countryside, somewhere east of Billings. There was no town, not even a ranch in sight. The train stopped on a curve so we had a clear view from the left side of the train of what was transpiring up ahead. Men in western hats and gear were removing horses from a flatcar. We had no idea how long they had been on the train, but obviously it had made a special stop to accommodate them. Like something out of a Western movie, once the horses were on *terra firma*, the men mounted and the train moved on.

We were in some rolling hills and the train moved at a more rapid rate. It was downhill all the way to the Mississippi, or so the saying went. As we rolled, Huck added to my freight-riding education—although we agreed that too much knowledge of the subject could be *prima facie* evidence of wasted time or a wasted life. However, we rationalized that this ride was necessary, an exception to the rule.

I was initiated into the mysteries of "riding the rods," the most danger-ous ride of all on a freight car, but one fading as the old cars built with steel rods slung under the floor, creating a kind of hammock, are removed from service. Another travel mode is "riding the blinds," denoting the space between the coal car and the first baggage car on passenger trains, out of sight of the engine crew, where the rider is forced to stand the entire trip holding onto or tied to a handrail. "Riding the reefers" means traveling in refrigerator cars which are easy to enter but difficult to exit; there were instances of sleeping or drunk stiffs freezing to death in reefers loaded with perishables. Huck warned me to avoid these dangerous rides. Since I never intended to ride the freights again, I happily agreed to follow his advice.

Miles City gave us no problem. Once more the dicks were lax and we were lucky. We remained there for a comparatively short time and again we rolled, headed now for Glendive, a small Montana city that remains large in my memory. The trip had gone unbelievably well so far; we were making good time and were not too far from Jamestown. But first there was Glendive. As the train slowed, entering the yards, the riders began jumping from the train. There must have been fifty or more who quickly hit the ground while the train was moving and took off for the jungles. We got the message they were sending: get off before the bulls grab you. But we could not respond fast enough.

The trouble lay in my comparative immobility. The Glendive officers must have had fearsome reputations with the stiffs! And there they were, two of them brandishing clubs. Their voices, behavior, and armament spelled big trouble for Huck and me.

It was only natural that he would want to follow the other travelers to safety, but my gimpy leg prevented rapid flight and the bulls spotted us. We were ordered off the train. Harold jumped off and helped me down. We began the march to their office, prodded along by their nightsticks, their barked commands in our ears. I felt guilty that I had been the cause of this debacle and was not helped by the fact that the police were in the right, that we had been caught trespassing on railroad property, and that we had been riding illegally on the train.

Different from me in temperament, Huck immediately launched an ar-gument: we were not habitual stiffs; we had definite destinations to achieve definite purposes; circumstances forced us to ride freights for transportation; we were truly honorable young men caught up in difficult times, etc., etc. All his persuasiveness seemed to fall on deaf ears. The dicks single-mindedly escorted us to their quarters. Huck must have be-lieved that the best defense is a strong offense because he never let up.

He was still going at it, with my occasional reinforcement, when we reached the office.

Inside, there was a lot of loud, tough talk by the two officers. They took turns lecturing us and threatened us with dire consequences for our transgressions on NPRR property. They manhandled us a little, not roughly, because by then they were beginning to realize, I think, that we were what we claimed to be.

In the near distance we heard the familiar sounds of a train in the yards—smashing of couplings locking together, wheels grinding and shrieking, whistles hooting, and men shouting. The train crew was detaching cars, adding others, rearranging our world. And time was fleeting. If we missed that train we would have to wait twenty-four hours for another fast freight, and waiting that long or trying to hitchhike, dirty as we were, was not appealing. The only alternative would be to ride slow-moving locals or milk trains, not a happy prospect. We did not want that delay, late as we were already for school enrollment, with about 375 miles to go to reach Jamestown. We knew that when the reassuring sounds coming from the train yard ceased we would be in real trouble.

Huck and I never let up. I joined him in fervent pleas for leniency. We really worked on those two bulls. I think they got sick and tired of our yammering. They were now willing to let us go provided we went out to U.S. Highway 10 and thumbed our way east. Huck wouldn't hear of it. He wanted their permission to get back on that freight. He actually grew a little indignant (or pretended to) at their effrontery in taking us off the train in the first place. Somehow we put them on the defensive. The obvious leader kept an eye on the train even as he was exhorting us to get out to the highway. The freight wasn't quite assembled as he opened the door and pointed to U.S. 10. There must have been a conscious acknowledgement on his part that we were right—weren't dressed properly and were too dirty for anyone to pick us up on the highway. I think he finally believed us—we were heading east to go to school. Urgency had made us persuasive and convincing. We spoke only the truth, and the truth came through.

The leading officer said "hit the highway" once more, turned, and closed the door. Both dicks knew we wouldn't. They knew we would get back to that train as quickly as we could, and we understood, somehow, that they would not prevent us from doing so. They just turned their eyes from us and let us go our way. I like to think they had a spot of softness in their hearts, and perhaps they did, but more likely they were delighted to free themselves from two relentless yappers.

We made a few tentative steps toward the highway and then turned back to the rail yards where the train, rearranged and reassembled, was about to depart. Time to board it was getting very short. The train began to move while we were still a short distance from it. We had no time to be choosy—we had to get on it and search later for an empty boxcar. Running alongside, Huck grabbed the vertical handrail, swung up onto the ladder bars, keeping the lowest one free and turned to me. Running as fast as I could, I lunged for the rung. I missed. My awkward gait and inability to run fast enough almost cost me a leg and possibly my life. I lost my grip on the handrail and fell under the train. Luckily, I sprawled clumsily and my legs did not go under far enough to be sliced by the wheels. Picking myself up as quickly as I could, I started to run again. I was close to panic. How could I get onto that car? Huck was about to get off, to give it up as a bad job.

Inexplicably the train, rather than picking up speed, perceptibly slowed as I limped alongside the car. Huck reached out again and shouted some encouraging words, and I lunged again for that elusive handrail. This time I grasped it more firmly with my left hand. Huck reached down, grabbed my right, and between the two of us I managed to get my good right leg onto the bottom rung of the ladder. After catching my breath I pulled myself up and planted my left foot securely on the rung. I'd made it! The train immediately increased its speed. With Harold ahead of me, we climbed to the top of the car and onto the catwalk.

Looking back, I can't yet quite believe I accomplished that feat with that bad left leg. Why should the train have slowed at the moment of truth? As I recall there was no grade that would cause loss of speed. I can only believe that the fireman in the engine cab saw my fall and told the engineer, who obligingly stopped accelerating for a minute or so. If that was the case, I give him a belated salute and my heartfelt thanks.

We found ourselves on a car about a third of the way back from the engine. That, too, proved fortunate chance. Back along the top of the train, we saw other stiffs riding as we were, but none ahead. If we had been closer to the engine, life on the walkway would have been very difficult, if not impossible, for any length of time. The great Baldwin locomotive gave off smoke, soot, and cinders that would have driven us off. We were just far enough to its rear to avoid much and tolerate the rest. Traveling at sixty miles per hour while hanging onto a freight car catwalk with no windbreak or shelter except a blanket roll is not fun. It is dangerous. Our first business was to secure ourselves. Huck removed his belt and told me to do likewise. We had to strap our thighs to the walkway. It seemed we should have come better prepared for this emergency, but we were traveling light. Even the vital blanket roll was considered an impediment by some; this was September in Montana, and yet I had seen stiffs in shirts, no jacket, no blanket, no hat, nothing. I supposed they found warmth at night around a fire in a jungle, but that was traveling too light for my greenhorn taste.

It was late afternoon. We were hastening the coming of dark by speeding east, but twilights are long on the northern plains. Even this late in the year, the gloaming lingered. Still, inevitably, night was coming and with it safety and protection. There were bound to be stops in North Dakota at Dickinson and surely at Mandan, a division point. Would we be pulled off the train again? We would soon reach Dickinson, we were traveling in the open with no place to hide, and the train crew knew we and other illegal riders were aboard. Our only protection was the coming darkness.

We had seen, far to the east, some heavy clouds. We might run into rain, but I couldn't worry about that. I had to hang onto that catwalk come what may. I hoped my strong, stout belt would hold because the engineer was "rambling" the train (opening up the throttle). Incredibly, I dozed. The rocking of the train, the grinding of the wheels, the distant sound of the engine and its whistles for grade crossings lulled me to oblivion. It had been an exhausting, nerve-wracking day, but all that and my present discomfort disappeared for about a half hour.

The absence of familiar sounds woke me. We were on a siding between Dickinson and Mandan, Huck misinformed me. In the eastern distance, above the remote idling of our own engine, I heard a train whistle and then a growing thunder. The westbound North Coast Limited, the NPRR's crack train, rushed by at about seventy miles an hour in all its majesty. Its passage was enhanced by the Doppler effect of its imposing whistle, which always makes a train seem faster than it really is. How I envied those passengers, secure and snug in compartments, reclining chairs, or lounge, protected from the elements, even coddled by the considerate and competent care of a skilled train crew. I almost wept with envy.

A receding roar and distant whistle ended the Limited's rapid passage and we were free to proceed. With all the grunts, groans, and shrieks of a mythological monster we got under way. That had been a scheduled, necessary stop; nevertheless, I think that trainmen hated them. Now they had to get up steam and speed again, costing time and much labor on a coal-driven engine. It also caused a lot of black, heavy smoke that did nothing to improve our appearances or lungs. But there was precious little we could do about it. In addition to the smoke, our discomfort, and distress, we were hungry and thirsty and there was little we could do about that, either. We had to be stoics until we got to Jamestown, now only about 125 to 150 miles down the track. If we could hold on against the filth, the discomfort, and the elements we would be home free.

In about ten minutes we were up to speed again, pouring through the night. We were fortunate again in Dickinson, where the train stopped only briefly. Our last danger point lay ahead in Mandan. If we were to be removed from the train before we reached Jamestown, it would happen there.

Earlier in the day we had seen heavy clouds in the east. They were moving across the state from the northwest. We had hoped the belt of clouds, dark and foreboding, would have dissipated before we reached them, but for once our luck failed us. Our position, exposed and uncomfortable, became a living nightmare. Clothes and blankets quickly became soaked. The rain captured soot and smoke and dumped the mess on us. In the dark we could barely see each other or anything else through slitted lids. The rain and wind combined to make me wish I had never begun this mad trip. Even foregoing a college education seemed little enough price to pay to have escaped this torture.

But, "Ill blows the wind that profits nobody." The weather conditions guaranteed our passage through Mandan. When we arrived in that city's train yards, the rain was still pelting with no sign of a letup. The crews, only human too, hurriedly replaced the engine with another and removed or added a few cars, all in record time. No bulls threatened us. They were intelligent men not about to arrest a couple of forlorn stiffs on top of a freight car in a driving rainstorm. Wisely, they stayed in their snug office, drinking coffee, no doubt, and chatting agreeably with each other. If we crossed their minds at all, they probably thought it served us right; anything they could do to us was as nothing compared to the punishment we were receiving from the cruel elements. We saw occasional flashes from the brakeman's lantern, heard the sounds of couplings, wheels, and whistles, and felt accompanying jerks and tremors, but no one came near us, no one intruded upon our isolated misery.

The train soon started on our last lap, but not very fast. Bismarck, just across the Missouri River from Mandan, is practically a twin city, and there was no point in gaining great speed until the state capital was behind. All this slow movement was scheduled, of course, but we wished the engineer would get a move on—time was passing very slowly, it seemed to us. Finally, clearing Bismarck, the train gained speed.

We estimated we had been perched on that unforgettable roof top for six or seven hours, which made it around nine or ten o'clock, local time. We should arrive in Jamestown no later than midnight if there were no more stops or delays. At the moment we were moving pretty fast—that fresh monster of an engine was not to be held in check, and that was all right with us—the sooner we arrived, the quicker our reprieve from our punishment. Meanwhile, we hung on and endured, half prone and half crouched on that catwalk, catching the full brunt of the slip-stream.

Our patience was rewarded. About thirty miles east of Bismarck we ran out of the rain. The clouds must have passed to the southeast. One less torment, but we were thoroughly soaked and sodden. We couldn't discuss this blessed phenomenon. There had been very little conversation since Glendive—shouting was exhausting and, besides, we had little need, desire, or strength to do so. We simply toughed it out. The end of the tunnel, so to speak, couldn't come soon enough for either of us.

As I have said, our brother George was new to Jamestown, settling into his job and seeking suitable quarters for his family, still in Iowa City. Meanwhile, he was batching it in housekeeping rooms in the Pulsher Hotel. How to find the place would present a small problem, but I couldn't think about that now—I had enough on my mind.

Although we still had soot and wind to cope with, the rain was gone, the sky was clearing, and conditions were improving. Emerging from the storm seemed an auspicious sign of things to come. We felt a bit more comfortable even if our clothes were ruined and the wind still biting, knowing our ordeal was soon to end. Jamestown was just ahead where, Harold assured me, the train had to stop.

We felt the train slowing and saw the glow of Jamestown's lights. It wasn't long before we entered the yards, lost speed, barely moved and finally came to a grinding halt. Immediately we unbuckled our heavy, sodden belts, and then slowly, with grunts and groans, we got into kneeling positions and restored them to our waists. Now to get off that hateful car top. Huck groped for the top rung of the car ladder by slithering on his belly, while I held onto his legs, until he found it. He swung down onto the ladder and then guided my legs to it. When I was securely on the rungs, he went down and off the car. I dropped our blanket rolls to him and slowly climbed down and off our rapid but very uncomfortable train. The movement was painful. We were both stiff and cramped from our long confinement, but we had little time for thinking about it. We were congratulating each other for reaching Jamestown in record time when we heard voices. We were still tresspassing on railroad property, and we had to get out of the yards. We walked at an angle toward distant street lights away from the voices and were finally free of the tracks. Now we were just two exhausted and sodden citizens. When we looked at each other near a street light we were jolted at each other's appearance. Black and grimy, worse than any chimney sweep, two more frightening apparitions probably had not been seen in Jamestown since its founding. Truly shocking specimens of humanity, we were fortunate that it was almost midnight and very few people were on the sidewalks.

Now my little worry became a problem. Where was the Pulsher Hotel? How would we inquire without making people flee in fright? After inspecting each other, we agreed it would be wise to avoid the police, or we might spend the night jailed for vagrancy. We were immobilized by indecision. We had to do something, but what? While we were standing in the shadows, a pedestrian or two passed us. We decided we had to ask someone to save needless, pointless wandering.

A young man, about my age, probably returning home after a date with his girl friend, came toward us. We decided he was the one to ask our question and stepped out to meet him. His pace slowed just a bit, but he kept coming. He had courage. As he neared us, Huck asked him very politely where the hotel was located. The young fellow looked at us, decided we weren't going to beat and rob him, and told us what we wanted to know. As it happened, we were not far from the Pulsher Hotel. Thanking him and walking as fast as we could, we reached the hotel, which was located on a side street just off Main and had only one light to illuminate the lobby.

There was no clerk in sight. There was a night bell, but we thought it best to ignore it. We knew the number of the suite George occupied, went directly to it, knocked, waited, knocked again more loudly, and waited. I was about to rap on the door again when the door was unlocked and opened a few inches; there was our brother, ready to go to bed.

Before he had a chance to close it again, we greeted him, and the door swung open. Later on George maintained he knew us at first glance, but I don't believe he did until we spoke. I couldn't hold that against him because not only did we look like wrecks but we must have reeked, too.

The first thing Huck and I did was shed our filthy clothes amidst much catching-up talk. George discarded them or had them burned, along with our blankets, all beyond redemption. Huck and I took turns in the tub, enjoying renewing, refreshing, long yearned-for, and much needed scrubbings and began to look and feel ourselves again. It would take another bath or two to remove all traces of grime, but at least we were acceptable. By now it was about 1:30 and, after stuffing ourselves with whatever George gave us to eat, we all went to bed, one of us with George and the other on the sofa. Oh! What comfort, what luxury! I fell instantly to sleep—the talk could wait.

When I awakened, I was alone. Ravenous again, I raided the larder and made a small meal. After another luxurious bath, I opened my homemade chest, found some clothes, and dressed, but wondered if it was worth the effort, I could have slept another twelve hours with very little encouragement. Huck was gone, but George would be back after business hours, and I could find out what had been happening.

When he returned in the late afternoon, he caught me up on the day's developments. Huck had slept until late morning, had been awakened by George who lent or gave him some fresh clothes, took him to the NPRR depot, got him a ticket, and saw him off on the east bound Limited. My guide, escort, and companion was gone, and I wouldn't see him again for at least a year.

The next morning I got my $35.00 from George, who pointed me in the direction of Jamestown College. The campus is sited on a hill in the northeast part of the city, quite a little distance from the Pulsher hotel. As I reached the top of the long flight of steps leading to the campus,

I was struck by the absence of mature trees on that windswept height although there were many slim saplings. The buildings stood stark against the horizion. I felt a touch of loneliness.

I found my way to the Bursar's office in Taber Hall, a classroom building that also housed the administrative offices. There, at the counter, I was approached by a small, gray, self-contained man who identified himself as Prof. Fulton, the college Bursar. Plunking down $25.00 in cold cash, I asked to be admitted as a freshman, even though, I acknowledged, I was two weeks late for the fall semester. He looked at me briefly, not at all *non-plussed,* and said "yes." Assured my high school credentials were acceptable, I completed the necessary forms and promissory notes and thereby was an enrolled student in Jamestown College. Prof. Fulton turned me over to Prof. W. B. Thomas, Registrar, who completed matters by assigning me to classes, enjoining me to secure the necessary books and informing me that my attendance would begin the next day. My journey to Jamestown was completed.

The
Electric
Way

The conductor and possibly two patrons
pose with interurban car #101 in DeKalb,
Illinois, ca. 1920. This eight-mile "juice"
line, the DeKalb-Sycamore & Interurban
Traction Company, connected the two
communities in its corporate name.
Opened in 1902, the road closed on August 31, 1924, an early victim of automobile competition.

The Cincinnati & Lake Erie Railroad proudly illustrated its public timetable of October 12, 1930, with interior and exterior views of its state-of-the-art interurban equipment.

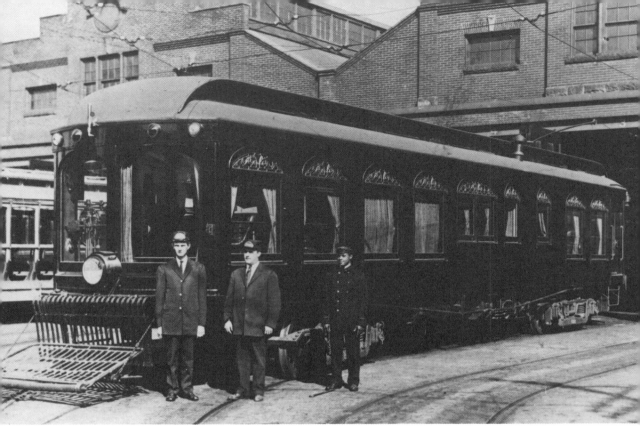

Large interurban companies frequently maintained private cars for the use of company executives and important clients. The pride of the Northern Ohio Traction & Light Company was the Josephine. This photograph, taken about 1910, catches the car in front of the Akron barns. The three-member crew, including a porter, awaits orders to take the Josephine out on the road. (D. S. Weaver Coll., University of Akron Archives)

By the twilight of the interurban era in the 1930s, often equipment grew shabby and the track weed-choked. This view of car #6 of Ohio's Toledo, Port Clinton & Lakeside Railway dates from the mid-1930s.

12 Riding the Interurban

J. S. Moulton

One resourceful individual, J. S. Moulton, a lawyer for the Interborough Rapid Transit Company of New York City, demonstrated early in the twentieth century the growing maturity of electric intercity railroads—"interurbans." In an August 1909 letter to the editor of the Electric Railway Journal, *he claimed to have been the first person to use traction for a trip from New York to Chicago. But this document holds even greater significance; it reveals the expansive nature of electric railway construction since the first carriers appeared in the late 1880s. While Moulton's motives are not known, it is easy to speculate about them. In writing to the leading trade publication, he surely sought to underscore the obvious possibilities of long-distance interurban travel. In the same vein, he likely wanted to propose that traction treks would be greatly facilitated if better connections were made at junctions and if companies offered complete information regarding times and costs to potential patrons. Moulton probably also hoped to pressure promoters to close gaps within the existing network. Obviously, a more direct route between Toledo, Ohio, and Fort Wayne, Indiana, was badly needed.*

Unfortunately, interurban enthusiasts, like J. S. Moulton, soon saw the automobile and bus fatally injure the industry. Although the nation's electric mileage peaked on the eve of World War I at 15,580 route miles, this total then dropped from 15,337 miles in 1920 to 10,422 in 1930, and slipped to only 3,197 in 1940. Today the Chicago, South Shore & South Bend remains as the lone survivor of the interurban era.

As far as I am able to learn from many inquiries this is the first trip made from New York to Chicago over electric lines for so large a part of the way. To be exact, the trip started from Hudson, N.Y., because the electric street railway service from New York City extends at present only as far as Tarrytown and the time lost in going to that town and then taking a train of the (steam) New York Central & Hudson River Railroad to Hudson would add nothing of value to the journey.

Leaving New York City at 12:30 A.M. by the New York Central road, I arrived at Hudson at 4:47 A.M., which gave me a full hour before taking the car of the Albany & Hudson Traction Company at 6 o'clock. I had breakfast at Electric Park on the line of the road and shortly after leaving there A. P. Deeds, general freight and passenger agent of the company, joined me and travelled as far as Albany. I took there the car of the Schenectady Railway at 8:00 A.M. and arrived at Schenectady, a distance of 16 miles, at 8:45. At 9 o'clock I took the car of the Fonda, Johnstown & Gloversville Railroad for Amsterdam. Arriving at 9:41 A.M., it is possible to go to Fonda by electric line, but the distance gained is so small that I took the New York Central road to Little Falls, a distance of 39 miles between Amsterdam and Little Falls. Leaving Little Falls at 12:30 P.M. on the Utica & Mohawk Valley Railway, the entire route of 23 miles to Utica was a trip that was made beautiful by the scenery. This trip was made in an hour. At 2:05 P.M. I took the limited car for Syracuse, a distance of 49 miles, which we travelled in one hour and 28 minutes. The country is fully as interesting as that between Little Falls and Utica. At 4:30 P.M. I took the car of the Auburn & Syracuse Electric Railroad for Auburn, 26 miles away, and a wait of 30 minutes gave me time for supper and to see a little of the city.

I left Auburn at 6:30 P.M. taking the Auburn & Northern road and the Rochester, Syracuse & Eastern Railroad, by way of Port Byron for Rochester, a distance of 66 miles. The train was on time at Rochester and, getting there at 9:45 P.M., I found I had travelled 387 miles, of which 233 miles were on electric roads. I was not fatigued in the least and, after going to the hotel, went out and walked about the city for an hour. Remaining at Rochester all night, I started at 9:50 o'clock the next morning, taking a local car to the city line, where the car of the Buffalo, Lockport & Rochester Railway started for Lockport at 10:20 A.M. J. M. Campbell, general manager of this road, met me at the Rochester end of the line and went with me to Lockport, a distance of 56 miles, and made my ride very enjoyable by explaining the signal system and the interesting points of the country through which we passed. Riding in the motorman's cab gives a much better view of the country. I arrived at Lockport at 12:18 P.M. within a few steps of the car of the International Railway, which leaves there at 12:30 P.M. for Buffalo, 25 miles distant. I reached the latter city at 1:25 P.M. It was remarkable to find that the electric lines, with their long runs and many stops in the different cities and villages, made almost exact schedule time. At Buffalo I called on J. C. Calisch, of the Buffalo & Lake Erie Traction Company. Mr. Calisch said he was glad to meet a man brave enough to undertake so unique a trip. He was wrong in suggesting that bravery was needed, because the trip affords pleasure all the time. At Buffalo I went through the city on a local car to the city line, now called Lackawanna City, where the Buffalo & Lake Erie Traction Company has its terminal. In this trip of 88 miles on the lines of this road to Erie, Pa., the cars pass through a great grape belt. After a beautiful ride of six hours, I reached Erie at 9 P.M., where

I remained all night, having covered that day 169 miles entirely on electric roads.

At 7 o'clock the following morning I started over the road of the Conneaut & Erie Traction Company for Conneaut, a distance of 33 miles, arriving there at 8:55 A.M. A wait of 30 minutes gave me time to set back my watch one hour, as I was traveling then on western (central standard) time. Leaving Conneaut at 9:30 A.M. on the Pennsylvania & Ohio Railway, I travelled to Ashtabula and there took a car of the Cleveland, Painesville & Eastern Railroad via Painesville, for Cleveland. The distance from Conneaut to Cleveland is 73 miles. Cleveland was reached at 12:50 P.M. and after lunch I left at 1:30 P.M. on a limited car of the Lake Shore Electric Railway for Toledo, a distance of 120 miles, via Sandusky, which was made in four hours and 20 minutes without change. After supper at Toledo, I went to the terminal of the Ohio Electric Railway and took the 8 P.M. car of that company for Fort Wayne, Ind., via Lima, Ohio. As I did not leave Toledo until so late, I did not stay on the car until Fort Wayne was reached, but thought it better to stop at Lima, where I arrived at 10:55 P.M.

On the following morning . . . [I] took the 10:15 A.M. [Ohio Electric] car . . . a distance of 60 miles to Fort Wayne, which was reached at 12:10 P.M. At Van Wert, Ohio, the Manhattan Limited of the Pennsylvania Railroad, which parallels the electric line at this point, came up, but we passed the steam train and kept ahead of it. At Fort Wayne I had dinner. . . . After supper [I] took one of the cars of the Fort Wayne & Wabash Valley Road to Wabash. . . . I remained at Wabash that night and started for Warsaw at 8:55 A.M. on the Cleveland, Cincinnati, Chicago & St. Louis ["Big Four"] steam road. After travelling a distance of 33 miles between these points I reached Warsaw at 11:36 A.M.[,] 30 minutes late. By this fall the road will be from Fort Wayne to Peru, Ind., on the Fort Wayne & Wabash Valley Traction Company road and thence to Warsaw by electric line, as the road now under construction will make the electic line route complete at that point, and therefore complete in the west.*

I left Warsaw at 1:30 P.M. for South Bend, Ind., over the lines of the Winona Interurban Railway and the Chicago, South Bend & Northern Indiana Railway, reaching South Bend at 3:40 P.M. I remained there until 5:30 P.M. taking a limited car on the Chicago, Lake Shore & South Bend Railway for Chicago, a distance of 90 miles, passing through the industrial settlements of Michigan City, Gary, and Hammond and reaching Pullman

---

*Although the Winona Interurban Railway finished its line from Warsaw to Chili, Indiana, in 1910 and thereby the all-important link between the Chicago and central Indiana electric roads, the Moulton trip never became much easier. Interurbans never connected either New York City with Hudson, New York, or Johnstown with Little Falls, New York, and no direct electric route ever tied Toledo with Fort Wayne and South Bend.

at 8:15 P.M. I took the suburban line of the (steam) Illinois Central Railroad to the central district of Chicago.*

It took me three full days and 21 hours from the time I left New York to get to the central (business) district of Chicago. The actual running time was 45 hours and 24 minutes. I travelled 1,143 miles, 956 miles on electric cars and 187 miles on steam roads. In one day of a little over 15 hours I travelled 298 miles on electric lines and the best of it all was that I saw the country pretty generally as well as the cities, towns and villages. These places are not seen by the traveller on steam roads. The electric lines pierce these places, the steam roads skirt them. About a year ago I made the trip by electric line to Philadelphia from New York, a distance of a little over 90 miles, and I thought I did well to cover it in nine hours.

The actual traveling time could be reduced several hours and as soon as I finished the trip and returned home I made a careful calculation and found that the actual traveling time could be reduced to 31 hours and 10 minutes. I had a fine and comfortable trip and shall certainly repeat it at the earliest practicable time.

The fare, including all steam fares from New York to Chicago, was $19.67 and the other expenses, including those for four nights at hotels, were $12.

---

*J. S. Moulton boarded a train operated by the Illinois Central's suburan division; the distance from Pullman to the "Loop" was fourteen miles. Later, in the 1920s, the Illinois Central electrified this busy commuter artery.

13 Riding the C. & L. E.

Editor, *The Deshler Flag*

*Although the interurban industry weakened substantially by 1930, not all compa-
nies readily accepted defeat. A few sought to respond to the
economic challenges in imaginative ways. A wonderful illus-
tration is the Cincinnati and Lake Erie Railroad. Organized
from several failing interurbans in 1930, this road linked the
Ohio cities of Toledo, Lima, Springfield, Dayton, and Cincinnati and also connected Springfield with Columbus. The
C. & L. E.'s head, Thomas Conway, Jr., a former professor
of finance at the University of Pennsylvania, believed (probably correctly) that there remained a place for the interurban
in the medium-distance range of passenger travel. (While
Americans like to drive, less than half of the nation's house-
holds owned an automobile until the early 1950s.) The
C. & L. E. bought twenty state-of-the-art lightweight high-
speed cars from the Cincinnati Car Company. Half were
coaches and half were coach-observation cars. They rode
smoothly over the company's deteriorating roadbed and were
popular with riders. "The comfortable car," extolled one pa-
tron, "goes kiting along sounding a fish-horn like schooners
on the Grand Banks." To introduce the new system and its
splendid equipment, Conway staged a race near Dayton between car No. 126 and an airplane in July 1930. Not surprisingly, No. 126 outdistanced its aerial competitor (at least for
the short mileage of the race course); this sleek car attained
a speed of 97 miles per hour. In a less dramatic fashion, the
C. & L. E. invited the press corps from throughout its service
area for an all-expense-paid outing to a Dayton hotel. The
editor of the Deshler, Ohio, newspaper joined the party and
then told his readers about the pleasant 127-mile ride to Dayton and the interurban's smart new rolling stock. Yet innova-
tion and good public relations could not save this mode of
transport. Conway's C. & L. E. failed in the late 1930s, a
victim of the Great Depression and ever-increasing rubber-
tired competition.*

With a clear sky and a clear track ahead about two hundred newspaper
men boarded special cars Sunday morning for a day's outing at Dayton,
Ohio, sponsored by the Cincinnati & Lake Erie Railway Company and

the Geyer Advertising Agency. Newspaper men from towns, villages and cities served by the C. & L. E. Railway all received invitations to spend the day, at the expense of the railway company.

W. T. Hager and F. L. Anway of Deshler boarded the special car at Deshler at 8:30 Sunday morning and were taken to Dayton in the fastest time ever made over any electric line. The car beginning its trip to Deshler with Assistant Superintendent C. O. Strait aboard to look after the comfort of his guests, was piloted by W. F. (Sparky) Hughes and Pressley Harris, both of whom are well known to nearly all Deshler people. The car stopped at Leipsic, Ottawa, Columbus Grove, Lima, Russel Point, West Liberty, Urbana, Bellefontaine, Springfield and Dayton to take on other newspaper men and women. Another car with Superintendent H. G. Mason and piloted by W. O. Daugherty of Deshler, left Toledo having aboard representatives of the Toledo press and picked up newpaper men and women at Maumee, Waterville and Weston and also at Springfield.

Other cars starting from Cincinnati and Columbus brought other representatives of newpapers in the towns and cities, all arriving in Dayton at about the same time. Nothing that could be done to enhance the comfort of their guests was left undone by the officials of the company, nor their employees. On boarding the car at Deshler, Messrs. Hager and Anway were greeted by Mr. Strait who proudly showed them over the entire car, taking great pleasure in explaining in detail every possible thing that he thought might interest his guests. Cigars and cigarettes were furnished very plentifully to the gentlemen guests, while the ladies were treated to candy.

Leaving Deshler, the trainmen demonstrated just what could be expected in the way of fast and comfortable service. In no time at all the car picked up speed of nearly ninety miles an hour and maintained this speed wherever the conditions were favorable, taking into consideration the sharpness of the curves and grades, always having the safety of their guests uppermost in their minds and speedy service next.

Arriving in Dayton, the guests were taken to the New Dayton Biltmore hotel where they were royally entertained. Luncheon was served in the grill room on the fourth floor. After luncheon, Franklin T. Dunlap of the Geyer Advertising Agency, acting as toastmaster, discussed plans for the future development of electric service.

And now, a word about the cars themselves. The cars are so constructed that there are no blind partitions to shut off any part of the view. One can look safely too, as both the front and rear ends of the car are completely enclosed with glass of the non-shatterable type, and flying glass and splinters are a thing of the past. Big, comfortable, low sitting, individual chairs with individual head rests greet one upon their first entrance to the car. Individual linen covers over the head rests insure cleanliness to all who ride on the cars. The cars ride along smoothly, easily and quietly on rubber insulated trucks which deaden the sound and smooth away the bumps and jars.

The windows along the sides are equipped with nickel plated brass sash and newly improved safety catches, and they raise and lower with scarcely any effort. The glass panes are cushioned in rubber to prevent rattling and they give an undistorted view obtainable only through plate glass.

Two twelve inch oscillating fans are directly overhead, keeping a nice circulation of air even while the car is not in motion or when all the windows are closed. The new small dome lights are located directly over each pair of seats which make reading a pleasure. The chromium plated bases are set in an artistically decorated ceiling of cream finish with green and gold striping harmonising with the other interior shades. The adjustable ventilators in the roof and the two systems of thermostat heat control for the front and rear of the car are so arranged as to provide the most comfortable temperature on the coldest or warmest of days. The floor is covered with battleship linoleum of special tile design. Walnut woodwork throughout the car enhances the refinement of the interior.

A cool refreshing drink may be had from the approved water cooler of modern design. The water cooler has two compartments, one for the water and the other for ice which insures a pure, cool drink at all times. Sanitary drinking cups, that cost you nothing are located conveniently near the drinking fountain.

The toilet is finished in light chrome green. Among its refinements is a neatly polished nickalene wash stand and large clear mirror. A concealed electric water heater insures warm water at all times.

The observation compartment is especially well equipped. Big comfortable overstuffed davenports and chairs make for very comfortable riding. Large clear glass in the windows gives a clear view from any angle. A writing desk is placed on each side of the aisle and two small tables with small table lamps finish out the luxurious fittings.

Following the dinner the guest were again taken aboard their respective cars and brought back to their homes. Messrs. Anway and Hager were especially well pleased upon arriving in Deshler to have Assistant Superintendent Strait invite them to make the run on into Toledo and return with him. The run was made into Toledo and return, arriving home at 10:35.

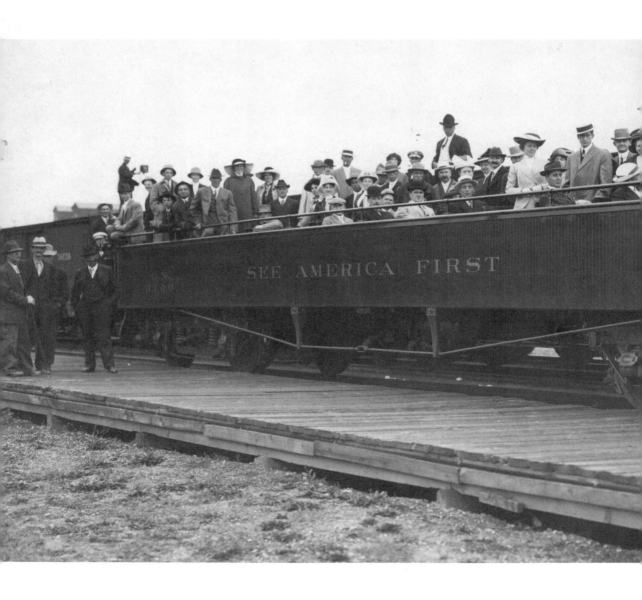

The Glory Years

The Great Northern Railway, a leader in promoting tourism in the West, made it easier for visitors to "See America First" when it attached open-top cars to passenger trains. Here a "special" prepares to depart from Kalispell, Montana, ca. 1915. (Don L. Hofsommer Coll.)

Throughout the Golden Age of rail travel, companies distributed a plethora of folders. The Seaboard Railway, for one, advertised heavily its quality Florida service.

Left. Travel on the Overland Route seemingly reached its zenith of comfort and speed with the splendid fourteen-car City of San Francisco. This widely acclaimed train posed for a publicity photograph in the mountains near Reno, Nevada, about 1940. (Union Pacific Museum)

Advertising brochure, ca. 1938.

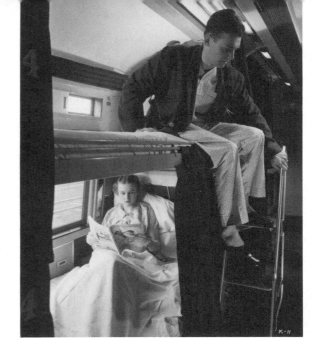

A good night's rest was part of a Pullman ride. Two travelers on the Overland Limited accommodate a commercial photographer, ca. 1935.

Railroad travel during the glory years meant more than superb equipment, it also involved outstanding service in the many passenger terminals. Dozens of "Red Cap Ushers" pose for a group portrait at the Chicago & North Western's Madison Street station in Chicago in the early 1920s.

Dinner in the diner might be the highlight
of a journey by train. Fine food became
the hallmark of the premier passenger-
carrying roads.

14 Traveling by Rail

Ellen Douglas Williamson

In the fall of 1887, three railroads, the Chicago & North Western, Union Pacific, and Southern Pacific, launched the Overland Flyer, offering daily service with through cars between Chicago and San Francisco. This crack train, which became the Overland Limited in November 1896, in time gained a reputation "with the single exception of its eastern counterpart, The 20th Century Limited, for being the most radiant and celebrated train in America."[1] It is little wonder that author Ellen Douglas Williamson (1905–   ) vividly recalled her childhood trip from Cedar Rapids, Iowa, to California in 1918, for traveling onboard the all-steel Overland Limited was immensely pleasurable. Known officially as "Number 1" westbound, it operated with a club buffet car, which included a barber and bath; dining car; standard sleeping car; drawing-room compartment car; and an observation car with rear platform.

All Aboard!

It was 2:30 in the morning, Tuesday, January 15, 1918, and the Douglas family, as usual, was leaving Cedar Rapids to spend the rest of the winter in California. The Overland Limited had left Chicago at 8 P.M. Monday for Omaha and points west but was to make a special stop in Cedar Rapids to pick us up.

The trunks had gone the day before, and the most exciting moment of all had arrived. Here we were with several friends to see us off, presents in our arms, luggage piled up on a cart beside us, standing in the freezing cold at this startlingly late hour of the night, and suddenly we heard the familiar far-off cry of the arriving train. It thundered into the center of town, stopped with steam and snow swirling about it, the porter of our assigned car descended, put down his familiar little yellow step, and up we climbed: Barbara and I scrambling up first, then sister Margaret and Mother and Danny, finally Rosie, cousin Aleck Douglas, my father, and of course the porter, who, after getting all the luggage on, slammed down the steel door covering over the steps we had climbed. The conductor,

---

1. Lucius Beebe, *The Overland Limited* (Berkeley, California: Howell-North, 1963), pp. 9–10.

still on the ground, shouted his familiar "All aboard," the brakeman waved a red lantern signaling the engineer to start, and they swung aboard somewhere up ahead as the train gathered speed.

Inside our car it was warm and the narrow hallway leading past the men's smoking room-washroom was dimly lit. However, our two connecting drawing rooms and compartment were blazing with light and the berths were waiting for us with snowy-white sheets, some even covering the windows, extra Pullman blankets folded neatly at the foot of the berths. It was so cozy and familiar and pleasant that we squealed with delight.

Danny shared a drawing room with me and Barbara, and as she was much the largest she always had the lower berth. Barbara and I drew lots to see who got to sleep in the magnificent upper berth where one could look loftily down on everyone. The loser got the hard little narrow sofa to sleep on, which was most uninteresting, especially as it had no hammock. The upper and lower berths always had small green string hammocks each stretched between the two little wall lights of the berth, into which one could put valuable things such as presents and handkerchiefs and books.

The first day on the train was just as exciting as getting on it. After we had taken turns getting dressed in our narrow floor space, and getting washed up in our small washroom with the shiny nickel- plated washbowl, and its toilet with a sign on it,* a waiter arrived all the way from the dining car, bringing us breakfast on a huge silver tray.

He and George, our porter, set up a table in the adjacent compartment. In case you aren't familiar with Pullman-car travel, a compartment is smaller than a drawing room, has no sofa and only an upper and lower berth. In the daytime the mattresses are locked in the upper berth, and the lower becomes a place where four people can sit facing each other. There is also a washbowl in a corner next to the door, and a toilet in the other corner by the door. It is discreetly hidden from view by a green plush-upholstered wooden cover, and can be used as a fifth seat if a poker game or party is taking place.

Another curious thing is that all Pullman porters were called George, unless you knew them personally from former trips. They were also always black, as were the dining-car waiters, and a nicer, more courteous and pleasant group of men never existed. I don't even remember one who wasn't cheerful and polite, and nothing was too much trouble for them.

The waiter spread a white tablecloth, unloaded his tray, and soon we were peeking into one covered silver dish after another and filling our

---

*The sign likely admonished the user not to flush the toilet when the train was in a station area. As is often the case today, human waste went directly onto the track; it was untreated in any fashion.

plates with hot corn muffins, bacon and jam. Besides that we poured hot cocoa from thermos jugs into our cups, and topped them off with whipped cream. Through the windows we could see flat snow-covered Nebraska. We were on our way!

Meanwhile George was busy "making up" our drawing room for the day. Away went all the sheets and blankets, and by the time we were through with breakfast we could move back into what was now our living room. There were two or three plump pillows on the sofa, our hats had been put away in paper bags, the luggage was all stowed away under the seats and in the overhead racks. It was our home, and we happily proceeded to open our going-away presents, and unpack our books and games and knitting. The presents were mostly candy and cookies, which we put aside. While sister Margaret read aloud to us we knitted our squares for the Red Cross.

The train stopped for a few minutes at Grand Island, so we put on our coats and ran down the whole station platform and back. It was freezing cold, and we were out of breath when we got aboard the train. By this time our parents were up, and cousin Aleck (who had a lower berth in the next car) joined us.

A word about Cousin Aleck that might interest you: he was unusually tall for those days, over six feet, so he had arranged to have lower berths No. 11 or 12, one of the two nearest the men's room. Why was this? These two lowers were always six inches longer than the others, and tall men could sleep without being squeezed between the headboard and footboard.

He was a great addition to our party, a bachelor in his twenties, who worked for Daddy's corn-starch company in Cedar Rapids, and who was a terrible tease and a practical joker and who taught us all sorts of strange and wonderful things: how to play mumblety-peg and how to palm cards and shoot craps.

How is that after over sixty years I am able to remember all these details of our trip so well? Because for a Christmas present on December 15, 1917, I received from some older relative (my grandmother, I think) a handsome gilt-edged leather-bound diary for the year 1918. I wrote in it faithfully every day, line after line, page after page, for just about six months. Then it evidently proved too much for me, for I began filling up space with an occasional place card from a luncheon that Margaret went to, and a postcard of the Busch Gardens in Pasadena that someone had sent Danny. Then in July, menus from hotels began to appear, church notices, and by August it was bulging with comic strips. By October it was filled to overflowing, and the rest of the pages remained blank, but I am happy that I kept it and I especially treasure the postcards of the Overland Limited.

The Overland Limited was an all-Pullman-car train, the word "Limited" meaning no coaches. Each Pullman car had a name painted on it in four different places; Lake Wales, for example, might be its name, and in large letters it always appeared on each side, and on each door just above the doorknob as you entered, front or rear. The Pullman cars were named after rivers, mountains, lakes, and I think national parks, and perhaps canyons, deserts, and maybe geysers. Anyway the name signified the kind of Pullman car it was. If the name was Lake Wales or Lake Okeechobee it meant that it had two drawing rooms, two compartments, and twelve sections (each with a lower and upper). And if it said Cedar River or Elk River it had all drawing rooms and compartments, and so on.

During the morning my father went to the barbershop, located up in the front of the train in the men's club, a car full of tobacco smoke and overstuffed leather chairs and brass spittoons (a horrid place, I thought), and eventually it was time for lunch. In our frugal Scotch way we had brought along a picnic basket filled with sandwiches wrapped in waxed paper, and there were hard-boiled eggs and apples.

After that it was more games, a fifteen-minute stop in North Platte. . . . Here another engine was hitched onto the long train to help us ascend the Rockies, and after we had freshened up, it was time for dinner in the sumptuous dining car, and by now the train was going around curves. Water was sloshing in the drinking glasses and the soup was spilling out of the soup plates unless one kept a spoon there, as a sort of anchor to windward (something one could *never* do at home).

By bedtime we were in Wyoming, and by the next morning we were over the Continental Divide, and coasting merrily downhill all the way to Ogden, Utah. After a long stop there in the midafternoon (after another now dried-out picnic lunch) came the most exciting part of the trip. We crossed Salt Lake! It was huge, and the Union Pacific [Southern Pacific] tracks went straight across the lake so close to the water that the train seemed to be riding along on the lake itself.

Before we reached the lake, however, we were prepared for it. We had our winter coats and mittens on, and walked back to the observation car (a kind of recreation car, in case you've never seen one, complete with bar, card tables, swivel chairs, and magazine racks). We hurried through this car to the end of the train and out onto the rear platform, and there we seated ourselves on green folding chairs, the porter covering our knees with steamer rugs, just as if we were in deck chairs on a ship.

When the train pulled out we got a wonderful backward view of everything, including the trip across the lake. We also got cinders all over us and in our eyes, but it was a splendid experience, and the clackety-clack of the train rattling over the rails and the whistle blowing and (after leaving the lake) the people to wave at as the train rushed through small villages were unforgettable.

We reached San Francisco the next day in time to have a late lunch at the St. Francis Hotel, all of us delighted to be off the train after such a long trip, and I remember that Mother took me to a perfectly fascinating oriental store called S. & G. Gump, on Post Street near the hotel.

Late in the afternoon the family met at the Market Street ferry, went back to Oakland, and took the Southern Pacific train known as the Lark to Santa Barbara, getting there the next morning at 6:30.

An overnight train trip such as the one on the Lark was humdrum indeed after the three-day voyage of the Overland Limited, and the procedure was entirely different. All the luggage except one little suitcase apiece was checked in the baggage car, not to be seen until we reached the Santa Barbara station.

A Ride in the Cab of the Twentieth Century Limited

15

Christopher Morley

Virtually every major railroad before the decline of long-distance passenger travel exhibited pride in its "varnish," and rightfully so. The New York Central, one of America's leading carriers, bestowed the "best of everything" on its Twentieth Century Limited, the road's flagship train. Introduced on June 15, 1902, on the New York City to Chicago "water-level route," the popular train immediately became a synonym for elegance and dependability. Residents of Albany, Utica, Syracuse, and Rochester proudly called the "Century" their train. Those travelers who had either a Chicago or New York City destination faced two opportunities for deluxe travel. In addition to the Twentieth Century Limited, there was its rival on the Pennsylvania Railroad, the Broadway Limited, which served Newark, Philadelphia, Harrisburg, Pittsburgh, and Fort Wayne. By the 1920s both name-trains frequently ran in several sections for their eighteen- to twenty-hour journeys.

The aggressive public relations office of the New York Central hired novelist-essayist-poet Christopher Morley (1890–1957) to write about his experiences in the cab of the powerful steam locomotive that pulled the Century between New York City and Albany in 1928. His comments soon appeared in an attractive pamphlet that the company distributed to riders and anyone interested in the "world's best train."

This was a little ceremony dedicated to Time; and as I came into the Grand Central Terminal the early afternoon sun slanted in bright diagonal from those high windows, exactly transecting the clock on the Information Desk in a clear swath of light.

Not less decorously than a bride made ready for her groom is the Century inaugurated for departure. A strip of wedding carpet leads you down into the cathedral twilight of that long crypt. Like a bouquet of flowers her name shines in white bulbs on the observation platform. In the diner waiters' coats are laundered like surplices. Mr. Welch, the veteran conductor, carrying his little box of official sancta, has the serene, benignant gravity of some high cleric. And as you walk by that long perspective of windows, you are aware they are not just a string of ten Pullman cars. They are fused by something even subtler than that liaison of airy pressure that holds them safe. They are merged into personality, become a creature loved, honored, and obeyed. This is a rite, you read it in every member of her crew. The blessed, the rich, the ultimate human faculty of Rising to the Occasion! And you can see them, porter just as gravely as conductor, each making obeisance to the little private deity ticking in his pocket. When railroad men compare notes on the time, they don't say (as you or I would) "two-forty," mean forty minutes after two. They know the hour, and take it for granted. It's minutes and seconds that concern them. Ask Mr. Brady, engineer of the electric that takes out the First Section, what he "makes it." He'll reply "forty fifteen," meaning forty minutes and fifteen seconds. There was a severity on Mr. Brady's face as he sat studying his watch. The time was close. It was 44-30, it was 44-45, it was 45. . . . Let's go!

Gently she steals out, along a corridor of that dusky underground forest where colored lights gleam like tropic birds. "Green!" "Green!" You hear Brady and his helper saying aloud to each other, checking up every signal as soon as it comes in view, each always verifying the other's observation. The electric engine has fascination and efficiency of its own, but in this ceremony one is bound to regard it mainly as the father who takes the bride up the aisle on his arm. Thirty-three miles the electric takes her to Harmon, where the bridegroom is ready, the steam engine; and (as the old rubric puts it) they are coupled together, to have and to hold. The father may be (I dare say usually is) more of a man than the groom; but the groom gets the romantic applause. So the electric is not a personality; just a miracle. Smooth and swift it toles you past those upper reaches of the city. Looking out you see the Second Section spinning along, just abaft your stern, on the adjoining track. There's a little boy, perhaps four years old, who comes down to Spuyten Duyvil station every fair afternoon, with his nurse, to see the Century spin by. It's a part of an engineer's job to know his roadside clients and salute them. When Brady waves, the nursemaid can set her watch. It's 3:05. The bell chimes musically overhead, and again one feels that there is some sort of religion in all this. And I suppose (come to think of it) that isn't a bad sort of religion either: Getting *There* when said you were Going *To*.

But what a moment, when you glide into Harmon and see waiting for you . . . what you came to see: one of the 5200's.* Of course, all that

---

*On February 14, 1927, the New York Central introduced the "Hudson"-type steam locomotives on its crack passenger trains. Built by the American Locomotive Company, these giant locomotives (each weighed 343,000 pounds with a 4-6-4 wheel arrangement)

talk about the groom is nonsense, for at once you adore her as She. There's only one phrase adequate for her: *Some Baby!* Sharp work here: it must have been a couple of minutes, but in memory it seems only a few seconds of golden excitement. They can grin as they like at your borrowed overalls, you're the one that's going to ride that roaring child for 110 miles. Have you seen the Central's 5200's? They've only been in commission a few months. This was 5217 and I shan't forget her. She seems as big as an ocean liner when you're in the cab.

They hand up a slip of yellow paper to George Tully, the engineer. If you're the engineer of the Twentieth Century they don't tell you to get anywhere by a certain time. They tell you not to get there *before* such and such. The message, signed with two sets of initials, was "Do not arrive Albany before 5:38." George Tully consults his watch (a nice, faithful old Hamilton; incidentally, he's carried it twenty-four years). It's 3:36 (or 3:35:50, as near as I could read my own Hamilton in my excitement) and we're off.

I suppose the greatest moments in life are those when you don't believe it's yourself. It *can't* be you, in that holy of holies of small-boy imagination, the cab of an engine—and such an engine. More than that, made so welcome and at home by George Tully and Tom Cavanagh that you feel you belong there. Perhaps the simple truth is that if men have something they're enormously proud of, it's pure joy to show her off. And they are never so lovable as in their honest rivalries. "Well," Tom roared in my ear, as he explained the automatic stoking, "I wonder if the Pennsy's got anything better than this!" For the first thing that puzzles you is two big canted cylinders in the cab. They revolve in spasms. These feed the coal into the firebox. A man couldn't shovel fast enough by hand to keep the pressure she needs (she eats up four tons between Harmon and Albany). The fireman sits comfortable, with his eye on the steam gauge, and regulates the coal-feed by turning a handle. I could tell you a lot about the marvel of that firebox, and the "butterfly-door" that opens in two wings to show you her fierce heart, full of flame and hardly anything else. The coal is practically consumed by the time it reaches the floor of the furnace. I fed her myself for quite a way. "Keep the gauge at 220,"* Tom said. "No black smoke, and don't let the safety valve lift. Every time she lifts that means twenty gallons of water wasted—costs three cents." "Keep her hot," George Tully shouted to me, grinning. "We've got five minutes to make up."

That was part of the fun of this ride: I had a chance to see how things

pulled such famous name-trains as the 20th Century Limited, Empire State Express, Southwestern Limited, and the Detroiter.

*The engine crew wished to maintain full steam pressure in the 5200-series Hudsons, and that meant 220 pounds of steam per square inch.

go when the breaks are against you. For there's a lot of work doing along the line: four-trackage being put in, the new tunnel at Storm King, and unavoidable slow-downs. "We'll be knocked out six minutes before we reach Beacon," Tully said. "We'll get it back."

Astonishing how soon one adjusts one's judgements. Leaning from the cab window, watching the flash of her great pistons, watching the 1,000-ton train come creaming along so obediently behind us, one soon began to think anything less than sixty mere loitering. All the imaginations that the cab might be uncomfortable riding are bosh. There is hardly—at any rate in those heavy 5200's—any more sway or movement than in the Pullmans themselves. The one thing a constant automobile driver finds disconcerting is the lack of steering. As you come rocketing toward a curve you wonder why the devil George doesn't turn a wheel to prevent her going clean off. And then you see her great gorgeous body meet the arc in that queer straight way—a constantly shifting tangent—and—well, you wish you could lay your hand on her somehow so she'd know how you feel. When George began to let her out a bit, beyond Beacon, I just had to go over and yell at him that I thought this 5217 of his was a good girl. With the grave pleasure of the expert he said, "They're right there when you need 'em." He let me blow the whistle, which makes one feel an absolute part of her.

Alive, shouting, fluttering her little green flags,* she divided the clear cool afternoon. Looking out into that stream of space I could have lapsed into a dream. I came closer than ever before to the actual texture of Time whereof our minds are made. This was not just air or earth that we flew upon, this was the seamless reality of Now. We were abreast of the *Instant.* It was Time that we fed into the flaming furnace, it was Time that flickered in the giant wheels. This was the everlasting Now, we kept even pace with it and so the mind was (literally) in its own element, motionless and at ease. Terribly great, senseless, ecstatic, mad with her single destiny, yet with queer pathos in her whole great mass, so much at our command. Her cab looked like a clock-shop, so many gauges and dials. But there is no clock in an engine cab. She makes her litany to one god only—the intent man who sits leaning forward so gravely. And he verifies himself by the other little god—the tiny one in his pocket. As you watch him you understand what he said—"There's no two trips alike. They're always on your nerve."

"Green!" "Green!" They kept repeating to one another across the cab; Tom and I sat on the port side where I could see the whole panorama

---

*When a railroad operated multiple sections of a designated train, something the New York Central did regularly with the 20th Century Limited, the first train displayed green flags in the daytime and green lights at night on the front of the locomotive. Green told maintenance crews, most of all, that a second section of the train would follow shortly and that they should take heed.

of the Hudson, and far down a curve of the river a white plume where the Second Section came merrily behind us, keeping her three-mile distance. And, with Tom, I waved to the regular clients, including the two priests in cassocks and birettas, near Poughkeepsie; and the Cleary girls in Hyde Park, whose husband and father is the flagman at that crossing. And then Tom said suddenly, after a glance at his watch, "We've got the dope on 'em now. Forty-nine minutes to do forty-five miles." I began to see that when chance works against him, the engine-man instinctively personifies the unforgiving minutes into mysterious enemies who are trying to spoil things. These mischievous divinities had been hovering about us, making us scoop up water (you have to slow down to forty-five for that) or what not; but now we had the dope on them. And the engineer has some very subtle inward correlation of the feel of things; so that even before he verifies his instinct by minutes and seconds, he knows how he's getting on. These men live with Time in a way we rarely dream of. Time is not their merry wanton, as she is to some of us. She's their wife, for better or worse. There was a truly husbandly grievance in George's eye when, just outside Albany, we had to slow almost to a standstill. Number 7—which left Grand Central forty-five minutes earlier—was right ahead of us. There was the accent of King Tamerlane in 5217's whistle as she shouted a blasphemy in steam. We came to a stop in Albany at 5:42. And as she wasn't due to leave till 5:49, everything was jake. I saw Tom, who is young and proud, taking a last look at his watch as he pulled his little black satchel out of the locker.

Even in spite of that fifty seconds just outside Albany, "they" hadn't been able to put anything over on us. We were on Time— spuyten duyvil!

16 I Travel by Train

Rollo Walter Brown

Rollo Walter Brown (1880–1956), a writer and educator who journeyed from Massachusetts to Texas over the New Haven, Pennsylvania, and Frisco railroads in the late 1930s, effectively comments on his fellow passengers. These trains carried a cross-section of types, including the ubiquitous business man. Before the dominance of automobiles and airplanes, executives, traveling salesmen, and the like regularly used passenger trains to make their business calls. Brown also reveals vividly one of the dangers involved with rail travel, not specifically to riders but to unsuspecting trespassers.

Nobody of consequence in Boston ever takes his train in South Station.* It is not so much of a station, as stations come and go, and it is surrounded by an atmosphere of leather, wool, roasting coffee, and dank sea water. But the traveler who is not too much in social bondage knows that it has its advantages. The sleeping-car is there in readiness—twenty minutes before leaving time. It immediately quiets the nerves to go into a car that is standing as if it meant to stay. And it increases a man's self-respect to walk in his space, see his luggage slipped under the berth, and then sit in the calm of green upholstery for ten minutes just as if only a half-hour before he had not been raging at everybody because his shirts had been smudged in the laundry. I had done pretty well in packing up—and so had my wife. I could think of nothing at all that I had left behind. Yet I pretended that I thought of something. Yes, it was something that would justify me in going to the rear of the train to telephone back to the house. I wanted my wife to hear me say in perfectly restrained voice that I was there and settled and all ready to go.

Even if it does sound like writing a testimonial for somebody, I must confess that I enjoy this traveling on a train. For a journey, as I like to think of it, consists not only of getting there, but of going. In the course

---

*South Station, located near Boston's central business district, served trains of the Boston & Albany and the New York, New Haven & Hartford railroads.

of a week, a month, I shall be able to use all my spare time in seeing what kind of country it is that I live in.

Immediately, too, I began to see it. For within five minutes after the engineer had given us the none-too-gentle jerk which assured us we were on our way, we were coming into the Back Bay Station.* Crowds of competently dressed men and women with dogs and children were saying good-bye on the plaltform. No fringes of any other classes of people were in sight. It was—and always is—America's best cross-section of a Brahmin population. In a crisp atmosphere that is a blending of the acquisitive and the intellectual, they are at perfect ease among themselves. Their language on such occasions, when they speak a little excitedly as if they were doing something unusual, has a flavoring that is more European than American. It is not precisely British—the British would be the first to tell you so—yet there is in it something that is more like Charing Cross or Bowness than Broad Street or Mackinac.

Only a few of them came into the car. They usually stick so close to the Atlantic seaboard that it is unnecessary for them to take a sleeper—except on those rare occasions when they go to Washington, and those rarer ones when they go to Miami. When they are sailing from New York they can ride down in a parlor-car. Yet when the last redcap had rushed from the starting train, our passenger list in the sleeper had been increased. In front of me was a little girl of four with her mother. They were going to Elizabeth, New Jersey, and thought a section in the sleeping-car would be more comfortable for so long a journey. Across the aisle a boy of six and his mother adjusted their belongings for a trip as far as Newark, Ohio. The mother was not a Bostonian; she had only married one.

I felt perturbed. I had had in mind looking over some jottings. There might not be great quiet. But I fortified myself. I like children. I recalled proudly how I had always been able to work with children playing—though not fighting—right beneath my window in Cambridge. And the little girl smiled at me with great blue eyes round the corner of her high-backed seat.

The boy saw her smile, and felt that he must participate. But he was less subtle. He walked over and wanted to know what my name was, and where I was going. His mother, who tried to look unadorned and sheer, very mildly reprimanded him. Then he asked the little girl. Soon they were playing in the aisle and looking out at my ⸱vindow, and the two mothers were discussing education—or rather, schools. The boy began

---

*Boston's Back Bay Station, about 1 1/4 miles from South Station, also served the Boston & Albany and New Haven roads. Trains to and from Boston customarily made this stop.

a demonstration of what his school had already done for him by swinging between his seat and mine and turning flipflops to the constantly accelerated accompaniment of a school chant. Then he began to yell very rhythmically as if he had learned that through teaching, also. I began to feel the least bit caged in. Instead of looking at my jottings, I concentrated on what was outside my window. The blueberry bushes were clumps of scarlet, the oaks beyond them were a brown that still somehow suggested life. It seemed a long hour before we had passed enough factories to be at Providence. I was on the state-house side of the train, and spent five minutes allowed for the stop in wondering why Providence, with all its many attractive spires and towers, would let somebody erect a great square hulk of a yellow building just across from the state-house and dwarf the graceful older building until it seemed to be shouldered off its hill.

At Westerly a little dried-leaf of an old lady who must have been at least eighty-five came shakily into the car. As the train started, it tottered her into a seat on the wrong side of the aisle.

"Oh," she exclaimed with a startling clearness, and rather eagerly, as if she were not always heard attentively, "I didn't mean to do that. I want over there, on that side—where I belong."

The very courteous, very black porter helped her over.

"Now!" she said. "Now! Now I can see them when we pass. It is so comfortable, too. So if it wants to storm now"—the sky was a little heavy—"we'll just let it storm."

The boy had watched her. He gave his upper lip a twitch of contempt. "She's an old devil, that's what she is!"

"Why, sweetheart, dearest!" his mother protested softly. "You shouldn't say that. Don't you see, she might be your own nice grandmother."

"I don't want any grandmother!" he shouted at the top of his voice.

A waiter came through from the dining-car hammering out some musical notes every so often and announcing that this was the last call for luncheon. I remembered that I had meant to eat a bite after I got aboard. Could there be a more appropriate hour?

A man can put in a lot of time in a dining-car if he is experienced. He can order item by item as he eats, and then eat very slowly, with full pauses now and then to read two or three consecutive pages in some interesting book, and with other pauses for the passing landscape. So for an hour and a half I sat and ate lettuce salad, and belated blueberry pie, and ice-cream, and read a little, and reordered coffee that was hot, and looked out at the sea, and heard, without trying, the conversation of the two youths at the other side of the table who professed ardently to believe that their prep. school had more class than either Groton or St. Mark's. One of them had just bought a yacht for which he had paid more that I in an entire lifetime had ever earned—or at least had ever received. He felt sure that his father would be able to stampede somebody into buying several blocks of stock at a good fat advance and by so doing pay for the boat without any drain whatever upon the established treasury.

Back in the sleeping-car I grew weary of the rhythmic jungle cries, and decided to seek out a place in the observation-car. I have made the test through a dozen years, but I made it again—with the same results: on these Boston-New York trains, as one walks through, there are more people reading books than on any other trains in the United States. It must be said also that there are more feet stuck out in the aisle, more people who glance up in disgust as you wish to put the aisle to other use.

There were no unoccupied chairs in the observation-car, and I immediately walked the full length of the train in the other direction. In the coach smoker close up against the section devoted to baggage I sat on the sleek oilcloth upholstery all the rest of the way to New York and enjoyed the bronzed reds of the Connecticut hills, the lighthouses on rocky points, the gulls flying everywhere, and listened with approval from some vague emotional depth of myself to two battered old pugs with heavy cauliflower ears while they declared with many variations that it was the good old sock right on the corner of the chin that made the world go round—at least for the other fellow in the ring.

Somewhere in the region of the Hell Gate Bridge* the train moved hesitantly for a time, and then made a broad sweep to the southward as if it were trying to find a way of getting around New York. It was exploring as it sped along. As it circled into open space, one of the fighters—they had both been silent for a time— looked off to the westward with a puzzled, interested stare as though he were seeing something that was beyond his understanding. Then I saw. The whole of New York from the region of Forty-second Street on downtown stood up in a leaden sunset sky like a dream of some brilliant madman. In a moment everybody in the car was silent and looking. It was something pagan, yet something unearthly. What had men been celebrating when they built it? A moment later when the train carried us along slowly where a veil of smoke in the foreground subdued the fading sunlight even more subtly than the clouds in the background had, the gray of the towers was less of the earth still. Soon afterward the train came to a full stop. There was no confusion near us outside, and everybody in the car for the moment was as silent as if he slept. We participated in something fantastic.

---

*Opened in 1914, the Hell Gate Bridge over Long Island Sound made possible a direct connection by the New York, New Haven & Hartford Railroad to Manhattan's Pennsylvania Station via Long Island. Using the "Hell Gate Bridge Route," through trains operated between Boston and Washington, D.C., over the New Haven and Pennsylvania railroads.

Evidently the train decided that there was no way of getting around. The only thing left to do was to go under. It gave us a violent jerk, swerved sharply to the right, and made a dive into a roaring tunnel which eventually brought us into the bowels of the Pennsylvania Station.

I went up for air. I bought the latest edition of three or four papers. I bought a magazine or two. I bought a book. And I received the welcome assurance that New Yorkers are just as childlike as anybody else, by watching hundreds of them solemnly ride a newly opened escalator down, since they were not going at the end of the day in the direction that would enable them to ride it up.

But it is never a journey until one is beyond New York. From New York it is still possible to telephone back home in a jiffy. And always among the pushing millions there are some of your friends. When I take a bedtime train in this direction I always find a vague inappropriateness in going to bed until we are past New York at two o'clock or so. And if I do go, I do not feel that I can settle down to solid sleep until after the long stop and the quick coming of the tingling pressure in the ears as the train drops swiftly beneath the Hudson. But when we are beyond the Hudson we are away—regardless of the hour. We have left behind everything peninsular and known. We are facing something vastly expansive. The train moves as if it had plenty of room.

The next morning when I awoke the light was squeezing in at my window. I pushed the shade up to see where we were. We were racing along a winding river among rounded hills, and two old women in sunbonnets fished from a flatboat. The maple trees on the hillsides beyond the river were as much green as yellow or red. When the train sliced off a piece of corn-field to save the trouble of keeping to the river, the ground from which the corn had been cut was matted with white and pink and purple morning-glories—and the fences were covered.

We swung out into more open country. Far in the distance I saw a dark train as long as our own, and racing as swiftly. I could tell by the design of the cars that they were sleepers. As day grew bright, today and every day, how many of them were there, racing everywhere in the United States, carrying whole towns of people along in their beds—and preparing breakfast for them? I tried to visualize a map of the United States with every long-distance train designated, as we mark the daily location of ships on the Atlantic. There they were, speeding everywhere—up from the South, across the Alleghenies, along the Great Lakes, down the Mississippi, across the Great Plains, through the Rockies, across the sands, up and down the Pacific coast.

When I was up and dressed and fed and ready to leave the breakfast table, our train slowed down and was cut over to the eastbound track. A moment later we passed scores of foreign-looking laborers who were busy putting down new steel on the track that normally would have been ours. Almost before we were at full speed again there were wild shrieks of the whistle, and a jolting, shuddering grind of brakes which brought us to such an abrupt stop that tableware crashed to the floor.

Since I had finished eating, anyhow, I went to the nearest open vestibule to lean out and see what had happened. There were fifteen cars or so in the train, and the diner was in the middle. I saw the conductor hurrying along on the ground from far in the rear, looking intently under the train as he ran. Far forward, the engineer in clean-looking striped overalls was coming back, looking under a bit more deliberately. Three or four porters had swung down and were standing back on the turf so that they might see farther alongside.

I swung down and walked forward toward the engineer. Before I came quite up to him, he stopped, looked back toward the conductor, and with a single easy lift of his stout arm signaled for him to come on up.

The conductor was there as soon as I was.

"There he is, under the front trucks of that baggage-car," the engineer said, without being quite able to be wholly matter-of-fact.

The conductor steadied himself by putting one hand against the lower edge of the car's body—which stood high above the road-bed—and looked under. A very black-headed Italian boy of about fourteen lay there limp and almost completely nude from having been dragged and rolled over the rough limestone ballast.

"He's not cut up to speak of," the conductor said. "We ought to get him out of there and be on our way in no time."

From somewhere a representative of the railroad company appeared. He glanced under. "That's easy. I'll look out for everything. You can scoot along."

From somewhere also—from the houses on the hillside just above the right-of-way—a number of dark-eyed children came running to see why the train had stopped.

"Any of you kids know who that boy was that was walking on the tracks bringing groceries home from the store?"

A cloud swept the faces of the entire group, as if they thought the boy had been arrested for something that he should not have done.

"Do you?"

"Yes," the oldest boy in the group said. "It was Fortunato."

"Fortunato? Your brother?"

"No, just my—friend."

"Well, he was walking on the tracks, and the train killed him."

In terror and helplessness the boy looked about at the rest of us as if we ought not to be there, twisted slowly away without moving his feet, lifted his hands to his face and then sank to the earth sobbing,"Oh, Fortunato!"

The other children stood speechless, except one boy who said half to the rest, half to the conductor, "The train was running on the wrong track."

"Yes, I know it was. But you see, he shouldn't have been walking on either track. He should have walked in the road."

"But there are automobiles."

I wandered back along the train. As I passed the dining-car it was still crowded with people who were obliviously enjoying their breakfasts and the bright morning.

I swung onto the train and walked all the way back to the observation-car.

There was only one person back there—a stout woman all freshly made up for the day, who was busy with a story in the *Delineator*.

She glanced up. "Can you tell me why this train is standing so long?" she asked. "We don't seem to be in any town."

"Oh," I replied, "we killed an Italian boy—up ahead."

"Why, how perfectly terrible!" she said in a voice so well modulated that she might have been reading from the story.

The train gave a little shrug of a lurch forward. "But I guess we must be going now."

Passengers began to come in from breakfast. Soon they had filled all the comfortable chairs. For two hours I sat with my back to the window and read. Periodically I let the book drop to the arm of the chair and looked out at the windows on the other side of the car past the heads of the solid row of those who sat across the aisle and did their own reading or smoked as if for once it would do no good to be impatient. Groves of maples, numerous in the hills and on the flat land alike, were splashed with fire. Occasionally some tree was solid yellow. Why had nobody ever said anything about the beauty of the hills between Coshocton, Ohio—or Athens—and St. Louis? Only Brown County, Indiana, has received any part of the praise due the entire region. And Brown County became known chiefly because a group of painters found it paradise when the genteel population of neighboring cities laughed at it because it was short on railroads and plumbing.

Within the train, too, a change had taken place since yesterday. Most of the New Englanders had gone on to Washington—if they had not taken a boat at New York—and the transcontinental passengers had already been outnumbered by energetic Buckeyes, who are always going somewhere, and who are not troubled in the least by getting up and taking a train at five or five-thirty in the morning. They sat wherever there was room, smoked cigars, talked pleasantly with some half-recognizable remnant of New England or Virginia in their speech, and felt that the world was not such a bad place, after all.

One of them left the chair next to mine. It was promptly taken up by a rangy, bony man whose heavy dark hair was loosely combed over the side, and whose brows were shaggy. "Did you ever think," he began rather promptly as if he were in great need of expression, "of taking a straw vote of all the people who travel on a train like this to find out how many of them are running away from something—the same as we are?" He gave a single ha of a silent laugh. "They might not tell you what they were running from, but they might be willing to say whether they were running."

I twisted a little in my chair to look him in the face. His eyes were very wide open, like those of a maniac occupied with his favorite hallucination. But there was a trace of a smile close round his lips and under his eyes and in front of his ears. It spread till it covered his face.

"Maybe you think I'm crazy," he said as he tried to make out the expression on my own face. "And who knows, maybe I am."

"And maybe you are only another Hoosier poet."

He laughed his single ha of a silent laugh again.

"Maybe I am that, too. You know, there's a mighty thin shade of difference. And I come from Kokomo, if there's anything in a name."

His face spread in a new smile. "And I'll be coming back from St. Louis by way of Paris."

I must have seemed puzzled. "Paris, Illinois," he added. "Don't you remember? That's where lots of American girls have got their French."

We talked about Booth Tarkington, Meredith Nicholson, James Whitcomb Riley, Lew Wallace, Theodore Dreiser, George Barr McCutcheon, Gene Stratton Porter, and a dozen others of the older generation of Hoosier writers. Of course, he had known them all. He paused sometimes to speak of the sumac in the ravines in southern Illinois, or nod for my benefit toward the men in small towns who were selling late roasting-ears, and apples fresh from the tree.

As we came into the smoke of East St. Louis, the train moved cautiously. It was above the housetops. It seemed to be getting ready for something important.

"Old Man River!" the man from Kokomo announced. "I find something to come over here for every once in a while just to see this."

He glanced at the man opposite us who had his face buried in a copy of *Liberty*. "It must be a hell of a good story he's reading if he means to pass this up for it. Or maybe he's just afraid he'll fall short three seconds of the prescribed reading time."

There was quiet as we moved deliberately above the last houses—frowsy affairs of tarred paper, corrugated iron, and oddments of boards—

and out over the east bank of the spreading river, over the resistless, eddy-
ing, boiling middle of it where we could look down through the steel
of the bridge into it just as if nothing much supported the train, and
at last over steamboats moving in to the western waterfront. Then everybody scrampled forward to be ready by the time we were in the station.

But for me St. Louis was only a pause—not long enough to rob me
of my sense of motion. My next train stood ready. I was on it so soon,
and it was so soon away, that I had difficulty in feeling that I had made
a change.

After a late luncheon I sat in the lounge half of the cafe-car and stud-
ied the world outside. Without effort, even in spite of myself, I heard
the conversation of two men who had lingered, after everyone else,
at the luncheon table nearest me. One had a heavy roll under his chin;
the other, on the back of his neck. They talked and ate and drank time
away.

Within two or three hours we were climbing toward a ridge of the
Ozarks—over sharp curves and counter-curves, and on and on, up and
up. Close beside the long train, which moved a little below speed yet
resistlessly, thin-looking cows picked grass from steep rocky hillsides under
good-sized papaw bushes that were just beginning to lose their greenish
yellow leaves and reveal fat clumps of green fruit not yet quite ready
to fall. The only bright color anywhere was the red of some gum or persim-
mon tree.

How many railroads are there in the world that spurn the valleys, as
this one does, and follow low mountain ridges for a hundred or a hundred
and fifty miles? In these ancient worn-off hills the valleys were too complicated, too stuffy, for some dreaming surveyor, and he took to the hills.
Now, after the engine's long steady climb that seemed to be taking us
across a county or two, we were up on them ourselves. We swept round
long curves from which we could look down over ranges of hills on both
sides of the train; we took long straight-of-ways on the comb of water-
sheds; we described letter S's; we made sharp hair-pin turns—all in an
effort to keep to the ridges. Once we passed a freight train that was
taking water at a tank and filling the air with surplus steam. Several minutes later I saw the same train not more than a mile or two from us
across a wooded valley. We had followed a wide round horseshoe in order
to get where we were.

The two men had been drinking steadily while they discussed the economic ills of the country, and their eyeballs were getting pretty yellow.
But they could still see what the train was doing.

"I bet you, by God," one of them began easily as if he were established
in a point of view that enabled him to see whatever was wrong, "that
the fellow who had the contract for building this railroad got paid by

the mile. Just look there, will you? There's that same damned freight train that we passed a half-hour ago. Why didn't they come straight across there? It wouldn't have required a trestle more than three or four hundred feet high—or maybe five hundred. If we were building her today, that's the way we'd do her."

Once, to the southeast and east, as far as eyes could see detail, the sun was on billowing woodland; and at the horizon there were dark, indistinguishable ridges. There seemed to be no houses. One felt a thinning-out of telepathic ties. Man had not yet done enough to the region to make his kind feel at home in it. Once, to the west, for a memorable second, the red sun shone full in our faces through a gaunt and abandoned old log tobacco-house just above us.

All the while, the steward, a slender youngish man whose hair was thinning, stood at the buffet end of the car, neat and official in his blue suit and white vest, and looked at the floor as if nothing of grandeur were to be seen. Only occasionally did he glance up to learn if the two men were signaling for further drinks.

The two talked on—in cumulative friendliness. One of them was interested in oil. The other was the head of a dozen factories. They talked in millions—regardless of what they discussed. One of them said the most valued thing he possessed was his acquaintance with nice people. "If there are any nice people in town, we know them. I wouldn't take five million for that—just that. Honest to God, I wouldn't."

They grew confidential. They discussed their wives. For ten minutes their wives would have been in heaven if they could have heard. Then one of them set forth a list of his wife's deficiencies that would have made her stick her fingers in her ears and run if she had been secretly present. The other admitted that his was sometimes a little hard to manage. But he was gleeful over the birthday present she wanted. He was getting off with nothing more than a trinket of a ten-thousand-dollar necklace. "I said, 'All right, if that's what you want, you shall have it.'" He chuckled. "The jeweler is making it up."

They returned to the state of the nation. "The real trouble with this God-damned government," the man with the roll on the back of his neck said finally, "is that there's too much extravagance among the higher-ups." He was now in the stage of inclusive, graceful gestures, and set out to discuss the matter in detail. But something interrupted his flow of thought, and he ended up by insisting that he pay for the luncheon—now four hours agone—and for the drinks.

His friend would hear nothing of the kind, "Or at least we'll go Dutch." But the other was insistent, and held on to the slips which the steward had very tactfully presented face downward. He looked at the bills. Then he fumbled for his large-style reading glasses. The luncheons were $3.50;

the drinks thus far, $14.25. After swallowing once in consternation he said, "You see, I'll just put it on my expense account."

The other showed a ready acquiescence, "Oh, well! That's different. If you want to let the stockholders pay it, O.K. But I won't let you pay it yourself—wouldn't think of it."

One of them begged the other to see the gorgeous sunset. It was not gorgeous. In fact, it was a washed-out, pale blue-green affair hardly deserving of a glance. But it was a sunset. The sun was going down. So the two of them decided just to stay right on where they were and eat their suppers. They ordered sirloin steaks and French fried potatoes and apple pie and cheese and ice-cream and coffee. An hour later, when I had finished my own meal and was thinking that I might go early to bed, they were having a little drink together as an aid to digestion.

The next morning I was awakened by inescapable early risers. I am sure they never get up early at home. They probably are very lazy. But on a train they talk across the aisle to each other about whether they should set their watch forward an hour, or back an hour, or leave it just where it is. Then after they have awakened everybody in their end of the car, they call to the porter to come and make up their berths right away so that they may sit in them. One of the upper berths sticks, and the porter has to do some hammering. But eventually he has all in readiness for them, and they then sit dumb for two hours. In the wakefulness that these on our train brought to me, I had a drowsy memory that we had stood still for a long time in the middle of the night. Then I heard a porter explaining in subdued tones why we were hours late.

But when I lifted the shade to see where we were, I was glad we were nowhere else. A clear sun was coming up over low wooded mountains somewhere in eastern or southeastern Oklahoma. There were no accompaniments—no clouds, no mottled skies, no romantic haze; just hard outlines of gray-green flecked with settlers' unpainted low houses, and a great stark ball of deep red. I was blinded to the band of evergreen and white birches on bleak hills that stretched a thousand miles westward from New Hampshire, to the bronzing reds westward from Massachusetts and Connecticut, to the living brightness of Ohio and Indiana, to the billowing green merely touched with bright tips of red that extended from the Ozarks back eastward across Kentucky and Virginia. Here one was in the presence of nothing but fundamentals.

By noon I was off the train in northern Texas where the world bore yet another face. Cattle roamed in limitless fields, and the trees were still green.

"I'm mighty glad to see you," the hotel manager assured me as if he meant it. "I sure am." And Jake the black "boy," who according to his own testimony was just old enough to remember seeing soldiers coming back from the Civil War, remarked pleasantly as he shuffled along with my luggage: "Mus' a' been 'bout two years ago that you was here the last time, ain't it—Doctah?"

In the early 1950s the motorman of a Minneapolis & St. Louis Railway doodle-bug walks in front of his train at Ackley, Iowa, while a postal employee works the mail. (Dan Knight photograph)

Twilight
of
Rail
Travel

Right. Three railroads, the Chicago & North Western, Union Pacific and Southern Pacific, superbly maintained their fleet of "Cities" streamliners between Chicago and the westcoast. Similarly, crew members took great pride in their work. Many African-Americans worked for the railroads in service positions, and the conductor, as the "chief-of-staff," held a coveted position.

Below. Although most railroads had given up on long-distance passenger service by 1960, the Santa Fe had not. Indeed, the company's "Hi-Level" streamliner, the El Capitan, remained popular with travelers because of its quality equipment, its excellent service, and the fascinating scenery between Chicago and Los Angeles. The El Capitan makes a stop during the mid-1950s in Albuquerque, New Mexico, according to a public-relations writer, "[to allow] passengers a stroll on the platform."

Shortly before Amtrak emerged, some intercity passenger trains were skeletons of their former selves. A photographer for the Escanaba Daily Press on June 12, 1969, caught the diesel and car that was the Chicago & North Western's service between Green Bay, Wisconsin, and Ishpeming, Michigan.

A northbound Amtrak train speeds though Boylston, Wisconsin, in July 1978, seven years after this quasi-public corporation began a new era for intercity rail travel. (Don L. Hofsommer photograph)

17 Slow Train to Yesterday

Archie Robertson

Great Britain saw its first railfan groups form in the late nineteenth century, and America experienced a similar phenomenon in the 1920s. This love of trains knew no geographical bounds and attracted individuals of all ages and all walks of life. "Buffs" especially adored the old and the unusual—the more anachronistic and bizarre the more popular.

One early book designed for railroad enthusiasts was Slow Train to Yesterday: A Glance at the Local, *published in 1945. Its author, Archie Robertson (1906–1965), a professional writer and editor, provides a breezy account of a variety of railroad adventures. Only Lucius Beebe's heavily-illustrated* Mixed Train Daily: A Book of Short-Line Railroads, *which appeared two years later, enjoyed greater fame. The following excerpt from Robertson's work tells of what was surely the most highly esteemed of all rides, traveling aboard the narrow-gauge trains of the Denver & Rio Grande Western in Colorado and New Mexico.*

I looked out the window of a lower berth in Alamosa, Colorado, silent upon a peak in Darien.

We were in a railroad yard. The next track had three rails, and on the narrow, inner track stood a miniature train. She was the San Juan of the Denver & Rio Grande and I was going to ride her. I loved her at first sight. Her four cars were wooden, and have the pleasing curvatures of age, but they shine with paint. She is definitely a lady, an express train, with her name emblazoned on a shield upon her tail.

The Denver & Rio Grande, a two-thousand-mile system, most of which has been standard-gauge for years, is still a little touchy lest you think their remaining six hundred miles of narrow-gauge are typical. Over most of it they operate competing buses, and they have abandoned daily passenger service on all but the line between Alamosa and Durango.

In 1937, perhaps as an experiment, the company decided to do right by the passenger service on this one narrow-gauge division. The old seats were replaced by reclining, swiveled chairs; modern plumbing and steam heat were installed; and the schedule speeded up so that she takes only a couple of hours longer than the bus.

They may regret their passing mood of tender-heartedness, for now they are going to have a hard time giving up the San Juan. Almost every day pilgrims come, sometimes from thousands of miles, for the rail fans' ultimate experience.

After feasting my eyes upon her external beauty, I went forward to inspect the engine. This morning we had what the crew calls the sport model, the lighter of the two types of narrow-gauge engines used by the line. Many of the innards concealed by iron sheathing on larger engines are left exposed to view: for example, a counterbalance on the main shaft, a disk which follows the revolving drive-shaft like the moon around the sun. The crew, however, calls it the Monkey Motion.

We rolled off at seven, while I was breakfasting in the parlor-car cafe with an Indian, two beautiful and flirtatious senoritas, a businessman's wife with two small children, and a home economist of the Farm Security Administration. Mr. Lewis, the brakeman, is also correspondent for the weekly at Durango and asks all parlor-car passengers their names and business and prints them in the paper, a regular service of the line, no extra charge.

I opened the back door, spread my feet on the rail, and watched the tiny track roll back, to the south the Sangre de Cristo peaks, to the north the Rabbit-Ears, in between the sagebrush desert. Sheep grazed on one side, cattle on the other, and I was ten years old and eating peanuts, the piano playing a crescendo and the film itself, sharing the unbearable climax, flickering wildly. The galloping desperadoes overtook the speeding train, on which their leader was held prisoner, led his horse alongside, smashed a window, and he leaped into the saddle.

The captain of this ship of dreams is Conductor W. H. Hines, forty-one years of service with the D. & R. G., a small man, at once friendly and sharp. Eyes snapping behind his glasses, he fiddles with his watch-chain and waits for the moment when the traveler wants to talk.

"We cross in and out of New Mexico thirty-five times between here and Durango," he observed mildly.

The brakeman put in, "There's two places where a man can be in New Mexico and his wife be in Colorado, on this train."

I asked Mr. Hines for a knife to sharpen my pencil.

"Here's one I took off a Mexican the other day," he said, reaching up to the luggage-rack. "He stabbed me with it."

The day-coaches have a row of single chairs down one side, double on the other, and midway the line is broken by a long, springy sofa. At risk of his own safety, the conductor preserves Anglo-Saxon standards of decorum. There were no fights today, perhaps because the forward car carried a dozen young Navajo section hands, and the conductor felt called upon at each stop to leap down promptly and shepherd unattached females into the middle car.

"Would you like me to punch your ear?" he asked amiably of the grandchild of a harelipped old Mexican at Allison—"Le gusta el tren?" The child grinned with delight, just like an Anglo-Saxon. Only six families live here, but forty people were down to see the train. A businessman swung aboard to buy an ice-cream cone. The narrow-gauge still brings the amenities of life to this lonely sunbaked country off the highroad, as it did forty years ago when the fare was twenty cents a mile and a sleeper ran from Durango into Denver.

There are no more narrow sleepers in this country. One of the last was remodeled into the San Juan's parlor-car. As you might imagine, the berths were small, but they occasioned no apologies from General William J. Palmer, builder of the Rio Grande. "I intend," he said firmly, "to do away with this business of strangers sleeping in the same bed."

At Osier, sixty-eight miles from Alamosa, 9,637 feet above the sea, we looked down at the rocky, bright Las Pinas River, a favorite with fishermen. The San Juan brings them here at nine-forty-five in the morning and they take the evening train back at half-past five, giving the trout to Charlie the steward to fry for dinner. We passed fifty cars of sheep, with two engines in front and a pusher behind, on their way after lambing and shearing to their summer resorts in the high pastures. Our locomotive blew short, impatient blasts for a few strays on the track.

The passenger crew rustles business. "Well, did you get anything?" Mr. Hines asked hopefully at the next stop as the brakeman swung on. Lewis shook his head. At the next station he leaned out to call, "Better come ride with us!" to a pretty Mexican girl. The two elegant senoritas dismounted from the parlor-car to be embraced by their father, an old sheepherder who smelled bad and obviously loved them dearly.

We paused at Las Cumbres Pass, highest point on the line, 10,025 feet elevation, to check brakes and engine before starting down the four per cent grade. It was snowing. I opened a window to photograph the engine around the curve, a fascinating and provoking pastime, as the train always seems to straighten again before the shutter snaps. We emerged from a tunnel above the magnificent Toltec Gorge, where a sign read, "Passengers are requested not to throw rocks, as there may be fishermen below."

A trackside monument stands here to President Garfield. At the time of his assassination, the D. & R. G. had just reached Toltec Pass. Passenger agents of the line, hearing the news, held a memorial service here at track's end, taking a collection to build the shaft which seems now to memorialize less an all-but-forgotten President than the eternal simplicity and earnestness of railroad men.

"And that," said Mr. Lewis, the brakeman, with a sly grin, pointing to a monolith of sandstone, "is what we call the Brigham Young Monument."

At Garracas, New Mexico, the eastbound pulled into a siding for us; I stood on the platform and snapped a picture of fans on the other platform snapping pictures of me. There was general waving from the windows, we tossed them the Denver papers, the brakeman set the switch by hand, and we rolled down through the sagebrush flatlands toward Durango. It was a little like ships passing at sea, a point in time and space to remember.

"Ever make a study of birthdays?" It was the brakeman again. "I've got over nine hundred listed. Now, that fellow that lives there," he said, pointing to an adobe hut near the track, "he was born on July 18, 1903."

I must have failed to express proper interest, for he flushed slightly. "Birthdays are kind of important in the railroad business, you know, on account of seniorities and so on."

In the narrow-gauge yards at Durango we rolled past another going-going-gone train, the mixed freight and passenger which runs twice a week on the branch to Silverton. Once a year it takes the people at Durango on an excursion up the mountain in open gondola cars with benches. On another track stood the Grey Goose, of the Rio Grande Southern, the only other Western narrow-gauge still offering passenger service.* She is a Pierce-Arrow automobile, close to twenty years old, made into a combination bus-truck on rails and carrying a few passengers in front and light freight behind. But I did not feel like running down the last, lonesome narrow-gauge track to its ultimate destination. It was better to stop with the San Juan, old and mellow but still strong.

"Come ride with us again," said Mr. Hines, the conductor.

"Come live out here," said Mr. Lewis, the brakeman, as we looked up at the mountains above Durango. "All the room in the world."

---

*The narrow-gauge Rio Grande Southern Railroad, which operated a 172 mile line between the Colorado communities of Durango and Ridgeway, used a fleet of "Galloping Geese" in the 1940s to transport both passengers and less-than-carload freight. The Geese, which at one time totalled seven vehicles, were large, silver-painted rail vans. The Rio Grande Southern, a long-time affiliate of the Denver & Rio Grande Western, folded in 1952, and its tracks were then removed and its equipment sold.

18 Troop Train

David P. Morgan

While the following piece, written by David P. Morgan, (1927– 1990), long-time editor of Trains, *was aimed at the railfan audience, it still conveys the nature of the once-common troop train. Conditions on these wartime "moves" were not ideal for the men and women of the armed forces, yet mostly they were tolerable. Although a luncheon of franks and peas hardly ranked as an epicurean delight, it adequately filled empty stomachs. But because of expansion of commercial aviation and the decline of rail service by the 1960s, Vietnam era military personnel never saw a troop train; the Korean Conflict marked the end of that long-standing tradition. This surely pleased most military riders, but disappointed diehard railroad enthusiasts.*

Riding a troop train left a negative impression of the railroad industry for some Americans; they showed a strong desire to select other means of conveyance, usually automobiles and airplanes. Observed one railroad official in the early 1980s, "I believe for many GIs that being herded onboard troop trains during World War II convinced them that they never again would travel by rail." And he added, "Likely with the troop trains the industry planted some of the seeds that grew eventually into the demise of intercity passenger service."[1]

Anyone who has ever been drafted, no matter how distant the war, remembers the month, day, and year his civilian rights were arbitrarily waived. He remembers how his given and surnames were transposed and appended with a serial number, all eight digits of which he remembers too. He remembers being simultaneously immunized in both arms, coping with the incongruity of military courtesy, acquiring dog tags and an MOS,[*] hearing the Articles of War, and memorizing General Orders.

And, if he served during the Korean War or before, he remembers troop trains, or mains, as they were officially designated. Americans began riding trains to battle during the Mexican War in 1846 for the reason laid down by General William Sherman. "No army dependent on wagons can oper-

---

1. Interview with William N. Deramus III, Kansas City, Missouri, October 15, 1980.
*MOS stands for "Military Occupation Speciality," that is an individual's military job classification.

ate more than a hundred miles from its base because the teams going and coming consume the contents of their wagons."

The sheer statistics of rail troop movements during World War II beggar comprehension. During the period December 1941–August 1945, the railroads moved more than 97 percent of American troops—approximately 43.7 million military personnel. That figure excludes weekend passes, furloughs, and emergency-leaves. Also, POW's.

We must break down these figures to bring them into focus. For example, the carriers committed 1 out of 4 coaches and half of all Pullmans to troop transport. They operated more than 2,500 troop trains a month. In 17 of the months during 1942–1945, the 30-day troop movement exceeded a million riders. As many as 100,000 traveled in a single day.

The Pennsylvania Railroad boarded more than a hundred thousand troops an hour at the peak and had more than 2,000 of its coaches and over 65 percent of its Pullman space committed to the military. PRR fed the great, gray Cunard liners which ferried troops from New York to England. Filling the *Queen Elizabeth*, for instance, with 13,000 soldiers translated into 21 trains made up of 233 coaches or sleepers, 42 baggage cars, and 34 kitchen cars.

Of course, the GI does not equate troop trains with the statistics they produced. WWII vets recall instead cinders on the window sill, one to an upper and two to a lower, duffle bags in the women's room, slack action, the breadth of Kansas and the altitude of Colorado, USO canteens, waving girls, tedium, kitchen cars and paper plates and fruit cup, rumors, and—if you were bound for basic or a port of embarkation—the lonesomest whistles in the world.

For the railroad enthusiast, troop trains were a welcome diversion from the ominous implications of uniforms. In that season, draftees were fresh out of a prolonged economic depression. Troop trains visited a world previously viewed only in the pages of *Railroad Stories* or *TRAINS, High Iron* or *Trains, Tracks and Travel*. Me, for example. Before being drafted in July 1945, I'd never been west of St. Louis. . . . The Army's decision to give this Kentucky lad basic training in Texas changed all that. Our 13-car trooper ran Frisco all the way from St. Louis to Fort Worth, 734.6 miles, instead of taking the shorter, joint Frisco-Katy Texas Special route. We were hauled by three different engines—to Monett, Mo., by a lovely 4-8-2 of USRA pattern,* the 1505; beyond to Sherman, Tex., by a streamlined blue-and-silver Pacific, the 1026; then into Fort Worth by an unstreamlined sister 4-6-2, the 1021. The running was everything Dellinger's

---

*David P. Morgan refers to a "Mountain"-type steam locomotive. The 4-8-2 designation is the Whyte System of engine classification. F. H. Whyte, a New York Central System employee, used the number of pilot-truck wheels, drivers, and trailing wheels to identify most kinds of steam locomotives.

prose promised. While my fellow inductees dozed, read pocketbooks, or played pinochle, I scribbled notes:

"Nice stations, well kept trackage, pretty fair nonstop running. Good starts and stops . . . 4310 4-8-2 Boxpok driv. With auxiliary tank B161 . . . 4111 2-8-2. East on oil drag . . . 1031 4-6-2 east on Firefly; we went into hole for this streamliner."

In World War II America attempted the unprecedented. Its troops would go to war in sleeping cars. Technically, organized troop movements of more than 12 hours were assigned Pullman space, if available. What enabled Pullman to carry 66 percent of all troops (loading a sleeper every 2 minutes 48 seconds in 1944, sleeping 30,000 men a night) was a prewar surplus of approximately 2,000 cars, mostly tourist sleepers, which the company had stored instead of scrapping.

By 1943, when troop movements were exceeding a million a month, the Government broke its ban on new passenger-car construction and ordered 1,200 troop sleepers from Pullman-Standard and 400 troop kitchen cars from ACF; in 1945 the orders were repeated. Both types of cars were based on the AAR standard 50 1/2-foot box car, modified with steam and communication lines and mounted on unique Allied "full-cushion" trucks tested "at speeds approaching 100 mph."

The center-door sleepers, numbered 7,000 up, slept 30 men in three-tiered, crosswise bunks. Toilets and wash basins were located at each end of the 76,300-pound, 51-foot 8 1/2-inch cars.

Former Pullman Conductor William Moedinger [once remarked]: "I never could quite understand . . . why the Pullman Company allowed its name to appear on the sides of these rattletraps. In a day when Pullman was a household word that stood for the finest in everything, applying the name to the sides of a windowed box car struck me as sacrilege."

Pullman itself was concerned enough to issue a bulletin to employees which read in part: "These cars will bear the name Pullman. They will be serviced with linen and other supplies in the same manner as all other Pullmans. There will be a berth for every man and bedding will be changed nightly by the porter. The kind of service on which we have built our reputation will be the same in every possible respect."

I rode Pullman 7007 in a troop train from Sheppard Field, Tex., to Lowry Field, Colo., in September 1945, and I thought the car fun. The presence of the porter was sufficient authorization for the name PULLMAN on the car sides; sleep came easy in the third bunk up over a flat wheel; and during the day the open-windowed vehicle was a breezy railfan's delight. Of course, a transcon ride in the winter might have altered my opinion. To this day, I look for Moedinger's "rattletraps." Declared surplus in 1946, they were sold off for service as M/W bunk cars,* baggage

---

*An "M/W bunk car" is a sleeping car used usually by a railroad's maintenance-of-way

cars, and cabooses—and apparently the unsold leftovers were shipped to the Government-owned Alaska Railroad for conversion into box cars. . . .

In the twilight of the troop train, in May 1953 (I did not know it then, but signing of an armistice to end the Korean War on July 27 of that year was—for all practical purposes—to write finis to mains), photographer Philip R. Hastings suggested that *TRAINS* report this special breed of train. He was an Army captain based at Fort George G. Meade, Md., a reception center for draftees. He proposed that, with the Army's blessing, we accompany a trainload of these men on the first leg of their journey to basic training.

I accepted with misgivings. Any draftee, once discharged, is reluctant to enter military property again lest he be again serialized, immunized, uniformed, and shipped out to one of those posts whose names once filled three pages of 5-point type in the back of the *Official Guide*. Instead of incarcerating me, though, the CO bid me welcome, explaining how Meade processed 12,000 draftees a month. For 202 of the recruits, the ritual of clothing issue, reading of the Articles of War, loyalty oath, tetanus and typhoid shots, $20 partial pay, haircut, and films was over by the morning of Wednesday, May 20, 1953. They were bound for Camp Breckinridge, Ky., for 16 weeks of infantry basic, and their transportation awaited them at the gate.

Main 2805 . . . consisted of eight Pullman heavyweights dating from the 1920's . . . spliced midtrain by Army kitchen car . . . and coupled behind . . . Pacific 5040. The train of sleepers had departed Camden Station, Baltimore, at 6:30 A.M., arrived at Meade at 7:30, cut in the kitchen car there, and been spotted for a 9:30 departure. At 9:20, eight buses of recruits drew up at trackside. The draftees got off and assembled into columns of twos; the buses pulled off; and, on instructions broadcast by a corporal on the roof of the boarding-area building, they climbed aboard the Pullmans.

I was impressed. The band was playing, the waiting Pullman was air-conditioned, the p.a. system was audible. The only element this operation had in common with my own departure for basic back in 1945 from Camp Atterbury, Ind., was a 4-6-2 up front.

Once underway, Main 2805 became a consist any draftee from 1940 on would have recognized. Extra 5040 West, to employ its train-sheet designation, was making time—and a new GI does not need to be hurried toward the great unknown of basic training. It was always thus. The great leveling effect of the Army fell early upon selected soldiers in a sleeper

---

workers. Old passenger equipment, especially coaches, diners and sleeping cars, commonly found extended life in M-of-W service.

adjacent to the kitchen car; they were ordered to don fatigues and report to the cook—no letters home or card games for them. The only men smiling in the train were gathered in the lounge of the Mt. Baker—the train commander, the train conductor, the Pullman conductor, and the railroad passenger representative. For them, civilian and military, Main 2805 was good duty, a straight shot west, no pickups or setoffs, and a prompt turnaround home.

Lunch. Noon. The classical menu: 2 weiners with ketchup sauce; 1 piece bread; 1 pat butter; peas; 1 boiled potato; fruit cup; iced tea. A fare indelibly inscribed in any serviceman's mind. Served to the troops, porters and trainmen, the train commander—in that order. Served in the Army tradition, which in this instance is the obvious procedure, i.e., all the GI's on one car (or in all the cars on one side of the mid-train kitchen car) walk to, through, and beyond the galley, picking up plates and utensils en route, then the troops do an about-face and return through, being served food on the second trip. Works like a charm.

Main 2805 rolled into Grafton, W. Va., about 4:15 P.M. . . . Captain Hastings and I remained in Grafton, he to catch the Metropolitan Special east, me to ride the National Limited west. As darkness descended, I made some notes . . . about the platform-level station restaurant where a cup of coffee still sold for 5 cents. . . .

I also thought that somewhere west of Grafton berths in rocking heavyweights were being made up for occupancy at 2130 hours, followed by a bed check and lights out at 2200 hours. I knew what must be running through the minds of the new troops. I was glad I was back in Grafton, watching No. 1 slide in. . . .

"Car 15?"

"That's right, Roomette 5."

"Right in here, sir."

The civilian life. You don't appreciate it until you don't have it.

19 A Dirge for the Doodlebug

William D. Middleton

Some memories of railroad travel involve utilitarian and at times dingy branch-line, local, or commuter trains rather than crack limiteds. The once ubiquitous self-propelled passenger cars—popularly, even affectionately, called "doodlebugs"—served hundreds of communities throughout the country with dependable transportation from the early twentieth century to the early 1960s. Unlike steam locomotives, classic Pullman cars, and even day-coaches, scarcely any doodlebugs have been preserved, although their "first-cousins," light-weight rail diesel cars (RDC's), in a few instances remain in revenue service.

William D. Middleton (1928–), a civil engineer and railroad historian, describes his rides in April 1959 on doodle-bugs in their last great bastion, the Upper Great Plains. Middleton correctly recognized that this transport vehicle was about to become extinct.

Chances are good that most of us who grew up in rural America before World War II remember the gas-electric motor car. Of course we never knew it by that name. It was always the "doodlebug" or the "galloping goose," or some equally derisive, yet affectionate, nick-name.

During my own somewhat nomadic boyhood my family lived in a good many out-of-the-way places, but no matter where we went there was nearly always a doodlebug local that showed up every day down at the depot. I was only six years old when we lived in Hayti, way down in the southeastern tip of Missouri, but I can still remember the day the whole family went down to the depot to meet my mother who was return-ing from the East aboard the Frisco's gas-electric local that came down from St. Louis daily. This was the first time I'd ever seen one, and it seemed a formidable machine, with red and white stripes on the front end. And I recall the long summers on the Montana prairies, when we went down to the Wolf Point depot almost every day to watch the Great Northern's galloping goose pause to load and unload its cargo of mail, milk cans, baby chicks, and assorted merchandise, and perhaps even a passenger or two.

The most impressive gas-electric of all those I remember was the Omaha Road's Namekagon which used to come through Hayward, Wis., on its run between the Twin Cities and Ashland. It was painted in bright green and yellow, and its name, which was taken from the local river, was proudly displayed on the rear of the trailer car, just like a mainline limited.

The first really successful internal-combustion rail car, developed by the Union Pacific's William R. McKeen, Jr. in 1905, wasn't a gas-electric at all, of course, but instead was a machine which used a complicated mechanical drive. The true gas-electric car, employing a gasoline-engine-driven generator and traction motors, had been tried as early as 1891; but not until 1908, when General Electric introduced a line of gas-electric cars, did the idea reach the practical state. By this time reasonably reliable heavy-duty gasoline engines were being manufactured, and rapid development of the electric railway industry had made the necessary motors and electrical equipment available. General Electric sold over 100 of its gas-electric cars to U. S. railroads, but the most successful builder was the Electro-Motive Company, which sold around 500 of them during the '20s.

Many of the gas-electric original proponents saw it as a means for the steam railroads to compete with the frequent passenger service offered by their interurban competitors, but as it turned out, the car was rarely used in this manner. Instead, low operating costs found a far wider application for the gas-electric as a means to economically operate lightly patronized local and branch-line services. Most important of all, perhaps, the gas-electric car pioneered the principles that made the diesel-electric locomotive possible a few decades later.

The gas-electric was what you might call attractively homely. Aside from the earliest McKeen and General Electric cars, which had knife— and bullet-nosed front ends respectively and were exceedingly dashing in appearance, most gas-electrics were built without the remotest concession to streamlining. They usually had a front end that was chopped off square, with such locomotive appurtenances as bells, headlights, markers, and air horns more or less haphazardly mounted on them. On the roof in disorderly array were located complicated-looking pipe radiators, mufflers, and exhaust stacks. For winter operation a sturdy snowplow frequently replaced the locomotive-type pilot.

The gas-electric was not a quiet machine. From a distance the snorting exhaust sounded something like that of a large tractor, but from within the engineroom, where the unfortunate engineer rode, the clatter of the engine was something frightful. An engineer who valued his hearing always plugged his ears with cotton before setting out. The gas-electric's air horn was, in prediesel days, a distinctive feature that earned the car its widespread "galloping goose" title.

What with the generally low estate of branch-line and local passenger service during the post-World War II years, little has been seen of the doodlebug recently. But in the late '50s a notable exception to the widespread disappearance of such schedules was the Northern Pacific's network of branch lines in North Dakota. It wasn't that NP was doing any better with this kind of operation than anyone else, it was simply that the obstinate North Dakota Public Service Commission refused to have any part of NP's proposal to substitute less costly highway services. By early 1959, however, NP—with the assistance of the 1958 Transportation Act—was finally getting somewhere with its efforts to discontinue almost all of its branch-line motor-car and mixed-train schedules in North Dakota. This seemed to be a good time for a last fond look at the once familiar doodlebug, and I promptly invested $15.62 in a round-trip ticket between Minneapolis and La Moure, N. Dak., that was good for a 24-hour circle tour comprising 278 miles of travel aboard two doodlebug locals and a mixed train, not to mention another 371 miles aboard the North Coast Limited and the Mainstreeter.

At 7:45 one April evening I departed from Minneapolis, and a few minutes before midnight the North Coast had me into Fargo in royal style. I was back at the depot shortly after dawn next morning, for motor-car train No. 139 was scheduled for a bright and early 5:50 departure on its 147-mile run to Streeter, N. Dak., over the Fargo & Southwestern branch. Motor car B-21 was already in the depot, and the assorted contents of a string of baggage trucks were rapidly disappearing into the mail and express compartments at the front end.

Except for the corporate title displayed on the letterboard, the B-21 had little in common with the glossy Loewy-style North Coast I'd stepped off a few hours before. The B-21 was a plain-looking, utilitarian vehicle, finished in serviceable Pullman green, with a bright red and white front end for visibility. There were comfortable leather-upholstered seats for 22 in the mahogany-paneled rear passenger compartment, and roomy express and RPO compartments up ahead.* A builder's plate identified her as a 1929 Electro-Motive product with a car-body built by St. Louis Car Company. Like all NP gas-electrics, the B-21 had long since been dieselized—in this case with a Sterling diesel.

Engineer Ed Williams poked around the journal boxes, then climbed up beside the noisy diesel to start the B-21 on its way across the prairies. It was early spring, after the snow had gone and before the fields had turned green again, and I had forgotten how lonely the empty, treeless plains could be. The towns along the way—Woods, Coburn, Sheldon, and Buttzville—seemed little more than a few houses and grain elevators, and perhaps a long row or two of shiny corrugated bins for the surplus grain, huddled close to the track. At almost every one a station agent, elderly and dignified in a trainman-style cap with a metal AGENT badge

---

*Doodlebugs typically contained a section for a Railway Post Office. Prior to the demise of this service in the 1960s, postal employees sorted mail en route, at one time an extremely effective way of moving the mails.

on the front, waited for us in front of a weathered yellow frame depot. Usually the local mailman was there too, with his battered sedan pulled close to the platform and the trunk lid raised in anticipation of a few sacks of mail. The plain little train order signal above the station's bay window was invariably set clear, for ours was the sole train on the line.

Lisbon was the only town of consequence all the way from Fargo to La Moure and its superior status as a county seat was clearly established by a neat stuccoed depot, larger and more substantial than the frame structures elsewhere along the line. The few passengers who remained from the half dozen or so who had boarded the B-21 in Fargo left the car here. Engineer Williams inspected a newly overhauled power truck for signs of overheating, while the agent and baggage-man manhandled a heavy head-end business. Then we headed westward across the Sheyenne River and out onto the prairie again, through more of the lonely little towns—halting momentarily at each to take care of the modest mail and express business, and at Independence just long enough for No. 139's Conductor C. L. Manro to register at the junction with the Oakes branch.

Le Moure was the end of my ride on the B-21, which paused briefly at the brick depot and then trundled off across the James River toward Streeter. Mixed train No. 154, scheduled daily except Sunday over the 69 branch-line miles between Jamestown, up on the NP main line, and Oakes, provided the next leg of the circle tour. If the black and yellow Geep* that brought No. 154 into town over the James River branch more or less on the 9:55 A.M. advertised seemed modern indeed, its consist was very much in the tradition of rural mixed trains of an earlier time. A long string of box and cattle cars was trailed by a big combine that clumped solidly along on 6-wheel trucks. Arch windows and truss rods marked it as a period piece. The interior decor was equally passé, with dusty leather walkover seats, oil lamps, and a pot-bellied stove. Just ahead of the combine, which accommodated No. 154's express and passenger trade, was a "peddler" box car for l.c.l. freight traffic.†

The mixed stayed in La Moure only long enough to switch a few cars and to handle a little express and l.c.l. business. Then the combine jerked forward as the Geep took in the slack and headed east. We retraced the route of the Fargo-Streeter motor car for some 5 miles, stopped to register at Independence, then headed south over the 15-mile Oakes branch.

Oakes proved to be the center of a considerable branch-line activity.

---

*A "Geep" is a general-purpose diesel locomotive. Initially diesel-locomotive manufacturers produced "road" units and yard switchers. But after their introduction in the 1950s, Geep locomotives were used to operate either on the road or in yards, shunting cars. The Electro-Motive Division of General Motors referred to this breed as "road switchers."

†Until the 1960s, most railroads offered "less-than-carload" freight service, so-called "l.c.l." traffic. Usually this freight traveled in a designated boxcar or "peddler" car, placed either at the front or rear of the train.

The town is the terminus for both NP's Oakes branch from the north and the railroad's Fergus Falls branch from the east. Chicago & North Western is represented by a branch which extends northward to Oakes from Huron, S. Dak.—the only North Western penetration into North Dakota— and the Soo Line by its Hankinson (N. Dak.)-Bismarck branch. The arrival of the NP mixed shortly before noon marked the beginning of a flurry of activity. Soon afterward NP motor car B-18 rolled in from the east on its daily-except-Sunday round trip from Staples, Minn., then the North Western came to life with the arrival of mixed train No. 1 from Huron behind a green and yellow 12-wheeled Alco road-switcher. Only the Soo remained quiet.

There was time for lunch at the cafe down the street from the depot before the B-18's 12:20 P.M. departure for Staples on the final leg of my branch-line tour. In appearance the motor car was little different from the one I'd ridden over the Fargo & Southwestern branch. Like the B-21 it was an Electro-Motive product—in this case with a carbody built by Standard Steel Car in 1926—and subsequently was re-engined by Caterpillar.

Staples was 170 miles away, and train No. 112 had a relaxed 5-hour 35-minute schedule in which to make it. For the first few miles east of Oakes the motor car traveled with a strange bounding motion over nineteenth century rails laid with opposite joints when the branch was built, then the B-18 settled into a more orthodox gait as newer rail was reached. At Wyndmere, Soo diesels waited impatiently to the north as the agent and crew loaded mail and express at a small depot tucked into one corner of the crossing. By midafternoon we were passing over the Red River into Minnesota on a curious humpbacked trestle, and finally, beyond Fergus Falls, the monotonous prairie landscape was replaced by Minnesota hills, trees, and lakes. At Wadena the motor car rolled onto heavy rail and crushed stone ballast, and followed the semaphores of the NP's main line into Staples.

The sun hung low in the western sky as the B-18 slipped past a long line of dead steam power and then between the platforms at the Staples depot. Baby chicks, crates of eggs, trees from a Minnesota nursery, cream cans, and mail was transferred from the motor car's head-end compartments to baggage trucks to await the eastbound Mainstreeter. Across the tracks an already shiny Budd car was being washed down preparatory to beginning its nightly journey to Duluth. With another 12-hour, 340 mile day behind it, the 33-year-old motor car rolled off to the enginehouse.

20 Mr. Frimbo on the Metroliner

Tony Hiss

For years Rogers E. M. Whitaker (1899–1980), better known as "Mr. E. M. Frimbo," wrote for The New Yorker. *When away from the office, he managed to ride hundreds of thousands of miles of rail lines in the United States and throughout the world. As Alvin Harlow, author of popular transportation books, said of Frimbo in 1953, "[H]e would like to ride over every mile of track on the North American continent. He knows that this cannot be accomplished as to track currently in use, for every little while another branch or small railroad is abandoned. . . . These abandonments annoy Whitaker as much as anyone of his placid temperament can be annoyed. He has been nibbling away at his hobby at odd moments for 18 years, and at the last audit had racked up more than 400 railroads, big and little, and traversed some 900,000 miles of track, much of which he traveled in reaching other railroads which he wanted to add to his score."[1] Fortunately, Whitaker shared his favorite railroad-travel adventures with readers of* The New Yorker. *In 1974, he and Tony Hiss, also a writer with* The New Yorker, *collaborated on the well-received collection of essays titled* All Aboard with E. M. Frimbo: World's Greatest Railroad Buff. *In the following piece, which originally appeared as part of the "Talk of the Town" in* The New Yorker, *Hiss writes about traveling with Frimbo on Penn Central's new Metroliner.*

By the late 1960s riders of the rails in America did not have too much about which to cheer; yet, some, including Frimbo, took hope when Penn Central introduced a radically different version of "doodlebugs," high-speed electric "Metroliners," in the winter of 1969. This service proved popular and durable; more than twenty years later this genre of trains remains the pride and joy of travelers along the busy Northeast Corridor.

1. B. A. Botkin and Alvin F. Harlow, eds. *A Treasury of Railroad Folklore: The Stories, Tall Tales, Traditions, Ballads and Songs of The American Railroad Man* (New York: Crown Publishing, 1953), p. 283.

We spent a delightful day last week travelling to and from Washington, D.C., on the Penn Central's new non-stop, high-speed train in the company of our old friend Ernest M. Frimbo, the world's leading railroad buff. We met Mr. Frimbo, by prearrangement, at Penn Station at a quarter to seven in the morning, and he greeted us with his usual booming "Hello," adding "My, it's good to see you. Haven't caught sight of you since—Let's see, must have been my two-millionth mile. Well, it's up to two million eighty-two thousand three hundred and ninety-five miles now, and we'll add four hundred and fifty today. You are going to enjoy today's jaunt. The Metroliner, which is what the Penn Central calls this new high-speed train, is the first forward step taken by any form of transportation in this country in donkey's years." Mr. Frimbo was wearing a tweed suit from Bernard Weatherill in two hues of gray, a pink button-down shirt, and a stripy tie. On his head was his familiar black homburg, and he was carrying, out of pure devilment, a maroon Qantas Airways bag. He looked fit. We said hello as soon as we were able, and he told us that it was time to get going. "The train leaves at seven-ten, but I wanted you here a few minutes early, so you could get a good look at her," he said.

We followed Mr. Frimbo down a flight of stairs and gazed, with him, at a sleek and slightly convex six-car stainless-steel train that was humming quietly on Track 12. "Four coaches and two parlor cars," Mr. Frimbo said proudly. "Built in two-car units, and there's no locomotive. Each unit is really its own locomotive. For a faster getaway. The rounded shape is called 'tumble home' by designers. Each of the coaches has a snack bar in the middle, and the seats, as in every ordinary coach, are four abreast, with an aisle down the middle. On an airplane, they call four abreast First Class. Huh! The parlor cars on the Metroliner have one seat on each side of the aisle. That's what *I* call First Class. Each of the parlor cars also has a small kitchen at one end, and for that reason the train crews call them galley cars. The Penn Central people don't call them parlor cars, either, by the way. They call them club cars—or, to be precise, in the present instance, Metroclub cars. That's an idea they borrowed from the Canadian National Railways. The people up there decided that 'club' sounds more modern and more tony. You know—'I belong to an exclusive club.' They thought 'parlor' sounded Victorian and fusty. Of course, I myself have spent many an enjoyable hour in parlors. And many an enjoyable hours in clubs, too, for that matter."

Mr. Frimbo went aboard one of the parlor cars, and we followed him. He called out a good morning to a porter, and the porter said, "Good morning to you, Mr. Frimbo. Glad to have you aboard, sir. We'll be serving breakfast soon."

"Good," Mr. Frimbo said.

We found our seats—Nos. 24 and 26. They were salmon wing chairs with the wings slightly raked, and they had pea-green paper antimascassars on them. We sat down, and agreed that our chairs were very comfortable. "This is the first high-speed train to be built by someone who knows how to build railroad cars," Mr. Frimbo remarked. "They had some models run up by people who built buses, and they put in—What do you think? Plastic seats. It was awful. The Penn Central people, be it said, have gone about this in the right way."

It was now seven-ten, and, right on the dot, and very smoothly, the Metroliner began to move out of the station. A voice said "Good morning, ladies and gentlemen" over a loudspeaker, and wished us a pleasant trip. The voice was replaced by soft music, which wobbled slightly as the train picked up speed. Mr. Frimbo caught our glance. "I know, I know," he said. "Just like the airlines. Oh, well, people probably wouldn't feel comfortable without it these days. You'll find it isn't obtrusive. This is my sixth trip on a Metroliner, and it hasn't been late yet. One day, we *were* six minutes late out of Philly, and everyone said, 'There we go,' but we were two minutes early into New York. We had made up eight minutes."

The train passed through Newark at that moment, exactly on schedule, and Mr. Frimbo started counting heads in the two parlor cars. Both were nearly full. "The Metroliners are doing a rocketing good business, and I'm very pleased," he said. "All in all, it's a damn good train, and two hours and thirty minutes from New York to Washington is a speed to be proud of. The first time I rode a Metroliner, the run took just a minute less than three hours. When I worked in the Pentagon, in the Transportation Corps, back in the Second World War, I used to come up to New York on the Advance Congressional Limited. It ran out of Washington Friday afternoons, and made one stop—at Newark, where it did not pick up passengers. That train carried ten of the heavy old ninety-ton parlor cars and a ninety-five-ton diner, and it was scheduled to arrive in three hours and fifteen minutes. One glorious day, we made it in three hours and ten minutes. So, despite all the streamlining and yelping, the Metroliner had cut eleven minutes off the run in twenty-five years. Today's run—two and a half hours—is all right, though. But that Turbotrain to Boston—running on the schedule of the Merchants Limited of twenty years ago, and not even going into South Station!"

The porter now appeared with two small trays, which he placed on two small tables by the sides of our seats, and Mr. Frimbo paused to eat breakfast. Our breakfast consisted of a dish of orange slices, a plate of corned-beef hash with grilled tomato, a piece of Danish pastry and a croissant, and a pat of butter, a jar of preserves, and a cup of coffee. We noticed that the porter had brought Mr. Frimbo a glass of iced tea, instead of coffee, without his having asked for it. Mr. Frimbo always starts the day with a glass of iced tea.

After breakfast, we leaned back on our pea-green antimacassar and asked Mr. Frimbo if he didn't think that transportation in the United States was improving. When he didn't reply, we looked at him and saw that he was sitting with his head propped on one arm, staring out the window at New Jersey. We repeated our question, thinking that perhaps he hadn't heard it, and he looked at us. "I heard you," he said. "That's a good question, I guess, and I was just thinking up the best answer to it. Yes and mostly no is the right answer, I think. The Metroliners are what we need, and if they have one every hour, as they keep saying they're going to, things will be moving in the right direction, but the truth of it is that transportation in this country is in one hell of a mess. I'm not talking just about the railroads this time, either. You've heard me often enough on the subject of the chicanery of railroads. It's the airlines and the bus companies, too. But I'll start with the railroads, as usual. In the first place, the railroads are hard-pressed, to give them their due. When an airline wants a new terminal, it gets the government to build it, and the men who run it are all government employees. When a bus company wants a new stop, it approaches the proprietor of a local hotel and tells him, 'We'll give you five per cent of the revenue we make on our ticket sales if we can use your hotel as a depot.' A railroad, on the other hand, is expected to build its own station, staff it, and pay real-estate taxes on it. It doesn't make much sense, does it? You and I would both do very well if we were tax-exempt, like the airports. The railroads would do very well if all the signalmen were paid by the government, like the air-control staff. Of course, there are—well, I won't call them rascals but people in the railroad business who would just as soon forget their responsibilities to the public, cut out passenger service altogether, and go into the real-estate and hotel business. Some of the railroads are already part of these giant new conglomerates, and are doing just that. There are even some people in the Penn Central hierarchy who are nauseated by the smell of success of the Metroliners. People like that are responsible for the fact that you can't get a train out of New York for Hartford on a weekday after 6:05 P.M. Imagine! A town the size of Hartford, one hundred and nine miles from New York City, and you can't take a train to it after 6:05 P.M.! This is curfew transportation. It's back in the nineteenth century."

"But *how* do they get rid of passenger trains?" we asked. "Doesn't public necessity count for anything?"

"I'll give you a primer," said Mr. Frimbo. "You have a fast train from New York City to upstate New York at half past four in the afternoon. You push its departure time up to two o'clock, and business falls off so fast that you can ask the Interstate Commerce Commission for permission to take it off. You schedule a train to arrive in Chicago an hour and a half later than it used to, thereby missing a dozen good connections. You take off the dining cars— that's the Penn Central's favorite stunt— and make the travellers pay as much for a couple of sandwiches as they used to pay for lunch. The Pennsylvania wasn't so bad, but then after the merger the New York Central men moved into the hierarchy. Now the trains are later than ever, dirtier than ever, less air-conditioned than ever, and more expensive than ever. The poor customers of the New Haven! It can cost you up to twenty per cent more to ride the coaches on what New Haven trains are left, the parlor-car fares have gone up twenty-five per cent, and now they want to end the service at the Route 128 station, a dozen miles this side of Boston. The argument is that in five or six years there will be a rapid-transit line from Boston out to Route 128. So the passengers can get off there and wait five or six years. The same sort of scheme is on the books for Washington. Those scoundrels are such . . . "

We observed a growing empurplement of Mr. Frimbo's countenance, and we sought to divert him. Remembering that he had persuaded us to make the final run of the Twentieth Century Limited, a year ago last December, we asked him whether he had a new favorite means of conveyance.

"I'll be riding the Century again in a couple of weeks," he said, subsiding.

We goggled.

"Oh," Mr. Frimbo said, "the Penn Central sold it all, and a lot of other cars besides, to the National of Mexico, and now it runs every night—and all-Pullman, too, the way it used to be—from Mexico City to Guadalajara, only it's called El Tapatio now. A great train! At ten at night, the diner is so full of happy customers that you have to be a regular rider to get a table. It's Mexico's most popular night club, you might say. When I see people standing up on Penn Central trains, I ask an official I know why people have to stand all the time. 'Shortage of equipment,' he says. 'Why don't you buy some of that stuff back from Mexico, then?' I ask, and he pretends that he doesn't know what I am talking about."

Mr. Frimbo shifted in his seat. "But now let's take the other forms of public transportation in this country," he said. "Let's talk about all those towns with one train and one bus a day—or none at all. What happens is that the railroads give up when the airlines move in, and then the airlines discontinue. I can tell you a horror tale or two. I remember flying to Grand Forks, North Dakota, one night some years ago—there was no suitable train—and asking the stewardess about bus service from the airport. 'Oh there isn't any bus service, sir,' she said. I asked about taxi service. 'Oh, there isn't any taxi service, sir,' she said. I asked her what I was supposed to do to get into town. 'Oh, well, sir,' she said, 'you *could* talk to the airport manager, and he *might* be able to persuade someone to drive you.' Of course, you can always fall back on the rent-a-car, but not at that hour of the night. And buses! I was stuck in Aberdeen, *South* Dakota, once, and the only thing for me to do was to catch the through bus from Seattle to Chicago. It got to Aberdeen six and a half hours late. Those are just examples that spring to mind. Everything that can be done in this country is being done to force people to get on the highways. And where will they all be when we have weather like the weather we had this past winter? Buses and airlines are fine, but in proportion. I fly to the Coast myself. No one would take the train nowadays, except on holiday. But once you get rid of the trains, just where are you in a bad snowstorm? Buses simply quit; the airlines are helpless. Only the train limps through. There was hardly a day last January and February when there wasn't something wrong with at least one airport in New York, Baltimore, Washington, Philadelphia, or Hartford. Ninety per cent of all inter-city traffic is already in private cars. But what's the answer? Get rid of the trains? The National Transportation Safety Board said that last year fifty-five thousand people were killed on the highways, and one million nine hundred and thirty thousand were injured; the amount of money lost in highway accidents was three and a half billion dollars. *Three and a half billion dollars*! And that doesn't include job loss or hospitalization. There isn't a country in the world whose transportation is as disorganized as ours. If that three and a half billion were spent on transportation, maybe we could approach the standards of civilization."

Mr. Frimbo glanced out the window. "The crews call this stretch of track, between Wilmington and Baltimore, the race track," he said. "We are now doing a hundred and ten miles an hour."

Just then the voice on the loudspeaker announced, "We are now travelling at a speed of one hundred and ten miles per hour."

"We'll be in Washington soon," Mr. Frimbo said happily. "Then we'll have time for lunch at the Occidental Restaurant and perhaps a short visit to Railroad Hall of the new Smithsonian Museum of History and Technology. They've got a Southern Railway old Pacific-type passenger locomotive, No. 1401, there, and she's painted the proper lovely shade of Southern Railway green. Haven't seen her in a number of years. And then we'll catch the afternoon Metroliner back to New York. It should be a *very* pleasant day indeed."

Rolling Home for Christmas

21

Riding Amtrak in the 1980s

Eric Zorn

In some ways, travel by train is timeless. This contemporary essay by Eric Zorn about riders on Amtrak's California Zephyr indicates that people still find pleasure with long-distance rail trips. Undoubtedly they will for the foreseeable future.

The California Zephyr, or "CZ" as it is sometimes called, operates daily over the 2,422 miles between Chicago and San Francisco (Oakland). Introduced on March 20, 1949 by the Chicago, Burlington & Quincy; Denver & Rio Grande Western; and Western Pacific railroads, the CZ instantly became a favorite with the public for its quality service and outstanding scenery which could be easily viewed from its "Vista-Dome" cars. When Amtrak started in May 1971, it altered the train's name to the San Francisco Zephyr and routed it over the Union Pacific from Denver to Salt Lake and then on the Southern Pacific to Oakland. The Rio Grande refused to join Amtrak and continued to operate its CZ equipment between Denver and Salt Lake City on a limited basis. But when the Rio Grande stopped this service in the early 1980s, Amtrak rerouted the Zephyr, once more called the CZ, from the Union Pacific to the more scenic Rio Grande.

There is nothing to see out the window of the train but visions of the girl, of the family, and of Christmas.

Pfc. Ken Worthington is coming home from the Army for the first time. Night has fallen across the Illinois prairie, and a train they call "The California Zephyr" is rolling west across America fully loaded with passengers, presents, and holiday hopes.

"It's going to be like the old movies," says Private Worthington, passing time in a window seat in the club-car lounge. "You know, when the soldier gets off the train and his girl and his folks are waiting for him? It's going to be the ultimate."

He is 25 years old. He was working on the family farm in Roseville,

Illinois, earlier this year when he decided he "wanted a different way of life," he says.

He left his girlfriend, Jenelle, and four siblings, and ended up stationed in San Antonio at Fort Sam Houston.

"Homesickness hits a lot of guys hard in the Army," he says, not talking about himself, exactly, but sort of. He flew up from Texas and caught the train in Chicago's Union Station. He is in uniform, on two week's leave, having a Coke, getting nervous and, now, less than 100 miles from home. It is the Saturday before Christmas and nearly all of the more than 400 passengers on the California Zephyr are headed home in one manner of speaking or another.

Debbie Perryman has lived in Little Rock, Arkansas, for many years, but home for her is still the family home in Denver where she is taking her husband, Rick, and daughter Emily, 7, for the holidays. The national rail network is now so thin that the Perrymans have had to go the long way around the farm belt and are now even further from their destination than they were when they left Little Rock.

"We wanted family time for just the three of us," says Rick Perryman, who is sitting on the arm of a chair in the club-car lounge and has his arm halfway around Debbie. "We can read. We can sightsee. We can get right back into the heart of this country."

"The train is so nostalgic," says Debbie. "And Christmas is such a nostalgic holiday."

She is a 1st grade teacher and speaks with a professionally honed enthusiasm. "You fly, you miss it all," she says. "This is an adventure, like a cruise."

The lounge is halfway back in the 14-car, quarter-mile-long train. A woman in a red vest stands at a counter in the middle and sells snacks and drinks. The windows are huge, curling into a partial dome on the roof of the car, but at night they reveal only what the imagination supplies.

"We'll go to services in the church I was brought up in," says Debbie Perryman, anticipating the holidays. "And, of course, we'll have to have oyster stew on Christmas Eve. It's an old tradition that I'm trying to break. I detest it."

"My family never experienced me being gone for so long," says Private Worthington. The train is running 20 minutes behind schedule and he knows people are already waiting for him at the station in Galesburg, Illinois, "It was a dramatic blow when I left."

In the next couple of days, he says, he and his neighbors will drive around in a pickup truck, caroling from door-to-door. "Then we'll have a bonfire," he says. "We used to have what they call barn dances, but they don't do so much dancing anymore. Now they're just get-togethers."

Down the line, the old-fashioned Amtrak station in Galesburg buzzes with the anticipation of those waiting to get on and of those waiting to meet loved ones. When Ken Worthington steps onto the platform, at first he cannot see anyone he recognizes. He can't hide his disappointment. He hitches his bag and trudges toward the station.

But then, from out of the darkness . . . .

He is home again. Jenelle is waiting. And behind him the train lurches and rolls away.

*D*ana Meyer is writing a short story.

"It's kinda dumb," she says. "Kinda hard to explain. I write a lot of morbid, depressing, horrible types of things. This one is about someone following someone down a street."

She is a junior in high school, sandy haired, coltish, eager. Her friends in Mobile, Alabama, have given her a blank, clothbound book to write in during the family train trip to visit relatives in the San Francisco area.

But the writing is not going well. The joyous spirit of the holidays has made it difficult for Dana's muse to sustain a dark mood.

"Christmas is special, the whole day," she says, casually draping a hand over the book to hide what she has written. "It's not what you get, it's the event itself. For our family it ties in with the train trip. Flying is too quick; we don't like it. The journey is just as important as the destination."

She is an actress in school and seems to have a gift for talking in quotes.

"I'll give you more," she says. "I love the train because you meet people. When I was 6, I met a lady on a train from India in full Indian dress. She said she was a princess. She said that I was a fascinating person."

*P*aul Michels hasn't taken a train trip since World War II, when he rode a troop transport from North Carolina to Washington, D.C., standing the whole way.

He and his wife, Agnes, now live in Rhinelander, Wisconsin, way up there, and are headed west to spend Christmas in Fort Collins, Colorado, with their two daughters and their 11-year old grandchild.

"We hardly know her," says Agnes of her grandchild. Agnes is wearing a black sweater with a sparkling Christmas tree pendant on it. She and Paul are in chairs facing the window, keeping an eye out for the occasional small town with multi-colored lights.

"In Rhinelander," says Paul, "people have really gone all out. You see thousands of lights on houses."

Many holiday traditions in the Michels family are fluid, as they are for most families that are scattered geographically. Some years the girls come back to Rhinelander. Other years Paul and Agnes celebrate with their son, who still lives near home.

But every year, no matter what, family members aways eat rutabagas with dinner on Christmas Eve.

*L*ittle Emily Perryman has written 13 letters to Santa Claus, each of them different. "The one thing that came up in all of them is that she wants a My Little Pony Perm Shop," says her father.

"With a Little Pony," adds Emily, a forward and wide-eyed child. She climbs around on her parents while they sit and talk, and the California Zephyr blows across the Mississippi River into Iowa.

"I was trying to explain to Emily about all the farmland we've been seeing out the window," says Debbie Perryman. "These people are feeding the United States. We're going through the breadbasket of America."

Rick Perryman, who is an executive with a power company in Arkansas, expresses more interest in the small towns and backyards he has seen. "You see the old taverns," he says. "Not bars, taverns. Every old neighborhood has its own tavern. So peaceful. So neighborly."

Emily says, frankly, she preferred the first train—the one the family took from Little Rock to Chicago. On that train, people in the club lounge sang Christmas songs. On this train, people in the lounge are silently watching the movie "Mannequin," which has just started showing on TV sets at either end of the car.

Emily and Debbie get up to take a walk. Rick stays behind.

"Santa's going to bring her that My Little Pony Perm Shop," he says in confidence. "Plus more than she can imagine."

*A*gnes Michels gets sad when she thinks of trains. When she was a young woman in the Upper Peninsula of Michigan and working as a telephone operator, she and the other local girls would go down to the station to see the boys off to the war.

"That whistle would blow and everyone would cry," she says.

But the train also brought young Paul Michels back from the war. The two then met in a dairy bar where Paul says with a wink, he had actually gone to hunt up an old girlfriend. Someone introduced him to Agnes instead. Forty years ago.

"Hard work, that's the secret," says Agnes.

"Hard work and compromise," says Paul.

"For example, usually he makes the decisions," says Agnes. "But making this a train trip was my idea. Good idea I had, huh?"

She nudges him gently and he nods.

*I*n the dining car, John Cahall has ordered the vegetarian entree, pasta shells stuffed with ricotta cheese and splashed with marinara sauces.

Vegetarianism is part of the Indian philosophy of Vendanta, which he is studying at a small rural school in Pennsylvania. He is traveling across the country to be with his brother and his brother's family in Ukiah, California, 100 miles north of San Francisco.

"I'm not a big Christmas person," he says. "It's no big deal to me. It's probably because of emotional hangups from childhood."

Cahall is 46 but looks at least 10 years younger. His hair falls to the top of his shoulders in back, he wears wire-rimmed glasses, and he carries a knapsack around the train.

He grew up on a dairy and tobacco farm in Ohio but ended up in San Francisco, where he worked for the city in a senior citizens escort program. But eventually he was so drawn to Vendanta that he signed up for a three-year intensive course of study.

He had planned to do some good reading on the train, but so far, he says, he's mostly been relaxing and looking out the window. He's been aboard since last night and will not reach his destination for almost two more days.

"I like riding the train," he says, a hedge in his voice. "I have gotten discouraged a few times. But I guess I'm just not real crazy about flying."

"Safety seems to be the big reason people ride with us," says Amtrak porter Robert Brooker. He is reading a paperback potboiler called *Rainbow Drive* as the passengers in his coach sprawl across their seats in the comical attitudes of sleep.

It is nighttime on the California Zephyr. The movie is over in the lounge car and stops are now more than an hour apart as the Great Plains spread out to either side of the tracks.

"A woman passenger last week took her own survey to see why people would ride the train," says Brooker. "I don't remember the percentages, but the reasons were safety, cost, convenience, scenery, and love of the railroad. The railroad still has a peculiar mystique and fascination for some people."

Holidays are alway busy and crowded on Amtrak, says Brooker, who quit a job as a restaurant maitre d' four years ago and joined the railroad to help get over a painful divorce. But despite the crowds this time of year, passengers are in a good mood.

He, too, is in a good mood. He, too, is headed home for the holidays. His four children and three grandchildren are waiting for him in Los Angeles. "The last one was born November 12," he says. "I haven't seen him yet. I'm dying to see him."

Sleep? No. Ron Patterson cannot possibly.

"I get all wound up," he says. "I get overwhelmed with it all."

He says he has not slept since getting on the train in Culpepper, Virginia, yesterday afternoon. He and his wife and daughter are going to Portland,

Oregon, to see his in-laws, and this will be the first Christmas in his 39 years that he will be away from Virginia.

He is in the club car on the lower level of the train, knocking back Budweisers with a kid named Scott Hohenshell from Omaha.

Hohenshell has gone by the nickname "Cricket" ever since he learned how to make cricket noises in junior high study hall. He demonstrates the noise repeatedly, to the evident distraction of the people up ahead in the club car who are having a loud argument about presidential politics.

"I've been trying to catch some city lights," says Patterson. He carries a portable radio to try to pick up some country music, but the bright orange earphone pads are sitting uselessly on his collar. "There's just not that much out here," he says.

Fifteen members of his wife's family will gather in Portland to feast and exchange presents. Patterson is hoping for snow "to make it feel like a traditional Christmas," but the forecast in the Pacific Northwest is not promising.

Cricket chirrups. At the other end of the car in a dense cloud of cigarette smoke, a big round guy in a military-style uniform that is not really a military uniform brags loudly to a circle of strangers about an expensive lighter he once owned.

The train crosses the Missouri River and rolls into Omaha. Some dude in an honest-to-goodness authentic relic of a leisure suit cackles that Nebraska women are the most wonderful women of all. For an awkward moment, his remark kills the conversation.

"My fault," says Robert Brooker, the porter. He is talking about his divorce. The reading lamp above his seat in the dark coach looks like a spotlight on him.

"But neither of us ever remarried," he says. "So every year at Christmas we get together with the family. It's like nothing ever happened. The kids really love it."

Christmas Eve will be at their son's house in suburban Los Angeles. They will open a few presents and have a quiet dinner.

"I haven't been to church on Christmas Eve for a long time, but I think I'm going to take my mother this year," he says. "She's 86. There aren't too many Christmases left for her."

The next day they will travel a few miles to their daughter's house, where they will have a major feed and open the rest of the presents.

Brooker rides the California Zephyr for six straight days when he leaves home. "You've got a lot of time out here to ponder life's problems," he says. "Sometimes you get a few of its answers."

Ron Patterson did doze off there for about two hours during the night. Then he woke up Shirley and Nikki, their 5-year old, for breakfast.

His watch said 6 A.M. but the train had crossed time zones and it was actually 5 A.M., an hour before the dining car opens.

"Man," he says later. "Come Monday I am going to be ready to be off this train for a while."

Nikki Patterson has made several little friends in the coach where Ron and Shirley have reserved seats. They play together while one of the parents keeps an eye on the group. A sense of community is building among the long-haul coach passengers who by now, half an hour from Denver, are nodding at each other when they pass in the aisles.

There is less familiarity among the first-class passengers, squirreled away in tiny sleeping compartments for which they have paid a premium of up to $200 each. The train is generally cheaper than flying if you don't get a sleeper, but it can take its toll in other ways.

"I just never could sleep in a moving car or anything," says Ron Patterson, who has reached the delicate state of fatigue where conversation begins to slide lazily here and there. "I've been that way all my life."

He is a groundskeeper on a private estate in Orange County, Virginia, and Shirley drives a school bus part time. They are getting Nikki a Barbie doll for Christmas. Ron has bought Shirley a diamond ring, but it is still on lay-away at the store.

"Lordy, Lordy, Rick is 40," sings Emily Perryman, nervous energy getting the best of her as the California Zephyr creeps the last mile toward the Denver train station. These words were written in icing on her father's last birthday cake and they have remained deeply etched in her memory.

"That's right, dear," says Debbie Perryman, somehow still euphoric after 33 hours on the train. She and Rick have packed up their sleeping compartment and seem almost as excited as their daughter to meet the family at the platform.

It has been Rick Perryman's first train ride. "I wouldn't have taken this trip any other way," he says. "It's been its own minivacation. We paid about what we would have to take an airplane, but we got more for our money this way."

When Debbie sees her mother and father waving on the platform, she looks happy enough even to eat oyster stew.

Agnes Michels slept the night reclined in an aisle seat and covered by her winter coat. But she is fresh, with new lipstick on, when the California Zephyr finally stops in Denver.

Granddaughter Allison is right there to greet her and Paul. The family embraces at more or less the same time that the Perrymans fall into delightful hugs with their family, bags and suitcases flying.

Funny thing. Neither little girl is too keen on kissing her grandfather hello. But both scrunch up their faces and go through with it. Once a year it can't hurt.

"Oregon!" shouts Debora Burd. She does not mean to shout, only she has earphones on and has been singing along loudly to a cassette tape of bluegrass music. "Dad is in Pendleton and we'll probably spend Christmas with my grandmother."

She takes off the headphones and turns off the tape player. "My train music," she explains. She has retreated to the lower half of the coach where she has found a door with an open window to lean out. The clean, cool mountain air blows her hair back.

"Last year, I met a guy from Paonia on the train," she says. "It was a railroad rendezvous. We drank a lot of beers and had a lot of fun. I was hoping it might happen again."

Burd is 31 and studying marketing at the Community College of Denver. She and two younger sisters are gathering at the family home for a quiet holiday celebration in honor of her grandmother, who is deaf, blind, and suffering from a variety of other ailments.

"I think it will be a sad Christmas," she says. "But I want Grandmother to be happy. If we can distract her from her discomfort for just a little while, it will be a good Christmas, I guess."

The skies are not cloudy so the lounge car has turned into a viewing salon. No seats available.

Dana Meyer, the short story writer, is curled up in a chair composing in a neat hand.

Insomniac Ron Patterson sits facing his wife who, to his annoyance, had a wonderful night's sleep.

John Cahall has taken a break from Indian philosophy and is reading *The Denver Post*.

And Trevor Copeland, a 16-year-old from Paragould, Arkansas, has fallen into a rambling discussion about Stephen King's horror novels with Mike Range, a college football quarterback from suburban Chicago.

Copeland is traveling with his parents and two sisters to Colfax, California, where some 25 members of his extended family are having their biggest family reunion in a decade. "Dad's the only one of us who's ever been on a train before," he says.

Range is headed to Salt Lake City, where his parents have just moved. He now lives with his grandparents in his Mom and Dad's old house.

"It's weird," he says, contemplating the concept of "home" in this context.

The train cautiously follows the grade along the Fraser River toward Granby, and the young men lean forward against the glass to watch water dance in the half-frozen rapids. To accompany the scenery, Amtrak has piped in orchestral versions of popular hit songs, with string parts as sweet as the strawberry pancake topping at breakfast.

Copeland turns and says to Range, "Did you know that Stephen King once wrote books under the name Richard Bachman?"

But of course he does.

Mary Lou Phillips has been interviewed before. Just last week, in fact, she was featured as the "Cook of the Corner" in the *Jefferson County Bee and Herald*, with a special focus on her Calico Beans Casserole.

"Oh, we love Christmas," she says. "We think it's a great time of year."

It is lunchtime in the dining car, and she and her husband, Robert, are both eating hamburgers because Robert is a cattle farmer and it's a question of professional loyalty.

Robert Phillips is an arresting sight in his red flannel shirt and his striped overalls. The couple—parents of six, grandparents of 10—are travelling to Pocatello, Idaho, from their home in rural southeast Iowa.

"The kids get together every year to buy us a gift," say Mary Lou. "One year it was wrist watches. One year it was a set of dishes. One year it was an exercise bike—we don't use that. And this year it's this trip."

They will spend Christmas in Idaho with their daughter and her family, whom they haven't seen in two years.

Robert Phillips flew for the U.S. Air Force in Europe during World War II, but has not flown since and will not fly now. "I still have the ulcers," he says. "The train is good enough for me."

"We've been watching the view and eating caramel corn," says Mary Lou, who works in a factory that builds washing machine parts while her husband tends to 90 cows and 5 bulls. "I brought along some magazines, but I haven't even read them yet."

Moses Green, a dining car waiter, regularly passes through some of the most magnificently scenic country in the world, the American Rockies. But he has never gotten off the train to look around.

"Someday," he says, "I should do it."

Today, though, Green's mind is on a different vacation—his upcoming visit home to Manning, South Carolina, where he will spend Christmas with his parents, four brothers, four sisters, aunts, uncles, and a variety of other relations.

"We always get a big pig, cut him in the middle and barbeque him in the yard," Green says.

Green has worked for Amtrak for four years. He now lives in the rough Uptown neighborhood of Chicago, but gets back south once a year. His work schedule will take him Christmas Eve back to Chicago, where he will hop another train as a passenger and arrive home on Christmas Day.

"Some people on the crew make a lot of friends," he says, stopping to talk during a lull between meals. "I tend not to socialize so much. My life is really off the train."

Nothing you can see from the windows of the lounge car can eclipse the beauty of the love between Hud Hudson and Tara Hughes. He is 23. She is 22. They are going back home to Boise, Idaho, with brand new, golden wedding rings on their left hands. Actually, they are not married yet. Not until two days after Christmas. "But we didn't want to lose the rings," says Hughes, almost apologetically.

They are graduate students at the University of Rochester in New York state, he in philosophy, she in English literature. They went to the same high school and have been dating for four years.

It seems like they have been on the train for four years, too. Actually, their trip is 38 hours, which is a long time to sit up in a coach car.

"I'm antsy," says Hughes. She will be wearing an old, ivory-colored bridesmaid's dress for the wedding ceremony, which will be simple and conducted in her parent's home.

Hudson will wear a suit. "This will be the most special Christmas ever," he says. "There will be the joy of our two families together and at least three big dinners."

He is concentrating in school on Spinoza's influence on Kant. She is focusing on 19th Century British novels. Right now, they are not making a lot of money.

"This trip home is our gift to each other and also our honeymoon," says Hudson.

Neither of them are quite used to wearing wedding bands yet. They are always playing with them, twirling them and looking at them.

Nighttime again on the California Zephyr.

Mary Lou and Robert Phillips are enjoying maybe their fifth nap of the day.

Moses Green is almost done with work and is listening to Nancy Wilson tapes while he helps count up the day's receipts in the dining car.

Tara Hughes and Hud Hudson have flopped their tray table down and are playing cards at their seats.

The TV in the lounge has crackled to life and is showing "White Christmas," which begins at almost the exact moment that a light snow begins to fall outside the train.

And the California Zephyr sweeps on through the Utah night, cleaving the flurries and leaving a trail of joy. It is headed to many, many different places, but, really, to only one place—

Home.

Acknowledgments

1. "Narrative of an Excursion on the Baltimore & Ohio Railroad." From the *Bulletin of the Railway & Locomotive Historical Society*, 6(1923):5–18.

2. Freeman Hunt, "Letter about the Hudson River and Its Vicinity." From Charles E. Fisher, ed., "Some Notes on Our Early Railroads," in the *Bulletin of the Railway & Locomotive Historical Society*, 81(1950):61–63.

3. Samuel Breck, "A Ride from Boston to Providence in 1835." From Richard Pike, ed., *Railway Adventures and Anecdotes: Extending Over More than Fifty Years* (London: Hamilton, Adams & Company, 1887), pp. 81–83.

4. Charles Dickens, "In America." From his *American Notes for General Circulation* (London: Chapman & Hall, 1842), pp. 80–84.

5. A. O. Abbott, "Sketches of Prison Life." From his *Prison Life in the South* (New York: Harper & Brothers, 1865), pp. 43–48, 51.

6. Florence Leslie, "A Pleasure Trip from Gotham to the Golden Gate." From her *California: A Pleasure Trip from Gotham to the Golden Gate* (New York: G. W. Carleton & Company, 1877), pp. 35–49, 51.

7. Linda Thayer Guilford, "A Winter Railroad Ride." From the Linda Thayer Guilford Papers, Western Reserve Historical Society, Cleveland, Ohio.

8. Robert Louis Stevenson, "By the Way of Council Bluffs." From his *The Amateur Emigrant* (Chicago: Stone & Kimball, 1895), pp. 102–34.

9. M. M. Shaw, "Nine Thousand Miles on a Pullman Train." From his *Nine Thousand Miles on a Pullman Train: An Account of a Tour of Railroad Conductors from Philadelphia to the Pacific Coast and Return* (Phildelphia: Allen, Lane & Scott, 1898), pp. 166–85.

10. Charles P. Brown, "Brownie." From his *Brownie the Boomer: The Life Story of Charles P. Brown as a Boomer Railroad Man* (Whittier, California: Western Printing Corporation, 1930), pp. 20–26.

11. Erling E. Kildahl, "Riding Freights to Jamestown in 1936: A Brief Memoir." From the *North Dakota History*, 55(1988):14–24. ©1988 State Historical Society of North Dakota. Used by permission.

12. J. S. Moulton, "Riding the Interurban." From his "New York to Chicago by Electric Railway," in *Electric Railway Journal*, 34(August 29, 1909):321–22.

13. "Riding the C. & L. E." From "Pressmen Enjoy Day in Dayton," in *The Deshler* (Ohio) *Flag*, July 3, 1930.

14. Ellen Douglas Williamson, "Traveling by Rail." Excerpts from her *When We Went First Class* (Garden City, N.Y.: Doubleday & Company, 1977), pp. 71–76. ©1977 by Ellen Williamson. Reprinted by permission of Doubleday, a division of Bantam, Doubleday, Dell Publishing Group, Inc. and by John Hawkins & Associates, Inc.

15. Christopher Morley, *A Ride in the Cab of the Twentieth Century Limited* (New York: H. W. Company, 1928), pp. 3– 20.

16. Rollo Walter Brown, from his *I Travel by Train*. Copyright 1939 by D. Appleton & Co. All rights reserved. Reprinted by permission of Dutton, an imprint of New American Library, a division of Penguin Books USA Inc.

17. Archie Robertson, *Slow Train to Yesterday: A Last Glance at the Local* (Boston: Houghton Mifflin Company, 1945), pp. 60–64. ©1945 by Archie Robertson and F. Strobel. ©renewed 1972 by Amy R. Previs, Martin Robertson, and F. Strobel. Reprinted by permission of Houghton Mifflin Company.

18. David P. Morgan, "Troop Train." From his "In the Twilight of the Troop Train," *Trains* 39(1979):44–48. Used by permission of Kalmbach Publishing Company.

19. William D. Middleton, "A Dirge for the Doodlebug." From *Trains*, 21(1961):26–28, 31–32. Used by permission of Kalmbach Publishing Company.

20. Tony Hiss, "Mr. Frimbo on the Metroliner." In *The New Yorker*, 45(May 17, 1969):29–31. Reprinted by permission; © 1969 The New Yorker Magazine, Inc.

21. Eric Zorn, "Rolling Home for Christmas." In *Lands' End* [Catalog], 24(1988):76–80. ©Lands' End, Inc. Reprinted courtesy of Lands' End Catalog.

Index

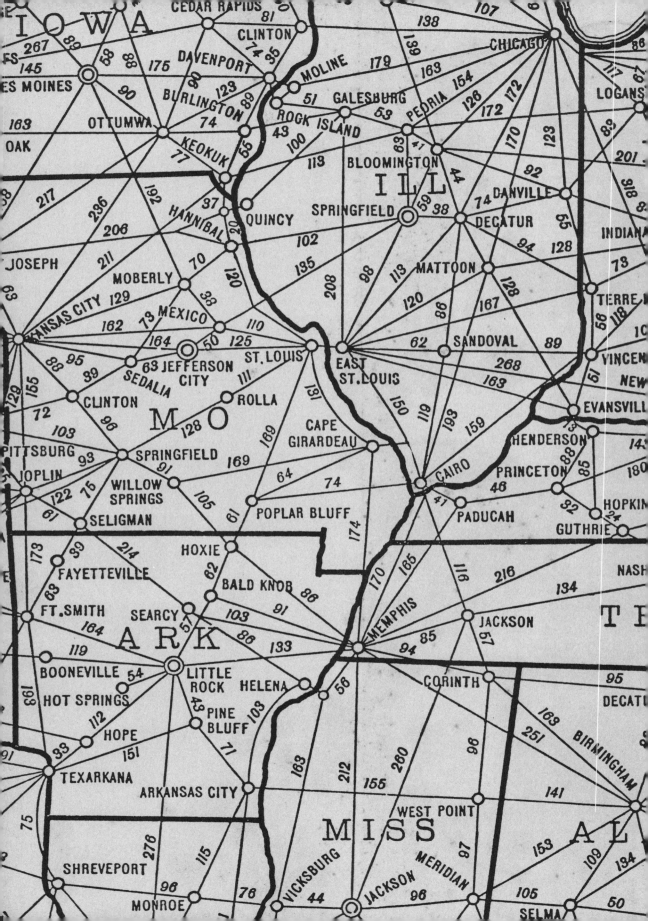